Paul Stephen Lundrigan

Treating Youth Who Sexually Abuse
An Integrated Multi-Component Approach

Pre-publication
REVIEWS,
COMMENTARIES,
EVALUATIONS . . .

"*Treating Youth Who Sexually Abuse* is a remarkably comprehensive and eminently practical guide. While much of the book focuses on residential treatment of these young persons, Lundrigan includes valuable information on outpatient treatment as well. The book also provides very useful program outlines, sample forms and guides, treatment program schedules, and other relevant resource materials."

Lloyd G. Sinclair, MSSW
Psychotherapist,
Midwest Center for Psychotherapy
and Sex Therapy,
Madison, WI

"At last! A book that addresses the full range of diagnosis and treatment for juveniles who sexually abuse. Lundrigan skillfully presents a comprehensive, useful, and highly readable overview of intervention with sexually abusive youth. This text provides a practical as well as clinically incisive resource for the practitioner and the layperson. The author uses his experience in the field and an obviously hopeful, caring perspective to shed light on a variety of extremely complex issues, from the challenge of working with these youths to explanations of a wide range of treatment approaches and the importance of staff training. It is a reading must for anyone in the field of child welfare and teaching."

Cynthia Crosson-Tower, MSW, EdD
Professor, Fitchburg State College,
Fitchburg, MA;
Author, *Understanding Child Abuse and Neglect* and *Exploring Child Welfare*

More pre-publication
REVIEWS, COMMENTARIES, EVALUATIONS . . .

"Paul Lundrigan has pulled together a resource that will be invaluable for all professionals who treat juvenile sex offenders, whether at the beginning, intermediate, or experienced levels. The book is outstanding because it is the first in years that brings together all of the latest practices and research for treating juvenile sex offenders in a comprehensive and detailed manner. The book clearly describes the role of the therapist, the offender, the family, the setting, and the community in a continuum of care.

If more juvenile sex offender treatment programs would put into practice this comprehensive approach to treatment, our communities would have far fewer juvenile, and subsequently adult, sexual offenders, resulting in far fewer children and youth becoming victims of sexual crimes. This is indeed a most welcome resource for those, like myself, who advocate on behalf of child victims of sexual abuse."

Patrick F. Guyton, MPA, MTS, MS
Executive Director,
Child Advocacy Center, Inc.,
Mobile, AL

"*Treating Youth Who Sexually Abuse* is a comprehensive, concise, easy-to-follow blueprint for treatment and should be required reading for all private and public providers of services to youth who sexually abuse. The field today must place an emphasis on a comprehensive continuum of services delivered locally if we are to successfully intervene in the lives of these most serious offenders."

Barbara Morton
Area Director,
Massachusetts Department
of Youth Services

The Haworth Press®
New York • London • Oxford

Treating Youth
Who Sexually Abuse
An Integrated
Multi-Component Approach

THE HAWORTH PRESS
New, Recent, and Forthcoming Titles
of Related Interest

Treating Children with Sexually Abusive Behavior Problems: Guidelines for Child and Parent Intervention by Jan Ellen Burton and Lucinda A. Rasmussen

Sibling Abuse Trauma: Assessment and Intervention Strategies for Children, Families, and Adult Survivors by John V. Caffaro and Allison Conn-Caffaro

Stopping the Violence: A Group Model to Change Men's Abusive Attitudes and Behaviors by David J. Decker

Stopping the Violence: A Group Model to Change Men's Abusive Attitudes and Behaviors: The Client Workbook by David J. Decker

Breaking the Silence: Group Therapy for Childhood Sexual Abuse, A Practitioner's Manual by Judith A. Margolin

From Surviving to Thriving: A Therapist's Guide to Stage II Recovery for Survivors of Childhood Abuse by Mary Bratton

"I Never Told Anyone This Before": Managing the Initial Disclosure of Sexual Abuse Re-Collections by Janice A. Gasker

Political Violence and the Palestinian Family: Implications for Mental Health and Well-Being by Vivian Khamis

Identifying Child Molesters: Preventing Child Sexual Abuse by Recognizing the Patterns of the Offenders by Carla van Dam

Patterns of Child Abuse by Michael Karson

Growing Free: A Manual for Survivors of Domestic Violence by Wendy Susan Deaton and Michael Hertica

A Therapist's Guide to Growing Free: A Manual for Survivors of Domestic Violence by Wendy Susan Deaton and Michael Hertica

Treating Youth Who Sexually Abuse
An Integrated Multi-Component Approach

Paul Stephen Lundrigan

The Haworth Press®
New York • London • Oxford

The Haworth Press, Inc., 10 Alice Street, Binghamton, NY 13904-1580

Cover design by Jennifer M. Gaska.

Library of Congress Cataloging-in-Publication Data

Lundrigan, Paul Stephen.
    Treating youth who sexually abuse : an integrated multi-component approach / Paul Stephen Lundrigan.
        p. cm.
    Includes bibliographical references and index.
    ISBN 0-7890-0936-6 (hard : alk. paper) — ISBN 0-7890-0937-4 (soft : alk. paper)
    1. Teenage sex offenders—Rehabilitation. 2. Youth—Sexual behavior. 3. Sexual disorders in children—Treatment. 4. Adolescent psychotherapy. 5. Child psychotherapy. I. Title.

RJ506.S48 L86 2000
616.85'83'00835—dc21

00-033532

CONTENTS

ABOUT THE AUTHOR

Paul Stephen Lundrigan, MA, has worked in various settings with adolescent offenders and their families. Beginning as a frontline staff member in a detention center, he has been employed as an outreach worker to inner-city youth, as a caseworker for the Massachusetts Department of Youth Services, and as a clinician and consultant. His experience working as a clinician in treatment programs includes locked psychiatric settings, secure facilities, residential programs, group homes, and outpatient clinics.

Brother Paul holds an MA in counseling psychology, is a Licensed Mental Health Counselor and a credentialed sex offense-specific treatment provider in the state of Massachusetts, and is a clinical member of the Association for the Treatment of Sexual Abusers (ATSA). He has presented workshops at state and national conventions and written several papers on topics of concern to those treating troubled youth.

Currently, Brother Paul is an outpatient clinician at AdCare Hospital in Worcester, MA. He continues to do some work with juvenile offenders in DYS facilities in Massachusetts.

Foreword

There are only a few good, well-written books on the subject of assessing and treating juvenile sex offenders, and *Treating Youth Who Sexually Abuse* is one of them. During the past twenty-two years, I have worked as a clinician treating both adult and juvenile sex abusers (JSAs). I have seen the number of programs grow from fewer than five specialized identified programs treating juveniles in 1978 to well over 1,000 identified programs in the year 2000. Treatment trends and new and better treatment modalities have grown simultaneously. New methods of assessing risk in JSAs are being developed as this foreword is being written. The field of treating JSAs has exploded during the past two decades, and signs point to increasing numbers of programs being developed in future years.

It is unfortunate in some regards that, in recent years, many of these programs are being either taken over or developed by profit-seeking corporations, which, in many instances, do not understand the complexities of JSA treatment and the need for vigilantly maintained and comprehensive treatment programs. In fact, many programs have begun to compromise treatment in the name of profit. In addition, surveys of professionals treating sex abusers reveal that many enter the field with no specialized training or experience in working with JSAs. Thus, they begin this work without a solid foundation and understanding of who JSAs are or what constitutes the best practices in treating these clients. They are treating clients, learning about programs, and understanding as they go.

Whether one is a seasoned professional with years of experience in treating JSAs or a novice looking to read and learn as much as possible, *Treating Youth Who Sexually Abuse* is a book that belongs in your library. The book is divided into five parts. Part I, an introduction to treating JSAs, addresses the many challenges we face as clinicians or administrators involved in JSA programs. Our expanding field and the development of new national laws affecting JSAs make our work ever more challenging. Part I also addresses one of the most important aspects of treating these specialized clients, the need for a continuum of care. Although this need has been recognized since the early 1980s, most states do not have such a continuum. Good treatment planning and the delivery of comprehensive services are enhanced when a continuum exists. Paul Lundrigan does an excellent job of describing what form a continuum of care should take and the importance of the many services necessary to treat this highly specialized population.

Part II addresses the variety of issues related to operating a treatment program. It clearly and succinctly covers both outpatient and inpatient treatment programs, with an emphasis on residential treatment. The importance of client and staff safety, residential standards of care, treatment components, multi-modality treatment approaches, and how to set up a treatment program from scratch are discussed. This part addresses the best practices in serving adolescents who sexually abuse and provides valuable information to both private clinicians and those working within residential programs.

Part III covers the basic components of treatment from group to individual therapy. It includes detailed information on parent education and family therapy, two important components in any comprehensive treatment program. In addition, Lundrigan covers the importance of setting up a milieu treatment program and how to maintain one to enhance the therapeutic setting. This part focuses on the basics of program design and implementation to help the reader understand and, if need be, develop a solid foundation for a good treatment program.

Part IV covers the issues of pretreatment and aftercare, two topics seldom written about in the literature but of vital importance to the running of a comprehensive treatment program. Anyone working with a residential program will benefit from Lundrigan's insights into initiating proper pretreatment and aftercare planning.

Part V focuses on staff training and development. In my experience traveling throughout the United States and overseas, I have observed staff training and development to be the first budget item cut when programs face financial difficulties. This leads to an undertrained and overworked staff. Part V helps the reader recognize the importance of staff training and development and the areas that should be addressed. Lundrigan also considers the issue of resident education and what a model program might look like. It is important to blend these two education areas in the running of a good program, and Lundrigan outlines the best practices in each area.

During the many years that I have spent in this challenging field assessing and treating sexual abusers, I have developed, consulted to, and evaluated specialized treatment programs for JSAs in the United States and overseas. In my work, I have consistently turned to the literature and other resources to support my ideas and to help create the best programs possible. I am excited to have *Treating Youth Who Sexually Abuse* as yet another resource to refer to in my work, and I recommend it to others who are developing programs or who simply want to ensure that they are running the best possible treatment program for JSAs.

This comprehensive book, filled with facts and current information, blends the knowledge in the JSA treatment field with the general literature about treating adolescents to maximize and enhance the sex abuse-specific treatment experience for clients. Lundrigan offers a detailed approach to assessing and treating JSAs. All sixteen chapters of this book are detailed, clear, precise, and easy to understand. *Treating Youth Who Sexually Abuse* includes over twenty-five figures and tables, several appendixes, and a comprehensive index. I am delighted that Paul Lundrigan has taken the time to write a book that serves as both a training tool and a ready-to-use reference in the treatment of juvenile sex abusers.

Robert E. Freeman-Longo
Sexual Abuse Prevention
and Education Resources International
Bomoseen, Vermont

Preface

I never planned to work with sexually abusive youths, nor did I, once engaged in that field, initially intend to write a book on the topic. After graduating from college, I was offered a job as a staff member in a juvenile detention center, which eventually led to doing outreach work with delinquent youth in the community, and then to employment as a caseworker with the Massachusetts Department of Youth Services. Although sexually abusive adolescents were part of my caseload, I was still naive as to the etiology and dynamics of sexual offending, and even less knowledgeable regarding the treatment of those who commit sexual offenses. It was as a graduate intern at an outpatient clinic that I received my first training and experience in clinical work with youth who sexually abuse.

After this internship, I began work as a clinician in a residential treatment program coordinating the treatment for those identified as "sex offenders." The program did not have a sex offense-specific treatment regime in place, so I immediately began to scour the literature and seek the advice of those I knew in the field to develop one. Although a good deal of information was available, no *single* resource provided a framework for incorporating all the possible components of treatment *within a unified scheme*. Thinking this unification important, I pieced together what I saw as the best in the sources (shaping the existing material and developing new resources where needed) and organized the information into a single treatment scheme.

This book is the fruit of that research, as refined and expanded by the experience of clinical work with abusive adolescents and their families (in secure, residential, and outpatient settings), study, supervision, trial and error, and grace. It is designed to present an overview of the treatment of sexually abusive adolescents, while encouraging the reader to delve into the other fine literature available for a more in-depth treatment of the topics discussed. Wherever possible, lists of such references are provided in the text for the reader's convenience.

The book presents both a broad view of treatment (i.e., treatment is conducted in a continuum of care composed of various programs) and a focused view of treatment (i.e., treatment is conducted in programs composed of various interdependent components). It is intended as a survey for training professionals to enter the field, and as a field manual for administrators and policymakers on the state and county levels, as well as program directors, clinicians, and other staff on the individual program level. The book was written with both inpatient and outpatient services in mind and attempts to provide information relevant to providers at all levels of care.

Readers should be aware that, as with the separate components of the multi-component model, each chapter is designed to work along with the others to contribute to the overall goals of the book. Therefore, some material that is applicable to more than one area or setting (and therefore could be included in more than one chapter) has been located in a single chapter to avoid repetition. By reading the book in its entirety, readers not only will gain insights into how different programs operate but also will find material applicable to their settings in chapters that seem to be written for someone else.

When speaking of clients, I have chosen to use the masculine pronoun for simplicity. Although adolescent females who abuse are an important population to consider, some of the models described have been used more specifically with males; modifications may need to be made to adapt the material presented for a female population.

In several instances, actual case examples illustrate the points being discussed. Although these examples are based on actual cases, certain information, including the names of the clients, family members, and staff, has been changed to ensure confidentiality. Where possible, clients were contacted regarding this project and were given the opportunity to request that they not be referred to at all.

The terms *sex offender* and *sex abuser* have been avoided when referring to these young people in response to the ever-growing belief that labeling them in this manner is detrimental. Such labels can transmit the message that this person is the equivalent of the stereotypic negative image of the sex offender prevalent in our culture. However, there remains in this book a mixture of terms. This has been done to reflect the continued use of many terms in the ongoing discussions regarding these young people, and also to reflect the continuing debate in some circles as to what terms should be used. Where the terms *sex offender* and *offender* do appear, their use was intentional (either for reasons of clarification, to distinguish two groups being discussed in the same sentence, or when the book speaks in a more general manner about persons who have committed sexual offenses).

I believe that these young people are not "bad," that (except in the case of severe psychopathy) they are treatable, that there is hope for them, and that they are redeemable—*regardless of what term we or anyone else uses when referring to them.* I believe that we must be careful not to add too much of a negative connotation to certain terms ourselves. We must be careful that by our use *or* avoidance of a label we do not convey the notion that the label put on them by the police, courts, family members, or others means they are bad. We must convey to our clients the underlying belief that regardless of what they did or what it is called or what we call them, they are not evil, hopeless, or unlovable. We must, through our words and agenda, uphold the notion that labels do not make people who they are, that "sex offenders" can and do change their behavior, that they have value as persons, and that they are loved by God.

Paul Stephen Lundrigan

Acknowledgments

I am deeply indebted to a number of people for their assistance and support during the shaping and completion of this project. Work on this book would never have been started, and could certainly not have been finished, without the support of Abbot Matthew Leavy, OSB, and Father William Sullivan, OSB, who gave me permission to undertake this project and allowed me the time and resources to see it through. I also extend thanks to my Benedictine confreres; my parents, Edward and Sandra; my sister Regina; and all those who offered words of support and encouragement to me during the past year.

Thanks is due to Ann Norton for reviewing the initial materials sent to the publisher, to Father Jerome Joseph Day, OSB, for his support and editing of the front matter of the book, and to Gail Ryan for emphasizing the importance of my use of labels. Essential to the shape, flow, and intelligibility of this work was the expert editing done by my sister Maria Gray. Any faults are mine to own and result from my failing to follow her thoughtful and carefully placed suggestions for revisions. Her reviews of the manuscript provided an invaluable contribution to the work as a whole and taught me to be a better writer in the process. Thanks also to Rob Freeman-Longo, who supported the project, read the manuscript, and provided input. I would not have had this assistance were it not for Steve Bengis, who placed me in contact with Rob and who has been supportive and helpful in his advice. Finally, thanks to Amy Rentner of The Haworth Press, who completed the final editing of the manuscript and prepared it for publication.

I owe a great debt to Kevin Creeden, who supervised me for three and a half years and who taught me from his expertise how one treats sex offenders. I am grateful to Kathy Kevil and Jim McKenna, who conspired to give me my first chance as a clinician working with sexually abusive youth, and to those professionals at the Massachusetts Department of Youth Services who consistently supported me, especially Barbara Morton and Ruth Rovezzi. I would like to thank all those who have influenced me over the years, especially Laurie Prehl, Bob Dube, Janice Marion-Billings, Kerry Fagan, Beth Flanzbaum, Denise Lavallee, Evan Graber, Paul Rosen, Phil Fokas, Wes Cotter, Leigh Curtis-Higgins, Joanne Schladale, Paul Finn, and Dick Hectl. A special mention is due to some of those who co-led sex offense-specific groups with me including Michelle Langlois, Joan Burke, and Joan Breault. Finally, I cannot forget to mention Mary Britt, who sat across from me in the group room for three years, who helped to shape the ideas expressed in this book, and who has been my most hearty fan, my most challenging critic, and a true friend.

An incalculable debt is owed to all the young men who taught me by their successes, struggles, and feedback how to better help those who would come after them in treatment. Some of them have been remembered in this book; others remain in my memory and in my prayers. And most important, a debt is owed to God; anything worthwhile I have accomplished is through his grace.

UT IN OMNIBUS GLORIFICETUR DEUS

PART I:
INTRODUCTION
TO THE TREATMENT
OF SEXUALLY ABUSIVE YOUTH

Chapter 1

The Challenge of Treating
the Sexually Abusive Adolescent

AN UNUSUAL LINE OF WORK

When people hear that an acquaintance treats adolescent sex offenders, they frequently shake their heads and fail to understand why someone would choose to do this for a living. To some outside the field, this work seems to be a great challenge filled with many obstacles, and to others, it is work that should be abandoned (in favor of permanent incarceration or castration). Many people tend to view adolescents as a difficult group to work with, and this is true enough. However, when the youth has molested and/or raped, the public also sees social stigmas and myths that have become part of our popular culture.

Those inside the field are aware of a great many challenges of which the average person is unaware. They know that a balance must be struck between vigilance in recognizing the danger possible from this youngster and openness to viewing the hurt person within. They are generally more aware of the truths behind the myths and have developed an ability to see the abusive youth as a person rather than just as a perpetrator of some of the most distasteful crimes in our society. However, they also know that one must always keep in mind the unhealthy person within, lest one lose perspective and thereby compromise effectiveness. Workers must be evaluating their own reactions to, and feelings about, offending behavior and the persons who perpetrate such acts. Also, they must be aware of how the typical thought patterns and potentially disturbing behaviors of sexually abusive youth affect them. This requires not only a knowledge of the clients they work with, but also of themselves.

The most frustrating aspect of treating the adolescent who commits abuse may be watching the very systems in which we operate, due to a lack of funding and resources or to inadequate knowledge, fail to treat offenders in a manner that our research has shown is the most effective. Encountering the difficulties of working with clients on one hand, and the limitations of the larger systems of care on the other, workers can feel boxed in and wonder if they are fighting a losing battle. Whatever the challenges, we must remember that the literature suggests that if the sexual offender is properly treated, he stands a very good chance of not reoffending, and in this we should take comfort. For if by our work we are able to reduce the number of those who are scarred by sexual abuse, then the challenge was worth it after all.

FOUR SOURCES OF THE CHALLENGE

The challenge of treating the adolescent who offends stems from four principal sources: (1) the client, (2) the intra- and interpersonal conflicts and struggles that arise in this work, (3) the limitations of the system, and (4) a society that promotes sexual misconduct.

The Client—The Initial Challenge

Authors employ many variations in their presentation of juvenile sex abusers (JSAs), including proposing various "typologies" that endeavor to sort JSAs into a taxonomic classification system. Despite these variations, JSAs commonly are a mixture of (1) fragility and emotional weakness (stemming from their own personal traumas) and (2) manipulativeness and/or aggressiveness (which they have cultivated to facilitate the inappropriate fulfillment of their needs).

The concept of the offender as possessing these two contradictory elements, a "victim-perpetrator" if you will, is not new (cf. Hunter, 1990), and this duality is a major challenge faced in treatment programs. One must be able to confront the more malicious and aggressive aspects of the youth, to cut through his manipulation, cognitive distortions, passivity, and denial, while dealing with his pain, trauma, and embarrassment in a more nurturing fashion (cf. Graham, 1996). This necessitates the development of strategies that are simultaneously "tough" and "tender" (cf. Ingersoll and Patton, 1990, Chapter 3). This is a difficult balancing act.

The clinician or child care worker also must be agile enough to work with the client on at least three overarching concerns:

1. Addressing and processing *overt behaviors* that are connected to the client's offending patterns. This includes exploring past behaviors to understand the client's offense cycle and relapse patterns, confronting and understanding present behaviors that are part of these patterns or are otherwise not adaptive, and working with the client to develop positive replacement behaviors for those which are problematic.
2. Examining, confronting, and working to modify distorted *patterns of thought.* This includes confrontation of these thoughts and careful demonstration of why they are maladaptive (using a whole host of cognitive therapy interventions). In addition, efforts should focus on understanding the client and assisting him in altering these thought patterns, so that they do not lead to problematic, unhealthy, or dangerous behaviors, and in creating new patterns that promote healthy and adaptive ways of acting and meeting needs.
3. Giving attention to the deep *pain and trauma* of the youth, as this is most certainly connected to the offending. This must be done in such a way as to help the client work through these issues of victimization while not absolving him of responsibility for his offending behavior. The trauma must be seen as a part of the offending, *not* as an excuse for it.

Often the worker must use a skillful approach simply to motivate the client to engage in treatment. Very few clients are willing to do this painful work and may be uncooperative at the outset, and many who do invest themselves in their treatment will at times be reluctant to work. The inconsistency; avoidance of treatment; manifestation of denial, passive-aggressiveness, and hostility; and the presence of a host of thought distortions can pose a frustrating challenge to the therapist and anyone else working with the youth. Even though the worker knows that at the heart of these defenses lies a well of fear, guilt, shame, embarrassment, self-loathing, and past trauma, it is easy to focus too much on what is seen on the surface and be drawn into anger and despair. It is indeed a challenge to develop an approach that will enlist cooperation from the client. It is a greater challenge to do this in such a way that the client is not allowed to skirt through treatment without taking responsibility for his behavior and really doing the work. We *are* calling on these young people to perform some rather difficult tasks, but they must learn to alter their thoughts and behavior if they expect to refrain from hurting others in the future.

An additional challenge is to understand the sometimes very complex dynamics that underlie why people engage in sexually offending behavior. One must understand both sex-offending dynamics in general and the particular characteristics of a given youth to comprehend why he did what he did and how he can prevent similar behavior in the future. For an introduction to the dynamics of sexual offending, please see On the Dynamics of Sexual Offending, located in Appendix D.

The final challenge of working with the sexually abusive adolescent is the liability involved. These adolescents *are* potentially dangerous to others. Risks include their victimizing staff or fellow clients, and, perhaps even more frightening, they may offend someone in the community while in our care. At discharge, the funding source will expect the program to offer some assurance that the risk of reoffense has been reduced by treatment. What does the program need to know about the client to offer such assurances? What sort of ramifications can come back to haunt a program in which a client has sexually acted out? What are the consequences for a program if a treated youth reoffends? How do you recover from such a situation? We will explore these questions in more depth in Chapter 4 when we look at program liability issues.

Conflicts Between and Within Persons— The Somewhat Hidden Challenge

This category can be divided into two general classes: (1) intrapersonal challenges and (2) interpersonal challenges. These are conflicts that arise between and within persons. Each class has its own set of challenges for workers.

Intrapersonal

1. Workers must cope with their perceptions of sex offenders and sex offending and the feelings that arise when discussing sexually abusive clients or being in contact with them.
2. Workers need to process the internal repulsion, or attraction, connected to abuse perpetrators that stems from their own unresolved issues or biases. This is especially the case when workers are themselves victims (or even perpetrators).

3. Workers have to deal with the stresses of the difficult relationship issues that arise while working with this population, as well as the stress from dealing with the often difficult and dysfunctional families of perpetrators.

4. Workers burn out due to the negative effects of failing to attend to self-care issues.

5. Workers must cope with and effectively process continuous exposure to sexually stimulating and sexually abusive stories and materials.

6. Workers have to accept the internal conflicts that arise when reporting new disclosures to the authorities, potentially jeopardizing their relationships with clients, as well as the feelings associated with having to talk to the adolescents' families after such action has been taken.

7. Workers need to guard against adopting the same thinking errors clients use to minimize the significance of their thoughts and behaviors to reduce internal stress and conflict.

Interpersonal

1. Conflicts and disputes arise between workers (or between various departments in the program) due to ideological/theoretical differences.

2. Problems occur between people due to the conflicts going on within individuals, which they are acting out in their relationships with others.

3. Conflicts arise between persons with differing views of the potential of the clients to act out sexually, which can also make maintaining a safe environment for staff and clients more difficult.

4. Difficulties occur when some persons in the treatment environment, due to their own issues or due to a certain laxness, want to "let things slide" rather than address certain behaviors. Other problems may arise because staff believe some of the myths concerning sex offenders.

5. Challenges arise because certain staff are not responsive to supervision and/or they do not agree with the treatment approach and therefore do not support it.

6. Frustrations surface when people do not follow through with their responsibilities or with what they said they would do.

7. Challenges arise when new staff enter the program and need to be trained.

These are only partial lists, and the reader could easily expand upon them. The point is that we must be aware of the various intrapersonal and interpersonal challenges present in this work, and we must examine ourselves and our programs to determine if we are properly dealing with these challenges. Any such discussion should include consideration of specialized training for clinicians, direct care staff, teachers, and administrators. The presence of these challenges also highlights the need for good supervision (individual and group) by those who can help workers to cope and remain healthy and effective. Two publications relating to this area may be helpful: *The Difficult Connection* (Blanchard, 1998) and *Impact: Working with Sexual Abusers* (Edmunds, 1997).

A System Stretched to Its Limits and Pulled in Many Directions— The Bigger Challenge

How the larger systems in which we operate are set up and function can produce even more challenges. Frequently, in working with a single client, one must deal with several state and county systems that may have contradictory purposes and different rationales. In some cases, these separate agencies might not work too well together. The social service agency, the juvenile justice division, the probation department, the mental health system, and the police may all be involved with the youth, perhaps with contradictory effects.

The author has known many young people who were clients of more than one state or county department at the same time. This can cause conflict as well as frustrations, especially when, even with this combination of services, there is an inability (due to lack of funding or resources) to find appropriate services. One such case involved a mentally ill orphaned youth committed to the Department of Youth Services for delinquencies. Each meeting held regarding him required the presence of his Department of Social Services social worker, his Department of Youth Services caseworker, and his Department of Mental Health case-manager. When the time came for locating and funding an aftercare placement, the combined scramble by the workers to offer suggestions created a stressful and difficult process for the workers and the client, particularly because the various departments had somewhat differing ideas of what the next step should be. Problems arose in finding a program that could continue the work done to this point, while providing the needed level of intensity. The agents of all three departments had difficulty locating a program, not only due to the special needs of this youth, but because gaps existed in the continuum of care.

The lack of both a truly complete continuum of care and continuity of approach to treatment can make the search for the "logical" next step exasperating. Sometimes a group home simply is not available, or no outpatient therapist within 100 miles will work with a sexually abusive youth, or residential treatment is too expensive and only a limited number of slots can be accessed. Even if an appropriate level of treatment is located, differences in treatment approach and a lack of communication among providers in the various programs can leave the client feeling as if he is starting over, rather than moving on in his treatment.

Turf wars between systems can cause challenges as well. Whether the systems in question are state and county agencies or secure, residential, and outpatient treatment programs, these battles not only can be challenging and stressful, but they may not be in the best interest of the client or community. We as providers must recognize that although we become invested in a client—and this is good—he is not "ours" in a possessive sense. We must realize that although we may believe our program to be the best, having *the* most optimal strategy for treatment, this is a closed-minded attitude that places barriers to cooperation between agencies and programs. A spirit of cooperation must be present.

In many states the systems that treat adolescents who sexually abuse are overloaded and lack adequate funding and resources. This situation can be even more frustrating when an appropriate program does exist, but the problem is funding for a given youth or an excessively long waiting list. If we could cooperate on all levels in these larger systems, perhaps we could produce more ideal treatment conditions that would demonstrate a level of treatment effectiveness to justify an increase in funding. We have done well with what we have, but we must always ask if we can do better.

A Troubled and Troubling Society—The Ultimate Challenge

Another challenge concerns the impact of our society upon young people. Many believe we live in troubled times, and many blanch at how openly sexual material is displayed. We live in a society that prizes sexual behavior and conquest among its young men, often using such activity as a criterion by which to judge the "manliness" of its boys. The mass media, from movies to television to popular music, often feature references to (if not actual footage of) sexually explicit acts, many of these being representations of unhealthy and/or abusive sexual behavior. If this was not enough, the Internet now provides a new and powerful venue for persons to promote any sort of deviant sexual behavior they please.

The result of all this is that our children are constantly receiving a variety of conflicting messages concerning what is appropriate sexual behavior and how to express one's sexuality in a healthy manner. Young people in treatment will hold many deviant views of sexuality, inculcated by a society that in many ways promotes sexual misconduct. This makes teaching adolescents appropriate means of sexual expression that they will continue to use very difficult.

The person who is aware of all these challenges will work to limit conditions that produce unnecessary difficulties and will endeavor to provide the best and most effective treatment possible. Challenges are obstacles, but they are not insurmountable.

Chapter 2

Treatment Within a Continuum of Care

TIERS IN A CONTINUUM OF CARE

In his monograph *A Comprehensive Service-Delivery System with a Continuum of Care for Adolescent Sexual Offenders,* Bengis (1986) explains in detail the need for a comprehensive continuum of specialized care for adolescent sexual abuse perpetrators:

> [S]pecialized diagnostic assessments and treatment services are the prerequisites for successful work with adolescent sexual offenders. For these approaches to be truly effective, however, they must be implemented across a carefully constructed service delivery system with a continuum of care that guarantees both a range of residential and outpatient alternatives, and a consistency of approach across the treatment continuum. (p. 15)

In this view, (1) an effective continuum must possess a full range of program options, (2) these options must be specialized to work with this population, and (3) all options should utilize a consistent treatment approach.

Although not present in all areas at this time, a full range of treatment options must be developed in every locality. State and county agencies working together with various treatment providers and human service agencies have a responsibility to develop a variety of program types to ensure effective treatment for sexually abusing adolescents at all levels.

Once a full range of program options has been identified, the next logical step is to ensure that these programs utilize the specialized assessment and treatment approaches that have been found, through clinical experience and research, to be effective with this population. The last requirement of an effective continuum is the most difficult to achieve. How can we get various independent treatment providers to utilize a consistent approach? Perhaps if we bring providers together into a unified system of offense-specific treatment, they can work with one another to develop approaches that are consistent between programs. The value of such consistency is clear when one considers the difficulty some residents have in adjusting to changes in treatment approach in new placements. Some examples may help to illustrate this.

The author recalls having two residents enter a residential program from two different secure treatment facilities. Each was eager to show to his therapist the work he had done in his previous placement. Each previous program used a cycle or pattern of abuse model that differed from the one used in the residential program. Both clients wished that the model they were familiar with could be adopted in the new program, so that they could more easily continue their work. This was not possible because six other residents were already quite accustomed to the program's current model. One of the two new residents (John) was motivated and worked to translate the knowledge he gained previously into the new model. The other (Bill) was less motivated and used the inconsistency as a reason to complain about the program and to discount the value of his past treatment (since he believed he would have to "start all over again").

In another example, a youth (James) had attended a pretreatment group for several months while in a preplacement detention center. One of the group facilitators was also a facilitator of the group in the residential program he was to attend. The pretreatment group used the same model as the residential one and was designed to begin treatment while preparing clients to work in the given model. When James entered the residential program, he had one immediate connection, the common therapist, and he was presented with a model and terminology and jargon that were familiar to him. His clinical transition was by far much smoother than Bill's, or even John's. In a related example, an outpatient group at a clinic in a city followed the same treatment model as a nearby residential program. The providers in both programs maintained close contact with one another (in fact, one of the residential clinicians did fee-for-service work at the clinic). Adolescents sent to this clinic had a smoother transition than those sent elsewhere.

It is indeed difficult to establish a network of providers which uses a consistent approach and which provides programs of treatment designed to link and overlap with both previous and subsequent treatment environments. There is also the concern of establishing such consistency without constricting the field and thus causing a stagnation in the development of better strategies. Even considering these potential obstacles, the establishment of consistent approaches and interconnection of services should be the goal of an ideal continuum of care. Bengis (1986) continues:

> Consistency of approach and predictability, central elements in the treatment of these clients, can only be guaranteed when service providers at all levels of the service delivery system are committed to confronting the problems of adolescent sexual offenders in an identical manner. (p. 17)

Each regional, county, and state group needs to establish within its area as high a quality continuum of care as can be developed, and to present as many creative solutions as possible to work toward ideals that will maximize the treatment effectiveness of a given network.

Levels of Treatment Within a Continuum of Care

The continuum of care has several principal levels of treatment, typically categorized by the level of structure and security in the program, the intensity of treatment, and the level of contact with persons outside the program. Figure 2.1 presents a diagram of possible program options and pathways of progression through the continuum. The following descriptions differentiate one level and program type from another. For additional discussion of these levels, see Bengis (1986) and Perry and Orchard (1992).

The reader may note that not all possible program models are depicted in this continuum diagram. The environments listed were selected because they are the most appropriate to a discussion of the treatment of adolescents who commit sexual offenses.

FIGURE 2.1. Levels of Care in a Care Continuum for Youth Who Sexually Abuse

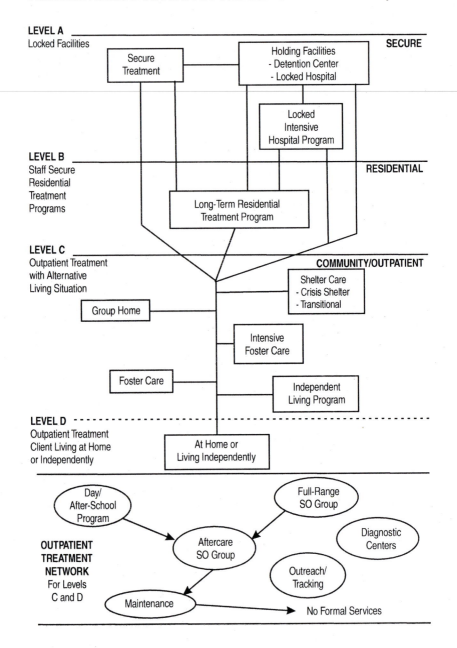

Locked Facilities (Level A)

Level A programs are of two general types: holding facilities and treatment centers. The holding facility category includes detention centers, which are juvenile justice facilities that do not conduct intensive treatment because the clients are usually placed there temporarily, and locked psychiatric hospital units, which are designed for stabilization and protective containment, but not long-term treatment, due to the nature and length of the clients' stays. Other programs in this level generally provide a course of treatment during the client's stay.

"Secure treatment" or "closed custody" programs are juvenile correctional facilities designed to provide intensive treatment services. They generally employ high staff-to-resident ratios, are quite structured, and have "hardware" designed to prevent client flight (e.g., locked doors, fences around yards, etc.). In these facilities, the youth is truly incarcerated and typically is quite restricted in his contact with the outside world. Characteristic features include high visual supervision, residents locked in bedrooms at night, and in-house school and therapy.

Locked intensive psychiatric hospital units are dedicated for long-term treatment but typically do not have the same level of facility hardware as their juvenile correctional counterparts. However, they still do use high levels of supervision and rigorous programs of clinical treatment, although the delivery of this treatment may differ somewhat from that provided in the juvenile justice secure treatment facilities. Some social service or child protective systems may not have direct access to locked facilities at all and will only be able to access them through their clients' involvement with the mental health or juvenile justice systems.

When the author refers in this book to a secure treatment program, he means any locked treatment program that intakes clients for an extended period of time for treatment, be they juvenile correctional facilities or psychiatric hospital units.

Staff Secure Residential Treatment Programs (Level B)

These programs are lacking the containment and facility hardware of secure programs yet they are generally quite intensive in their treatment, and utilize combinations of individual, group, family, and milieu therapy. Although they may vary significantly in theoretical approach and in treatment delivery, they are all designed to have residents living within a controlled setting for an extended period of time. They are also equipped to provide residents with increasing opportunities for contact with the community, in preparation for release from the structured environment of the program.

Two distinctions can be made regarding offense-specific residential programs. The first is between residences that treat only sexually abusive youth and those which have a mixed population of offenders and other troubled youth. As is discussed in Chapter 4, an ongoing debate rages as to which of these is the best arrangement. Those who are planning to establish or modify a program will want to take this distinction into careful consideration.

The second distinction is especially important for residential settings. Some residential programs have an in-house offense-specific treatment regime, and some send their residents to a community-based group or contract for someone to run such a group in-house. The programs with an in-house treatment regime have distinct advantages over those which use outside treatment. These programs provide a more intensive environment for the treatment of sex-offending behavior, they have potentially higher levels of treatment consistency, and the presence of offense-specific treatment staff can enhance safety, increase the efficacy of therapy, and reduce sexual acting out.

Alternative Living Situations (Level C)

Clients on this level need more supervision, containment, structure, support, and services than those who would be sent home to live or who would be living independently, yet they do not require the intensity of a residential program. Clients in these alternative living situations would generally be enrolled in outpatient groups and/or day programs at a local mental health clinic for their sex offense-specific treatment. Adolescents placed in alternative living situations are typically judged as relatively low risk to reoffend (when compared to their level A and B counterparts), but they are not yet ready to enter a less structured living environment. Indeed, to move them to a less restrictive environment would generally increase the risk for reoffense. The goal would be to use the alternative living situation to prepare the client for transition to home or independent living by helping him to acquire skills in the areas in which he is still deficient. This setting also helps ensure that the client's life is structured in such a manner that he can better follow relapse prevention plans, maintain a positive and healthy range of activities, and hopefully avoid further incidents of acting out or offending.

These environments offer clients many opportunities to be in contact with the community, while ensuring that the client is monitored in his living situation. Problematic behaviors are noted and reported to the outpatient treatment center for processing in therapy, and if the client appears to be decompensating and is becoming unmanageable, he can be referred to a more restrictive setting, or a higher level in the continuum of care. The two principal options used on this level are group homes and foster care.

Group homes generally provide structure through a group living environment facilitated by professional and/or paraprofessional staff members. Although clients typically go to school in the community and to outpatient therapy, group homes do provide significant supervision, advocacy, and tracking. These programs employ milieu treatment approaches, program groups, and other treatment measures, although in many cases at a lower intensity than in a residential program. Stays are typically short term but can be longer, and the goal remains to prepare the client to move to a less structured living situation as safely as possible.

Foster care is a potentially problematic living option for sex offenders. Many times foster care is utilized for the client who does not require the structure of a group home but cannot return home and/or may be too young or too immature to live on his own. The tricky part of these settings arises from the following serious concerns:

1. Foster parents are generally not as well trained as professional staff and may lack some of the insight into offending and methods of dealing with various behaviors.
2. The parents live day in and day out with the youth (not on eight-hour shifts) and can get too close to recognize the danger signs, as well as being prone to tiring out easily.
3. Foster parents are not generally provided with the backup and resources that a group home has.
4. There is much less structure in a foster home for those who need such structure.
5. Some agencies are not as careful as they should be when placing other children in foster homes with a sexually abusive youth, or with how much they tell the foster parents about the offender, thus increasing the possibility of reoffense.
6. Some foster parents are more concerned with the financial gains of being a foster parent and are not invested in providing ade-

quate levels of supervision or attention to the youth in their care. The result is that these children can feel uncared for and have more freedom to act out.

7. The presence of foster parents' biological/adopted children in the home can further complicate an already complex living situation, especially if these children are victims or perpetrators of sexual abuse themselves.

That being said, many agencies *do* provide excellent foster care programs in which dedicated parents are well trained. Some have support staff who regularly visit the foster homes to assist the parents, provide case managers to assist in community adjustment and school issues, and schedule regular group activities to add more structure and enhance the agency's ability to assess the youth. Clearly these types of programs are preferable for sexually abusive youth.

It should go without saying that foster parents who accept sex offense perpetrators must be (1) properly trained to deal with these clients, and (2) aware that a given youth is a sexual abuser. This last point may seem so obvious as to need no mention; however, until recently in certain localities, the Department of Social Services was not required to inform foster parents of a youth's status as a sex offender. Thanks to the dedicated work of many people a law is now in place requiring such disclosures.

Shelters, or transitional care settings are generally for clients awaiting placement in a program or for those removed from a more open placement in the community. These settings, similar to their locked counterparts, generally provide minimal clinical services due to the nature of the clients' stay. Independent living programs (or transition to independent living programs) typically have very little structure and supervision. They are for youth who are on the verge of living on their own, or for those moving to the next level in the continuum of care.

At Home or Living Independently (Level D)

The final goal following any out-of-home placement is for the client either to return to living at home with his family (or some other approved relative/guardian/adult) or to live independently (if he is of an appropriate age and possesses the necessary level of maturity). In such a case, the client is fully transitioned into the community.

However, many clients will not require out-of-home placements for treatment (or may need such placements only during assessment). As such, these clients essentially enter the continuum on level D. The hope is that they can remain at this level and need not be moved up the continuum to a more restrictive setting.

Clients at this level, as with the clients in level C, will receive their offense-specific treatment from an outpatient provider. Supportive services may come from a variety of sources, such as an informal support network (e.g., Big Brothers/Big Sisters programs), outreach and tracking programs, and other assistance provided by community and social service agencies.

It is important that clients at this level complete their course of treatment as prescribed by the outpatient provider, and that they recognize the possibility that they may need to reenter treatment after leaving formal services, if the need arises.

The Outpatient Treatment Network

As stated earlier, clients in levels C and D living situations will need to be enrolled in outpatient treatment. Outpatient programs are usually run out of clinics and consist of specialized treatment groups, individual and family therapy, and referral and advocacy services. The options available range from clinics running sex offender groups to those which provide structured day programs with many treatment and educational functions. These outpatient treatment options and the lines of progression through the outpatient network, indicated in Figure 2.1, are discussed in more detail in Chapter 5.

The day and after-school programs provide more extensive services than an offense-specific group alone, as well as increased clinical opportunities to impact the youth. These programs provide intervention components such as other groups, activities for socialization training, recreation, family groups, and other outpatient services in addition to the SO group.

Sex offense-specific groups run by an outpatient clinic should be of two general categories: Type (A) groups would be for those clients who, after diagnostic assessment, are entering the continuum of care at one of the two community/outpatient levels of service. These clients, having been deemed safe enough to begin their treatment while living in the community, would then progress through a comprehensive outpatient treatment program. Ideally, those in alternative living situations would be able to remain with the same clinic as they step down through the continuum to home or independent living.

Type (B) groups would be for those clients who are in the last stages of the outpatient program and for those returning to the community from residential or secure placements. These "aftercare" groups would serve as a stepping stone from more intensive therapy (e.g., day programs, outpatient groups, residential/secure programs) to maintenance treatment and eventual discharge from formal services. Using aftercare groups keeps clients with one to two years of prior intensive treatment from being placed in groups with clients who are just beginning treatment. Such groups do not need to deal with the basics of offense-specific treatment and offending dynamics, focusing instead on relapse prevention strategies and their application.

Diagnostic Centers

These centers may be run by outpatient clinics as part of their offense-specific complement, operated by state agencies, or included as part of a private or group practice. The point is to provide resources in the community to assess and evaluate adolescents as they are referred for entry into the continuum, and as they are moved through the various levels of the continuum.

In practical application, clients who are identified as possible sexual offenders would first be referred for a specialized assessment performed through a diagnostic center by a specially trained practitioner. This assessment may take place in a clinic, home, shelter, or detention center (depending on the client's requirements for security and where he has been placed). This assessment guides the case management team in determining (1) what type of inappropriate behavior has occurred, (2) if the youth requires specialized treatment and, if so, what type of treatment is appropriate, and (3) at what point in the treatment continuum he would enter. Generally, when a change in placement is anticipated or after an extended stay in one placement, the client would again be assessed by the diagnostic center to determine the appropriateness of the planned move to the next step on the continuum and to offer suggestions for future treatment. There is also the possibility of clients moving up the continuum if the assessment indicates a need for a more structured setting.

A PROPOSED SCOPE FOR TREATMENT

For the purposes of this discussion, it is necessary to divide the continuum of care into three main treatment categories. Referring to Figure 2.1, the reader will note the divisions between the Secure, Residential, and Community/Outpatient categories along the right side. A full understanding of the scope of treatment lies in the distinctions between the different treatments provided by each of these three categories. Considerable treatment overlap exists between these categories, with the principal differences being (1) what is covered in the course of treatment by each type of program, (2) where the principal focus of therapy is for each category, and (3) how and to what extent the different areas of treatment are addressed.

Phases of Treatment

The phases of sex offense-specific treatment are steps within the general scope of treatment that represent the changing treatment focus as the client moves from initial entrance into therapy to the successful completion of that therapy (regardless of how many programs on the continuum were involved in the process). Figure 2.2 illustrates the general phases of treatment for sexually abusive adolescents and the typical domains covered by each of the three main categories and an outpatient aftercare group. This scheme draws on Lundrigan (1996a), Barbaree and Cortoni (1993), and a document of unknown authorship listing the phases of sex offender treatment. What follows is a more detailed breakdown of each phase.

Pretreatment

1. Move past denial that the offenses happened.
2. Address minimization of the offense.
3. Cease to blame the victim for the offense.
4. Agree to participate in treatment.

22

FIGURE 2.2. General Scope of Treatment for Various Provider Levels

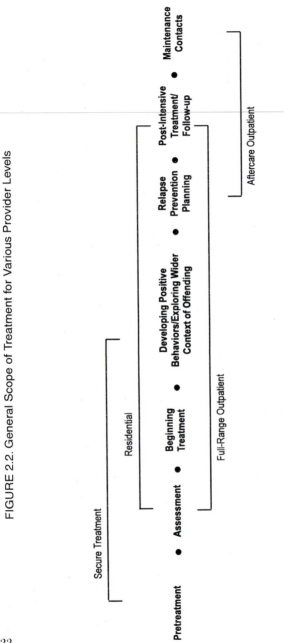

Assessment

1. Disclose offenses to therapist/evaluator.
2. Participate in exploration of deviant thought patterns.
3. Explore range of offending behaviors and other critical issues.
4. Develop an attitude of cooperation with treatment efforts.
5. Engage in the process of preliminary education.
6. Develop a treatment plan.

Beginning Treatment/Understanding Sexual Assault Cycle

1. Begin group treatment; disclose offenses to group.
2. Work to take genuine responsibility for offenses.
3. Develop understanding of own assault cycle.
4. Address own victimization in the context of offense-specific work.
5. Enhance healthy sexuality, increase sexual knowledge, and explore concepts of male and female roles.
6. Work to eliminate cognitive distortions.
7. Begin to see how the cycle affects everyday life.

Developing Positive Behaviors/Exploring the Wider Context of Offending

1. Increase quality of social skills and interactions.
2. Develop more prosocial means of relating to others and getting needs met.
3. Enhance communication skills.
4. Learn to recognize, identify, and express feelings.
5. Learn to be assertive without being aggressive.
6. Explore family dynamics and own role in family.
7. Develop empathy for victims and others.
8. Work on anger and impulse control skills.
9. Explore nonsexual precipitants to own offending.
10. Explore the role and function of fantasy and work to modify deviant fantasy.
11. Learn about and deepen understanding of grooming, maintenance, coercion/force, and preoffense patterns.
12. Begin family and victim reconciliation work.

Relapse Prevention Planning

1. Consolidate work done to date.
2. Develop a relapse prevention plan (RPP).
   a. Internal/self-management strategies
   b. External supervision and boundaries (avoiding/escaping)
   c. Positive behaviors and activities
   d. Plans to deal with various emotions and situations
3. Identify a support network after treatment.
4. Identify the next treatment provider.
5. Share the RPP with all concerned parties.
6. Involve the family in this process.

Post-Intensive Treatment/Follow-up

1. Follow the RPP and read regularly.
2. Make planned follow-up contact with most recent program.
3. Recognize availability of last therapist for emergency communication.
4. Continue in aftercare treatment as planned.
5. Participate in monitoring and ongoing assessment.

Maintenance

1. Utilize spaced contacts or "booster sessions" as needed.
2. Recognize availability of last therapist for emergency communication.

An Illustrative Case Example

A clinical example may help to illustrate the overlap and the differences in treatment focus possible at the various levels of the continuum. Tim is a fifteen-year-old adolescent sexual abuse perpetrator who is in denial and resistant to the idea of treatment. His multi-problem presentation, aggressiveness, sexually provocative behavior, risk for running, and multiple victim profile indicate the need for secure treatment. It is recognized that he will need to "step down" to a residential program for continued work on his issues before he will be ready to return home. The secure program would likely begin with pretreatment to bring Tim to a point at which he could begin formal treatment. After this, the program would proceed to work on the tasks in the beginning phase of treatment, moving on to introducing Tim to the more detailed work of the next phase before transitioning him to a residential program. Before and after such a transition, ideally, providers in the secure and residential programs would share information and records to aid the residential treatment planning. In addition, the two staffs could hold a transitional meeting, and Tim could visit the residential program.

The residential program would reinforce the beginning work done in secure treatment, but it would delve more deeply into the next phase of treatment by examining the more subtle aspects of Tim's offending, including work on many of his collateral issues. Some of these issues may include: difficulty in communicating his feelings, problems in socially engaging others, lack of vocational skills, poor time management, lack of self-esteem, etc. In Tim's case, the main focus of the residential program would be on the exploration of this wider context of offending and the development of positive behaviors (which would include extensive family work and work on the many nonsexual issues with which Tim presents). The program's focus would switch to relapse prevention planning at an appropriate point, in preparation for Tim to receive extended home passes, and in anticipation of Tim's eventual release from a staff secure setting to a placement in the community.

Prior to being transitioned to the community, Tim might begin work with his next therapist. Certainly the residential and outpatient clinicians should have shared information and records by this point, so that the outpatient provider is aware of all that has been learned about Tim throughout the entire course of secure and residential treatment. It is also possible that the residential program would collaborate with the outpatient provider in aftercare follow-up services to provide extra support through the difficult first months following release to the community. The outpatient provider would reinforce all that the client has done in previous treatment and would likely provide support and therapy to family members as they cope with reintegrating Tim into the home. The outpatient treatment in this case would likely focus on the application of relapse prevention and self-management strategies to everyday living in preparation for Tim's transition out of formal therapy.

There are many variations on this scenario (e.g., a client who enters secure treatment who will return home and bypass residential, or a client who is entering a residential placement without prior treatment who will be going to a foster home with a day program, etc.). Different variations will have different treatment plans for adolescents, and perhaps different foci for the programs on the various tiers of the continuum. Each program will vary somewhat with each unique situation. In the end, each program must assess client needs to determine what role that program will play in helping the client progress through the phases of treatment and toward the goal of safe and healthy living on level D.

PART II:
TREATMENT PROGRAMS

Chapter 3

Elements of a Treatment Program for Youth Who Sexually Abuse

SEX OFFENSE-SPECIFIC VERSUS UNI-MODAL VERSUS MULTI-MODAL TREATMENT

To discuss what is meant by the multi-component model of sex offense-specific treatment, and prior to a closer examination of sex offense-specific treatment programs, it is necessary to examine briefly the concepts of sex offense-specific treatment and uni-modal and multi-modal treatment methodologies. Although the distinctions are simple ones, and many will be readily aware of the differences, it is important to review these concepts to help remove misconceptions.

Sex Offense-Specific Treatment

Treatment is sex offense-specific not because it is treatment given to sex offenders but because it is treatment that is informed by, and conforms to, the large body of literature on the effective treatment of those who commit sexual offenses. The adolescent who commits sexual offenses tends to be different from other young delinquents (Perry and Orchard, 1992), and the types of treatment that work best with this population must likewise be different (cf. Heinz, Ryan, and Bengis, 1991; Ryan and Lane, 1998).

Traditional methods of psychotherapy are at times not effective with sexually abusive persons and other such special populations. Ross (1994) believes that to do offense-specific therapy, one must break with traditional therapy. He also cites research showing that ineffective psychotherapy can make the sex-offending problem worse (see also Prendergast, 1991). Table 3.1 is a comparison of the differences between sex offense-specific and traditional therapy, of anonymous authorship. Although this cannot be taken as a definitive or all-encompassing list, it does illustrate that a specific approach is required with this population. Just going on "gut feelings" and "traditional wisdom" (which in many cases is influenced by inaccurate societal concepts of sex offending and the people who commit sex offenses) is not adequate. The assistance of experienced persons with relevant training and credentials is vital for program design and improvement and for ongoing supervision of staff and clinicians.

Sex offense-specific treatment can be delivered by means of various treatment modalities. Most common are sex offense-specific group, individual, and family therapy. In addition, a variety of other treatment modes can be geared specifically to adolescents who abuse and their families (e.g., milieu treatment, aftercare services, educational groups, etc.). Some programs treat those who commit sex offenses by employing a single treatment modality to address the offending issue; others use a variety of treatment approaches to address the issue from various angles.

TABLE 3.1. Comparison of Traditional and Sex Offense-Specific Therapy

Traditional	Sex Offense-Specific
• Patient not responsible for behavior	• Patient is responsible for behavior
• Supportive	• Confrontative/challenging
• Trust patient	• Do not trust patient
• Believe patient	• Expect patient to lie, minimize, and justify
• Allow patient to set agenda	• Therapist sets agenda
• Follow patient's values	• Therapist imposes values
• Work to alleviate guilt	• Work to induce guilt
• Patient welfare is first concern	• Public safety is first concern
• Complete confidentiality	• Limited confidentiality
• Goal is to remove negative feelings from behavior	• Goal is to induce negative feelings surrounding behavior to motivate change
• Concern is how patient feels	• Concern is how patient acts
• Patient is accountable to self	• Patient is accountable to society

Source: Cusack, 1994.

Uni-Modal and Multi-Modal Treatment

References to a uni-modal method of treatment in this book indicate treatment using a single *sex offense-specific* clinical intervention. For example, the following are uni-modal treatment situations: a client who is placed in the community and who is attending a sex offense-specific group (the most common modality); a youth in a residential program who is sent to a clinic for a sex offense-specific group; and a youth in a group home or residential program who attends an on-site sex offense-specific group (and not other interventions).

The general consensus, however, is that such uni-modal approaches may be less than optimal (cf. Marshall and Pithers, 1994; Borduin et al., 1990). This is especially the case with adolescents who have a variety of developmental needs that must be addressed concurrently with, and as a part of, their sex offense-specific treatment (cf. Cellini, 1995). A program treating adolescents who sexually abuse must develop a wide approach to address the many areas that must be targeted for effective treatment to take place. We must look to treat the client in his entirety and not simply target "the problem."

In contrast to the uni-modal approach is the multi-modal methodology, which involves the use of several different *sex offense-specific* treatment interventions at the same time. Examples are a youth in a residential program who participates in a sex offense-specific group, individual therapy with a trained specialist, and family therapy, and an adult in a day program at a clinic who attends sex offense-specific group and individual therapy, and who participates in social skills training groups and sexuality education. For the purposes of clarification, we can divide multi-modal treatment into two general types: proliferation of services and the multi-component model.

First, multi-modal treatment conceptualized as a proliferation of services to the client that is a common approach involves case managers sincerely attempting to provide all the services they can to address a complex clinical problem. The idea is that by providing the client with several varied types of sex offense-specific services his chances for success will increase. Although this premise is correct, often in this approach, the client ends up receiving services from several different persons, sometimes at several different facilities, when he needs continuity, accountability, and stability.

Consider the case of the youth in a residential program who attends sex offense-specific groups at the local mental health clinic. He receives family therapy from a social worker at his program and sex of-fense-specific individual therapy from a therapist at the clinic (not one of his group leaders). The program aims at providing interventions to address collateral issues, and a sexuality, dating, and relationships group is run once a week by the staff in the program. While this youth is receiving a good variety of services, coordinating these services is a monumental task. In the author's experience in such situations, the dif-ferent providers are likely to have difficulty maintaining adequate con-tact among themselves to engage in a maximally coordinated treatment effort. The result is that the client (who may be all too quick to monop-olize on the inconsistencies of the situation) may fall through the cracks in some areas. It is also likely that the various service providers will have differing theoretical orientations, use different jargon, and perhaps employ different models of treatment. All this combined cre-ates confusion, lack of organization, and discouragement for the client. This is not to say that treatment delivered in this manner will not be ef-fective; indeed, in most cases, this may be the best option available. For the more difficult and/or serious offenders, however, the problems of not having the highest possible continuity and adequate communica-tion can be extremely significant.

In the second type of approach, the multi-component model, the various modes of treatment are linked and use a common treatment staff, common theoretical models, and common jargon. Many secure programs (which do not permit residents outside for treatment) have necessarily developed this form of treatment. Also, some residential programs and even outpatient clinics provide a full range of treatment modes that are unified as part of a coordinated treatment effort.

THE MULTI-COMPONENT MODEL

The multi-component model is an effort to maximize the range of ser-vices provided to the client, while allowing for the highest possible level of continuity and coordination among these various services. The term multi-component was selected to convey the idea of one single treatment program with organically united parts, or components. These compo-nents function much like the various organs in the human body, unable to stand alone or function as effectively without the presence and inter-action of all components.

Such a multi-component model must address a wide range of goals. Table 3.2 presents a scheme by Casella (1990) that lists the goals of a comprehensive program for adolescents who commit sexual offenses. As we explore the various components of the multi-component model, it should become clear how these goals are designed to be met as clients progress through the phases of treatment.

The interplay between the various components can be likened to a group of people on the beach who are passing two or three beach balls among themselves, trying not to let the balls hit the ground. They must all work together to accomplish their common goal, and each must have some degree of awareness of the position and strength of the others. This awareness of the others also means remaining somewhat vigilant of the movement of the balls, being ready for a pass from another player. This task is made more complex if we envision this game as a relay race in which the group of players must attend to keeping the balls aloft while they move along the beach toward a finish line, sometimes passing off the balls to another group farther down the beach.

TABLE 3.2. Casella's Goals of a Comprehensive Program

- The program should include a complete, individualized assessment and treatment plan.
- The treatment should assist the offender to
  — accept responsibility for his offenses; and
  — understand and be aware of his patterns of offending (e.g., sequence of thoughts, feelings, events, circumstances, and arousal stimuli).
- The treatment should assist the offender to
  — learn to intervene in or break into his offense pattern; and
  — call upon tools, methods, and procedures to suppress, control, manage, or stop the behavior.
- The treatment should provide reeducation and resocialization to
  — replace antisocial thoughts and behaviors with prosocial ones;
  — acquire a positive self-concept and new attitudes and expectations of himself; and
  — learn new social and sexual skills to help cultivate healthy relationships.
- In residential treatment, an offender needs a prolonged period to safely test his newly acquired insights and control mechanisms in the community.
- Each offender needs a posttreatment support group and continued postrelease access to therapeutic treatment.

Source: Casella, 1990.

Notice that the more people involved in the game, the easier it is to keep the balls aloft. Two or three can do it, but they have to work harder and be more agile.

This analogy sheds light on the operation of the multi-component model if we conceptualize the balls as the major treatment areas that are being addressed by the program and the whole constellation of balls as the client himself. Each of the players is like a different component in the program waiting for the time when the work on a particular issue will fall into his arena. When it does, each player will impact upon it and then send it off for further work by another component. With good communication and coordination the same treatment issues will become areas of focus for different components at different times, each component adding a little more to the work done each time it impacts that issue. The cumulative effect of these interventions is that the client can be moved, much the same way that our beach ball game (which represents the client in interaction with a given treatment provider) moves its way down the length of the beach as it is played).

The time will come when this game will encounter another group of players farther down the beach (representing a future service provider). The first group will carefully pass the constellation of balls on to the other group who will then assume the task of continuing the journey down the beach. This passing of balls is a process that is tricky and may require the work of both programs for a period of time to ensure that the transfer is done properly. Once successfully transferred, the first group can disengage its involvement and allow the client to move on with a new group to assist him. All these groups (i.e., different service providers) work together as a larger team with the ultimate goal of assisting the client to cross the "finish line" into an abuse-free lifestyle. Although this analogy inaccurately presents the client as essentially a passive entity being acted upon by the program (not the view of the author at all), it does give some sense of the dynamic nature of the multi-component model within a program and between programs.

What Components Can Be Included?

Many possible components of treatment may be used in any given treatment program. These components are the building blocks of the multi-component model. The most widely used components are the following:

1. *Sex offense-specific group:* a standard in the treatment of this population
2. *Family therapy education:* very important for adolescents in treatment
3. *Individual therapy:* has many important functions when used in conjunction with group therapy
4. *Adjunct/therapy treatment:* addresses wider issues and treats the whole person
5. *Milieu treatment:* an essential component for group care programs dealing with a treatment environment
6. *Assessment and treatment planning*: a component ensuring quality treatment

Two additional components encapsulate treatment and represent "bookends" to the client's involvement with a given program:

7. *Pretreatment:* prepares clients to engage in treatment (usually only needed in the first intervention setting with clients who are not yet ready to enter full-scale treatment)
8. *Aftercare/follow-up:* bridges the gap between programs on the continuum and ensures adequate supports for clients transitioning to their next setting to enable success

Two final components support the work of others:

9. *Staff training:* gives the staff needed tools to work with the adolescents
10. *General resident education:* assists group care programs with a mixed population to create a healthy, tolerant, safe milieu

Secure treatment, hospital, and residential programs (which ideally would have in-house SO treatment) should be able to include most, if not all, of these components in their treatment regimes. Day programs may have less ability to offer all the components, but they still are able to create a therapeutic milieu, and they should try to augment treatment with as many components as possible.

Full-range outpatient SO treatment programs (lacking a milieu and often having only clinical staff) would clearly not be using several of the components. However, they should try to incorporate at least assessment, SO group, family treatment, individual therapy, adjunctive treatment, and aftercare components into their program.

Integration of the Various Components

To this point we have considered the various components that can make up a comprehensive treatment program for adolescents who sexually offend. Chapters 7 through 16 discuss each component in depth, but it is important to understand at the outset how these components can influence one another.

Figure 3.1 presents a conceptual diagram of the multi-component model. The outermost oval represents the comprehensive program. Within it are contained the central treatment components under the direct influence of the assessment and treatment planning component aspect of the program. The ongoing assessment and treatment planning directs how the services of the other components in this arena are delivered. It unifies them under a common set of goals and guides them to work both individually and as one unit to address the various treatment needs of the client.

Individual therapy has a central place in this model because it serves as a focal point from which one person (the therapist) can monitor work done in the other components and individually guide the client as he undertakes the achievement of his varied goals. Individual therapy is a point of accountability for the client, and it is the place where his individualized treatment plan is discussed and strategies for its implementation are devised.

Sex offense-specific group, individual therapy, and family treatment all feed into the aftercare/follow-up component. These primary treatment settings will provide for the development of the resident's relapse prevention plan. Remember that they do not work alone. Important information and work from milieu treatment and adjunct treatment will be made part of the activities of aftercare/follow-up, as the issues raised in these treatment areas resurface in SO group, individual therapy, and family treatment. The aftercare component is the point at which present and future providers overlap; it represents the culmination of the client's work in treatment in preparation for discharge/termination.

Peripheral to the central treatment components are the treatment facilitating components of staff training and general resident education. Program administration is also included as a facilitating influence because its policies and actions will directly affect treatment

FIGURE 3.1. A Conceptual Diagram of the Multi-Component Model

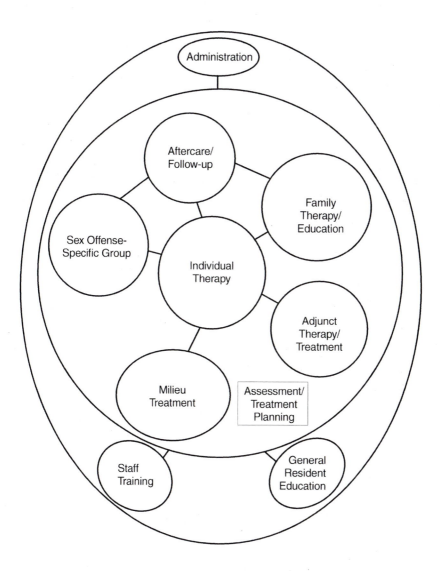

planning and service provision. Inclusion of the administration in this context also implies that administrators must understand and be supportive of multi-component treatment. The connections between the assessment component and the treatment facilitating components are bidirectional. The assessment component (embodied in the treatment team) influences staff training and the topics discussed in resident education, which enhances safety and quality milieu treatment. In addition, these structured contacts with staff and residents provide valuable information to aid in treatment planning for individual residents, and in the continuing work of program evaluation and improvement.

Let us look at a brief example of the model in action. This example focuses on a client in a residential program with the treatment goal of understanding his pattern of offending. Suppose that in his sex offense-specific group, he was examining his pattern of withdrawing and isolating prior to masturbating to fantasies about sexually abusing small children (SO group). The next afternoon he gets in an argument with a fellow resident and sits alone in the corner of the room. A staff member notices, speaks with him (staff training), and then engages him in some activities going on in the next room (milieu treatment). This behavior is communicated to his therapist who, remembering the group discussion, raises the issue in their therapy session (individual therapy), asking the client to look into the pattern and any thoughts he was having at the time and to bring this back to group. That night in family group, the client talks about his isolating, and his parents provide many examples and a better understanding of this pattern (family treatment). The staff realize that the client needs to learn to engage himself in more activities (assessment/treatment planning), so he is enrolled in an activity group they have started; in addition, he discusses his social awkwardness in another program group and receives helpful feedback (adjunct treatments).

In the following sex offense-specific group, the client processes what he has learned over the week on this issue (SO group). The residents suggest that he ask some questions of his parents (family treatment) then bring the issue to his individual session (individual treatment). While trying to engage more positively with residents a few days later (milieu treatment), he again has an argument with a resident and isolates during the activity. Another resident approaches and speaks to him. When he does not respond, the resident quietly informs a staff member (resident education). The staff member sits with him and tries to show him the appearance of the pattern (staff training). The client realizes that he has begun to have inappropriate fantasies and tries to change his thinking by playing cards with other residents (milieu treatment). The next day he explains this occurrence to his therapist, and the two work on some possible strategies that he can bring to his sex offense-specific group for feedback (individual therapy). And so on . . .

Remember that each resident may be working on several such issues collectively at any given time. This example has attempted to show how the same issue is addressed and augmented as it moves from component to component, and how the various components can provide effective unified treatment.

Chapter 4

The Group Care Program

Programs that treat offending adolescents in a group care setting face special issues and challenges. A group care program is defined here as one in which the clients in treatment live together and/or spend extended lengths of time together. This encompasses secure environments, hospital settings, residential programs, group homes, independent living programs, and, it may be argued, foster care. Given the amount of time clients in an outpatient day program spend together, they also share some of the same challenges addressed in this chapter, and much of this material is applicable to them as well.

Since this is a wide range of program types, and since individually discussing each issue in the context of every possible environment would be too time-consuming, this chapter will attempt to present the material by aiming for the "middle ground" of a residential program (level B in the scheme of Chapter 2). Providers at other levels should easily be able to make appropriate modifications to the information to suit their specific settings.

ISSUES TO CONSIDER
IN A SEX OFFENSE-SPECIFIC PROGRAM

What follows is a list of questions that group care programs working with sexually abusive adolescents should take into consideration. Most of these questions are also applicable to outpatient programs as well and can be used by them in program development. These questions are raised so that they may be discussed, researched, considered, and deliberated by individual program providers as they undertake the work of program design and/or ongoing development. The reader will note that each of the questions seems to beg other questions that also can be explored as part of this process. Looking into these questions and making use of recognized specialists and current literature in the field are important parts of making an informed decision as to how each individual program will address the challenge of treating adolescents who sexually offend.

Program Questions

1. Should our program treat sexually abusive clients at all?
2. Should we treat a mixed population of adolescents or sex offenders alone?
3. How will the program's physical environment be set up?
4. What will the daily schedule look like?
5. What will be the staffing patterns and level of client supervision?
6. How will educational services be provided to clients?
7. What will be the minimum training and qualifications for the various staff positions?
8. Who will make up the treatment team?
9. What will be the crisis intervention policies, and who will respond to various crises?
10. How will we ensure a safe environment for residents, staff, and guests?
11. What mandatory and ongoing training will we provide to staff?
12. How will staff communicate with one another both on and between shifts?
13. How will we respond to sexual behaviors exhibited by residents?
14. How will we evaluate our program for effectiveness and make improvements?
15. How will we respond to the multicultural issues of clients?
16. Will we engage in pretreatment?
17. Are we willing to make a commitment on all levels to the treatment of these clients?
18. What will be considered contraband items, and how will we deal with them?

Legal Questions

19. What are our liabilities if a youth sexually acts out?
20. What is our level of accountability to the court/state agency/ community?
21. What types of documentation or reports will we be expected to provide?
22. What sorts of things should or should not be included in such reports?
23. Wll our community accept a "sex offender" treatment facility in the neighborhood?
24. How will we establish rapport with community leaders and the local police?
25. When will we involve the police for assistance?
26. What will be the policies regarding client passes?
27. What sorts of activities will we do in the community with the adolescents?
28. How will these activities be supervised?
29. How will we handle new disclosures by clients?
30. What are we mandated to report to outside authorities?
31. What will be the expectations and limits of client confidentiality in therapy?

Admissions and Discharge Questions

32. What will be the criteria for acceptance of a youth to the program?
33. What types of subpopulations of offenders will we be able to service?
34. How will we determine if a youth must be removed from our program?
35. Can we manage dual-diagnosis clients?
36. What are the criteria for successful completion of the program?
37. How will we reintegrate the youth into the community?
38. What types of aftercare services will be arranged or provided for the clients?

Treatment Questions

39. What sorts of assessment procedures and instruments will be used?
40. What theoretical model(s) of treatment will we use?
41. What modalities of treatment will we employ?
42. How will we structure the various treatment modalities into a cohesive program?

43. What adjunct services and treatments can or should we provide?
44. To what standards of treatment and ethics will we hold ourselves?
45. What sort of follow-up services will we provide?
46. Will we use physiological measures (e.g., plethysmograph or polygraph)?
47. Will pharmacological interventions be used, and if so, who will monitor the use of the medication?
48. How will families be involved and engaged in treatment?
49. How will home passes be used as part of the treatment effort?
50. How will we handle victim clarification and family reunification?

STANDARDS FOR SEX OFFENSE-SPECIFIC RESIDENTIAL TREATMENT

For the past few years, an organization known as the National Offense-Specific Residential Treatment Task Force has been working to produce a set of comprehensive guidelines for the treatment of youthful sex offenders in residential programs. Their efforts have yielded a monograph titled "Standards of Care for Youth in Sex Offense-Specific Residential Programs." This document represents some of the most current thinking in the field. Information on how to obtain a copy of these standards is included in Appendix A of this book. Please note that the task force's concept of a residential program is somewhat broader than the narrow definition used in this book. These standards have a wide application in almost all group care settings.

DECIDING WHICH CLIENTS ARE APPROPRIATE FOR RESIDENTIAL TREATMENT

To determine which clients are appropriate for residential treatment, one must again view the continuum as having three main divisions. These divisions (secure, residential, and outpatient) are principally based on the level of structure and physical security placed on clients and their level of access to the community. By examining the criteria for admission to residential treatment, providers at the secure, residential, and outpatient levels will be able to judge which of these levels is appropriate for the client. Providers must gain an understanding of which adolescents are most appropriate for their programs and then establish criteria for admission that allow for maximum safety and treatment effectiveness for all clients.

The majority of clients referred for residential placement will fall somewhere between the typical profiles of adolescents in secure or outpatient settings. Such is the role of residential treatment: to treat clients who are too disruptive, disordered, delinquent, disturbed, or out of control to be placed in community, yet who are not so dangerous as to require the structure of a secure placement. When faced with the decision to admit a youth to a residential program, one must determine if he would be better served in a more restrictive or less restrictive setting. Such determinations allow providers to divert to community treatment those who can be so treated, thus avoiding unnecessary structure, while sending to secure treatment those who require such containment. This enables the preservation of residential placements as safe and manageable high-intensity treatment settings.

In general, some factors (expanded from Perry and Orchard, 1992) indicate that a youth may not be appropriate for residential treatment and might be better served in a *more restrictive setting:*

1. Eminent risk of running from an open program when confronted on issues
2. Refusal to admit to the commission of the offenses for which the youth is charged
3. Hostility toward treatment or refusal to participate in treatment
4. Significant aggressive behavior
5. Presence of an escalating pattern of sex-offending behavior that cannot be contained in an unlocked program
6. Occurrence of sexually abusive behavior in current residential or secure placement or has reoffended after previous offense-specific treatment
7. Demonstration that the youth does not want to change the behavior
8. Clear intention to reoffend or act out despite the limits of the program
9. Repetitive occurrences of sexually aggressive statements and/or behavior with residents and/or staff that are unresponsive to verbal redirection
10. Refusal to cooperate with the assessment and/or admissions screening process

Presence of these factors should cause residential program providers to consider carefully whether to accept such a client (unless the program is designed to deal with the concerns that are presented, or other overriding circumstances are present). The goal must be to maximize safety and treatment effectiveness, which means realizing that some adolescents are beyond the capabilities of a given program.

On the other hand, sometimes a referred youth is a low risk to act out, has few collateral issues and no prior history of delinquent behavior, has a supportive and engaged family, and presents as motivated and cooperative. In these cases, it is important to recognize some of the factors indicating that a youth could possibly be treated in a *less restrictive setting*. Kahn (1992) lists the following factors as indicating that treatment in the community might be appropriate (the tenth was added by the author):

1. Client has access to a specialized deviancy treatment provider in his area.
2. Client acknowledges some responsibility for offenses and voices a willingness to participate in treatment.
3. Client has never been caught or arrested previously for a sexual crime, nor has undergone sexual deviancy treatment.
4. Client has only one known victim (but may have had more than one sexual contact with that victim).
5. Offense involved client having circumstantial access to victim, as in baby-sitting, with no predatory or escalating pattern noted.
6. Offense did not involve violence or the threat or use of a weapon, nor did it result in serious injury to the victim.
7. Client has no other criminal history and seems able to learn from the consequences of his behavior.
8. Client has no known history of sexual abuse, nor other deviant learning experiences.
9. Parents or guardians indicate that the youth is stable and responds to their limits and controls.
10. The family supports treatment, and a stable living situation is present.

Factors from either of these lists in a client's history or presentation should not automatically indicate the need for a different level of structure. Clients must be judged on a case-by-case basis. Any automatic sorting system does not take into account the possibilities of client variability and other contributing factors, nor does it recognize that a large part of the client's offending history may as yet be unknown, or that the information presented may be inaccurate due to the client's (or the parent's) deception.

SAFETY ISSUES IN THE PROGRAM

Interactions with Others: The Forum for Unsafe Behavior

Sexual offending is only partly about sex; it is much more a function of the person trying to get his needs met in exploitative relationships. The youth's interactions with others will quite often be colored by the same dysfunctions of social interaction that have supported his offending behavior. Especially in the early stages of treatment (but certainly at any other point thereafter), he may seek to engage others in interactions that mirror his offending behaviors. To maintain program safety, staff members must monitor the clients' interactions with one another and report this information to the clinical staff for processing in therapy.

Clients Who Sexually Offend and Staff

Staff must never forget the offending youth's potential to manipulate them and to minimize the significance of his behavior. Staff members who fail to recognize the client's potential to reoffend, or who do not want to admit the possibility of the client acting out in the program, *are creating the potential for such behavior.* In many cases, these adolescents have been able to perpetrate sex-offending behavior by successfully lulling persons into complacency, or by presenting a façade that made them seem to be safer than they actually were. Persons working with adolescents who sexually offend must realize the ability of many of these clients to manipulate their relationships with staff so that they are able to gain sufficient trust to be allowed to "slide" on certain rules.

This does not happen because staff members are not intelligent or because they are "fools," but because these kids are very skilled at what they do. It happens because staff become too confident—"These kids can't put anything over on me." By adopting such a belief, staff become less vigilant and may even ignore evidence of their own mistakes or laxness. In his book *Without Conscience,* Dr. Robert Hare (1993), perhaps the world's foremost expert on the psychopathic personality, explains that *anyone* can be fooled by a truly skilled manipulator. He illustrates his point by relating a story of how he was manipulated by a man whom he was interviewing, even though he knew this man was a psychopath. His message was simple: If you think you cannot be manipulated, then you are fooling yourself.

To curb such manipulation, staff should *never* keep secrets with clients nor agree not to bring issues, events, or concerns to the attention of clinical staff. If staff members notice something that concerns them regarding clients' thoughts or behaviors, they should bring it to the attention of clinicians and all staff, *especially* if clients attempt to convince staff that they are wrong in their perceptions and should not inform others. This brings to mind the case of one youth who successfully abused several of his peers in a residential program. He had earned the unquestioned trust of all the staff, had the highest possible privileges (with corresponding loosening of supervision), and was even selected to supervise younger residents alone in areas of the program. When some of his inappropriate behaviors surfaced, he was able to keep the information secret by tearfully pleading with others not to say anything. He convinced staff and residents alike that (1) the behaviors were not as significant as they believed them to be, and (2) if they told anyone, the clinicians would overreact and have him unjustly returned to a secure placement. Not wanting to be responsible for doing such a thing to this scared and oppressed young man, both staff and residents kept the secret. In reality, he *was* sexually abusing other youth, and their keeping his secret enabled the continuation of his behavior.

A key to successful safety management is to identify and address behaviors as soon as possible. Many behaviors that will eventually result in sexually abusive situations start out as low-level, possibly harmless, and very often nonsexual behaviors. Training is needed to know what behaviors are significant. Staff should be aware especially of a client's use of sexually provocative comments (especially with female staff). Sometimes sexually aggressive comments will be disguised as a clinical discussion of issues. Other times a nonsexual behavior will parallel the client's pattern (that is, having essentially the same dynamics, yet operating in a non-sexually abusive scenario). Some examples of this are manipulative power struggles, dysfunctional relationship dynamics, and other behaviors specific to individual clients.

All inappropriate behavior should be addressed and documented. This documentation ensures that others are aware that this behavior has been addressed, it provides for the discovery of behavioral patterns over time, and it allows these behaviors to be processed in therapy as parts of the youth's cycle or pattern of offending. This enables staff to assist in helping the client stop his offending patterns (even if the client does not appreciate their efforts at the time).

Clients Who Sexually Offend and Other Clients

Staff should be aware of how and with whom the client develops relationships in the program. Particular attention should be paid to monitoring relationships that are unmatched in terms of age, social skills level, developmental level, size, intelligence, etc. In such relationships, the unevenness in relative "power" may be exploited by the stronger, smarter, or more advanced member. Such relationships should be discouraged. Relationships in which gifts (whether material or symbolic) are exchanged should be of particular concern, as this may indicate one person in the relationship grooming (i.e., preparing) the other for a potential offense. Residents who are unresponsive to suggestions to expand social contacts or who defiantly isolate with a particular client despite staff discouragement are a primary concern. Leaving two clients alone without adult supervision (regardless of classification as having sexual behavior problems) provides an opportunity for inappropriate behaviors. Incidents of sexually inappropriate comments and/or behavior should be addressed at once, and appropriate sanctions leveled. Also of concern are those clients who are being verbally abusive, belittling, making fun of, humiliating, or talking down to other clients. These behaviors should be dealt with accordingly.

Table 4.1 lists some behaviors indicating that a client may be grooming someone for abuse or sexual contact. Many of the behaviors may not seem problematic in themselves, but when fit into the client's overall pattern of offending, they become extremely significant. This list is by no means exhaustive, and providers will be able to add to this list both generally (behaviors applying to any sexually abusive youth) and specifically (behaviors that are unique to a given youth). These behaviors should never be "swept under the carpet"; they must be addressed openly and, if appropriate, publicly.

TABLE 4.1. Behaviors That Might Indicate a Client Is Grooming Others for Abuse or Sexual Contact

- Not respecting others' physical boundaries
- Talking about their sexual issues with other residents and/or outsiders
- Asking other residents about their sexuality, sexual behavior, or sexual history
- Trying to damage a resident's relationships with others (usually to the advantage of the offender's relationship with that particular resident)
- Encouraging other residents not to share certain information with staff and/or clinicians
- Having relationships that seem to be too intimate
- Making sexual jokes and/or talking about people as "sluts," "whores," etc.
- Telling another resident that he is "the only one who really understands" him
- "Flexing" his power (in size, status, intellect, favor with staff) in front of others
- Establishing negative contracts with others to keep secrets in exchange for the offender doing the same
- Collecting "dirt" or gossip on other residents that could be used to bribe them
- Spending a lot of one-on-one time with another resident (especially when this interaction is against staff directions)
- Giving presents to others for making special deals
- Making people feel that it is their fault when anything goes wrong for him
- Being "too good" or "too helpful" or "too complimentary" or "too willing" or "too quick to agree" with you
- Being exempted by many staff from certain rules and having special privileges
- Being able to back certain people down in conflicts especially when the reason for this acquiescence is not clear
- Acting "scattered," as if the offender is "just holding it together"
- Behaving in any way that does not seem right, even if you do not know why—trust your gut feelings

Notes on Contraband

All programs will define certain materials and possessions—in addition to weapons, drugs, and other obvious dangers—as inappropriate and not allowed on the unit for safety and/or clinical reasons. A list of materials that can be unhealthy for sexually abusive adolescents and possibly counterproductive to treatment efforts is presented in Table 4.2.

TABLE 4.2. Some Items Considered Contraband in a Sex Offense-Specific Program

• Any sexually provocative written or visual material, especially commercial pornography or material produced by the client himself • Visual material focusing on young children, e.g., children's underwear advertisements • Pictures of past victims, even if they are family members • Drawings of sexually explicit acts • Drawings that present persons in a sexually provocative manner • Posters whose sole purpose is to be sexually provocative or arousing, especially those that objectify women or present persons, regardless of age or gender, in provocative poses • Reading materials that focus on incestuous relationships • Reading materials that depict forcible sexual assault as being romantic or acceptable • Materials that the resident continues to attempt to possess even though this has been previously addressed

Other Safety Areas

Other areas to be considered when discussing program safety include (but are not limited to) the following: staffing patterns, program layout, floor supervision policies, bedroom assignments, showering and bathroom arrangements, swimming policies, grouping of clients for activities, extent of the use of interns and volunteers, transportation methods, assignment and completion of chores, types of recreational activities, selection of television shows, program schedule and use of downtime, methods for level advancement, decisions to give clients special responsibilities and privileges, using older clients to mentor newer clients, use of less trained relief staff, family visit policies and supervision, clients' access to potentially dangerous items, and the level of consistency and firmness in staff discipline.

Providers will ensure the maximum level of safety if they identify possible safety issues and develop reasonable methods of addressing them within the context of their program's treatment model.

TREATING A MIXED POPULATION OR SEXUALLY ABUSIVE YOUTH ALONE

The discussion on this topic in recent years has focused on one central question: Should a given program exclusively treat adolescents who sexually offend, or should these clients be placed within programs that treat young people with a variety of problems, many of whom are not sex offenders? Although this section refers principally to group care programs, outpatient providers may want to look at some of these same issues, especially as they relate to day or after-school programs.

Many providers suggest that mixing youth who sexually offend with nonoffenders may not provide optimal treatment. Although some programs put this belief into practice, the majority of programs do not have separate cottages or quarters for sexually abusive clients (Heinz, Ryan, and Bengis, 1991), possibly due to financial and practical constraints. On the other hand, some believe that the mixed-population model provides interesting opportunities for treatment. So the question is twofold: (1) *Can* the program (financially/practically) treat only offending youth, and (2) which is the better treatment environment?

Is a Sex Offense-Specific-Only Program Feasible?

Large programs with separate residences or cottages and a sufficient referral base of sexually abusing youth may be practically and financially able to employ a sex offense-specific-*only* model. These larger programs, with presumably a larger source of referrals in general, are in essence shifting all their youth who offend sexually to a single residence. In such programs, this consolidation of SO residents clearly makes sense. Smaller programs that have only one living unit would need to exclude all other referrals besides sex-offending clients to use this model, and for them, this may not be so easy. Although referrals of sexually abusive youth possibly would increase if a program was known as sex offense-specific, it is risky to place the program's future on the line without being sure.

A further matter to consider is the community's response to having a "sex offender program" in the neighborhood. Indeed, the financial and community concerns may severely limit a program's options. A final obstacle may be contractual obligations or the inability to determine exactly who is admitted (i.e., no or limited right of refusal). In such cases, providers *cannot* opt for this model on their own without a contractual change or approval and cooperation of the funding source.

If a program *cannot* practically or financially support the switch to sex offense-specific model, and providers still want to treat youth who sexually offend, then they must consider another series of questions:

- How many of the program's slots will be for sexually abusive youth? What will be the maximum number of offenders permitted?
- What are the special considerations in treating youth who are sexually abusive in a mixed milieu?
- Since the *whole* treatment regime will not be converted, how will sex offense-specific treatment be successfully incorporated into the program?
- Who will head the treatment of sexually abusive clients?
- Should certain types of sexually abusive youth not be treated in the mixed setting?

Discussion of these and other questions will enable the program to provide quality treatment to youth who sexually offend without compromising the treatment of the other clients.

For and Against Sex Offense-Specific-Only Treatment

The following is a brief exposition of the pros and cons of a program focusing on only sexually abusive youth. This exposition will contrast the recognized position for sex offense-specific-only treatment of Heinz, Ryan, and Bengis (1991) with some reasons why providers may choose to treat a mixed population.

The Case for Sex Offense-Specific-Only Programs

Some programs that have evolved from mixed population to sex offense-specific only have reported considerable advantages for both staff and residents. Many of these were larger programs that chose to house sexually assaultive youth in separate cottages or units. Before this separation, staff reported being intimidated by adolescents who sexually offend and their manipulative and victimizing behavior. Staff in the previously mixed cottages had been more easily divided on issues regarding treatment and seemed to have needed more intense training. Separating the offenders into fewer units meant a smaller staff needed to be trained to deal with these adolescents. Furthermore, this enabled selection of staff for the sex offense-specific cottages who (1) were better suited to work with sexually abusive clients and (2) wanted to work with this population.

Sex offense-specific only programs specialize in work with sexually assaultive youth, making it easier for providers to gear all aspects of the day to sex offense-specific treatment. Heinz, Ryan, and Bengis (1991) put it this way:

> Sex offenders in offense-specific units seem to create a stronger treatment culture when all the members are working on similar issues. In effect, it permits them to implement their program twenty-four hours a day. When all the youngsters are dealing with their manipulative and intimidating behaviors, they can recognize them more readily in one another and help one another to deal with them. (p. 195)

The other possible benefits authors offer:

> Because the treatment culture is stronger and the focus can be on the sexual or abusive issues all day, length of stay may be shortened and the supportive atmosphere ease[s] the difficulty of exploring such issues as homosexuality and masturbation. (p. 195)

This last point is particularly significant. In mixed programs, some clients have a difficult time feeling "safe" talking about their sexually abusive behaviors because they fear how the nonoffenders in the program will react to them and subsequently treat them. This presents a whole set of issues that mixed programs must continually struggle with to maintain a viable treatment culture.

Other reasons for creating sex offense-specific residences include (but are not limited to) the following:

- Low functioning and/or younger adolescents who are not sex offenders may try to carve out an identity and gain acceptance by imitating some of the undesirable behaviors of sex offenders.
- Seriously emotionally or mentally disturbed adolescents may not be able to protect themselves adequately from the aggressive and intimidating behavior of some sexually abusive clients, which can be detrimental to their treatment and potentially place them at risk to be victimized.
- In a mixed setting, clients who have sexually offended may require different levels of supervision and/or be under different policies regarding passes and other activities. These differences

can cause some degree of tension that would not be present in a sex offense-specific residence. (Heinz, Ryan, and Bengis, 1991)

The Case for Mixing Populations

In their treatment of this topic, Heinz, Ryan, and Bengis (1991) also note that there are "major residential programs for juvenile sex offenders that have remained committed to maintaining a client mix." Some of the reasons for maintaining this mix include (but are not limited to) the following considerations:

- A mix reduces the stigma of being in a "sex offender program," which may help some fragile clients more easily transition into their treatment.
- A mix may help the more resistant client who does not want to admit to his status as a client with sexual behavior problems to cooperate with the program. These clients, many of whom are blocked by guilt and shame, can in a way console themselves that this program is not *only* for sex offenders until they can take full responsibility for their behaviors.
- Mixing the population helps to "normalize" the group being served. This can help residents to break from the personality and behavior patterns that are typical to many adolescents who sexually offend.
- In a mix, sexually abusive clients can learn how to relate to peers who do not have significant sexual issues and problems. It can help them to observe and learn to interact with others in nonsexual ways.
- A mix reduces (ideally) the number of possible residents who would conspire to engage in sexual behavior in the program and (hopefully) provides more residents willing to report such behavior to staff.
- Sex abusers with significant issues in other areas will find more chances for therapeutic engagement with other residents.
- A mix presents to clients living proof that there is life without offending.
- A mix helps to ease staff burnout, from working with only offenders all day long, and provides them with a diversity of presenting problems, which is healthy for them both personally and professionally.

One program (Lundrigan, 1996a) has summarized its commitment to maintaining a client mix in the following way:

> It is our belief that by working with these residents in a setting that contains young men with a variety of backgrounds and problems we best serve their needs for growth by providing them with a more diverse group of peer role models from which to learn. This mixture also helps the offender to learn how non-offenders respond to their issues, thus better preparing them to deal with a society of diverse views and tolerances for sexual abuse and its perpetrators. Finally, the mix helps to provide a community with a low tolerance for sexually acting-out behavior and thereby serves to hold that behavior in check. (p. 1)

VISITS, PASSES, AND CLIENT CONTACT WITH THE COMMUNITY

An important area to consider is how the client will interface with the larger community (if at all) and the level of supervision that will be maintained during this contact. Some persons may advocate for the client to have *no* contact with the world outside the program. They want to protect the community by isolating the potentially sexually abusive client during the duration of his treatment, thus reducing the possibility that he will commit another offense. However, our goal is to prepare the client for a safe life in the community, and we must consider how best to do this.

Not allowing the client to have contact with the world outside is a bit short-sighted. With adequate levels of security (locked doors, fences, and alarms), twenty-four-hour supervision, and incarceration, we can bring to almost zero the number of offenses that clients commit in the community *during their stays.* But what happens after the clients are released? They have been so long deprived of normal age-appropriate experiences (e.g., dating, engaging in community social activities, etc.) that they have missed out on some valuable socialization. If we are to do our job well, we need to prepare clients to live offense-free lives *after* they are released from a secure, hospital, or residential program.

Isolating residents totally from the community is not productive because it does not benefit treatment. Those working with sexually abusive youth will no doubt understand the difficulties that clients face when reentering the community. Failing to allow clients to make contact with the community deprives them of the opportunity to properly anticipate the difficulties that they will encounter and to develop workable strategies for dealing with these situations. By the same token, however, we must be careful of the types and extent of contact we allow clients to have with the community as part of their treatment. We need to balance the clinical needs of the client, which will increase the chances for future safety, with the immediate safety needs of members of the outside community.

Visitors to the Program

Reception of outside visitors to the program is generally considered both important for the client and, especially in the case of the legal guardian, a right. This is not to say that adolescents should have free and unrestricted access to visitors, or that anyone who wishes to visit should be allowed to do so. Boundaries concerning who is allowed to visit and when should be clearly established in the program. A good clinical reason must exist to keep parents from seeing their children. Given the legal and procedural regulations of most programs, these restrictions likely will need to be documented and/or approved by others. However, such restrictions may need to be employed, especially if a parent is a sex offender and/or has sexually offended this youth. In addition to parents, visits by siblings need to be carefully considered, especially in cases of interfamilial victimization by the client. In these cases, clinical determination needs to be made as to what will be the appropriate time to allow such visits, and what types of clarification and reunification work must be done in preparation. Any visitors outside of the immediate family should be considered on a case-by-case basis. In making such decisions, providers should consider what possible positive and negative effects a given person's visit will have on the client's treatment.

Visits can have very important clinical benefits; however, too much visiting can become distracting. They should be seen as part of the clinical whole of the multi-component program, for they can be both an important adjunct to formal treatment and an important preparation for the client's receiving home passes.

Passes to the Community

Passes may be divided into three general categories: staff supervised, parent supervised, and unsupervised. For supervised passes a staff member, parent, or other designated person is present and maintains appropriate (often "eye-contact") supervision of the resident during the duration of the time out of the program. In addition to the previous categories, there are several *types* of passes. Passes can be "in the area of the program," "at home," "to foster home," "to next program," "to meet with future treatment provider," "for a medical appointment," "for shopping or other needs," "for family death or illness," or "for legal reasons" (e.g., court appearances, probation visits, etc.).

The critical concerns are what level of supervision (category of pass) the client will be given and at what point in the client's stay will he become eligible for passes. A further area of inquiry surrounds the establishment of policies for clients progressing through various kinds of passes, as is clinically indicated. Passes are an important part of treatment and also one of the areas most open to potential abuses and compromises of safety.

Clients should progress logically through the categories and types of passes in such a way as to approximate a gradual return to the home environment or next setting. For example, the residential client returning home would begin with no passes, then might progress to staff-supervised passes in the area (the option closest to being in the program), perhaps next to parent-supervised passes in the area, next to parent-supervised passes home (of increasing duration, up to and including overnight and weekend passes), and, if possible, unsupervised passes in the area, to unsupervised time in the home community when home on pass (the option most similar to being home). Some programs will add to this scheme staff-supervised home passes and/or staff-supervised outings with parents. The category and type of passes given may vary during the same point in the stay of a given client (e.g., alternating weeks of parent-supervised area passes and parent-supervised home passes). However, use of the less restrictive kinds of passes will increase as progress in treatment indicates. Clients can also regress in their progress to less freedom on passes if clinical or behavioral conditions warrant this. Thus, the pass system becomes a mini continuum of care bridging the client from the restrictive, protected setting of the present program to the less structured, freer setting of the next placement.

As with visits, passes have many positive clinical benefits. They can help facilitate adjustment to the next setting (be that home, foster home, group home, etc.) by introducing the client to increasing levels of exposure to that setting. This is especially important if the aftercare setting is different from the client's living situation prior to entering the current program. In addition, passes afford the client with exposure to a number of persons, places, situations, thoughts, feelings, problems, concerns, realities, choices, and pressures that he would not be exposed to in the residential milieu.

It is important that clients prepare *before* a pass to take note of these unique occurrences, and that they process their passes in therapy *after* returning to provide material for relapse prevention planning. Almost all clients have experiences on passes that they (and the clinical staff) never dreamed would arise. Clients, when processing their experiences on passes, will frequently say, "I never thought about that before," or, in the case of a concern raised by a provider that the client did not think was important, "I guess I better *really* look at that." Passes are approximations of life in the community that serve as an important part of the treatment process, and as such, they can be of tremendous clinical benefit. However, if they are not viewed in this way, they cease to be part of a larger treatment picture and simply become "time out of the program." This could conceivably be detrimental to treatment and compromise the safety of the client, family, and community.

Program-Related Client Contact with the Community

One final area of client contact with the community is the contact that results as part of the program's activities. Residential (level B) and community-based (level C) programs frequently bring clients into the community for activities related to education, community service, program functions, or recreation. It should go without saying that the level of supervision for such outings must be considered carefully. One rule of thumb is that the general level of supervision should be what is required of the client who is most restricted. The level of supervision that is prudent for safety should be weighed against clinical concerns, against the need to maintain a good image in the community, against the need to maintain an orderly and organized atmosphere for the activity, and also against achieving the goals of the outing. Different clients may be placed under different levels of supervision on the same outing, but this must be done with care and communication so that a client does not escape appropriate supervision. Since sometimes on outings the clients are excited and the staff is less vigilant, providers may want to lean toward a little more strictness in supervision. Remember, *never* think that it cannot happen because then you let down your guard and increase the possibility that it *will* happen.

NOTES ON PROGRAM LIABILITY

The specifics regarding program liability may vary from state to state and agency to agency, as the laws and regulations under which various programs operate may be different. The purpose of this section is to raise the question of liability so that it becomes part of the discussion providers undertake as they seek to create new services or to improve the existing services.

The situations of the most concern for program liability are when one client assaults another client in the program, when a client on pass assaults someone in the community, and when a client who has been released with a "clean bill of health" reoffends.

Providers need to identify the actions that might increase the risk of an incident occurring to minimize the possibility of legal action being taken. Bengis and Cuninggim (1997) provide a list of high-risk program policies, summarized in Table 4.3. This list should serve as a reminder of what actions might decrease program safety and open the possibility of litigation.

TABLE 4.3. List of High-Risk Program Policies

• Accepting sexually abusive youth into the program without having an offense-specific treatment approach
• Mixing abusing and nonabusing youth in the same residential or day program in the absence of very competent clinical understanding of the treatment and safety needs of both populations
• Sending youth home for visits either before they have demonstrated the internalization of self-control or in the absence of a family capable of managing a treatment contract
• Sending youth home when their prior victims reside there and prior to formal therapist-led victim-abuser reconciliation
• Having insufficient staff to be able to keep sexually abusive youth who are deemed high risk in sight at all times prior to their internalization of self-control
• Allowing non–sex offense-specific therapists to treat these youth
• Assuming that therapy alone is sufficient to treat abusers in a residential program (i.e., the program does not have an integrated offense-specific milieu)
• Treating sexually abusive youth in outpatient settings without any control over their behavior outside of therapy

Source: Adapted from Bengis and Cuninggim, 1997.

The issues of liability are programmatic, systemic, and legal. They are programmatic because incidents of sexual and violent aggression can have significant effects on the operation of the program and the treatment culture; systemic because they can effect the utilization of the program by referring agencies or cause the program to become the focus of child abuse investigations; and legal because they potentially can result in legal action being taken in the courts.

This final concern is the most frightening. To what extent are we legally liable for the behavior of our clients, and in what cases may we be held legally responsible? This is a complex question, and a clear answer would require the advice of a competent legal expert. However, Yorker (1997) provides some guidelines regarding determining negligence and malpractice in a program. In general, for such a claim to be made, it must be shown (1) that the program providers owed a duty to the plaintiff (in this case the abused and the parents of the abused), (2) that the providers breached that duty, (3) that the breach of duty was the proximate cause of the injury, and (4) that the plaintiff suffered damages.

In the case of one client assaulting another client, we know that the abused client was entitled to appropriate protection from injury while in the program, and we can say that the plaintiff suffered damages. What remains to be determined is whether the program providers breached their duty to protect the client, and if that breach was the cause of the injury. What constitutes such a breach? Perhaps appropriate standards of care and supervision requirements were not devised, and/or staff did not adhere to such standards. Perhaps the staff failed to properly contain an aggressive youth. The problem may lie in accepting and retaining a client who cannot be safely managed within the program. Perhaps it was a failure to utilize respected and proven treatment approaches.

If program designers wish to provide the safest environment for clients and staff they must understand what measures can be reasonably taken to ensure that safety and then apply them. Cohen (1995) states:

> Adherence to all required information gathering-studying-sharing steps will go a long way towards insulating clinicians and others who work with sex offenders from liability if a decision turns out to be erroneous or if there is misplaced trust. (p. 10)

In many cases involving assaultive events, either an appropriate standard or procedure was not in place, or someone was not following it. Both of these factors may be focal points in a potential legal action. Cohen (1995) continues:

> a basis for liability may be found where a law mandates a report and it is not developed, or where important diagnostic material exists and is not shared as legally mandated. (p. 10)

A prospective plaintiff may ask, "Why didn't you comply with that standard? Why didn't you have a policy to account for that? Why weren't staff supervising the clients at that time?" To answer, "We didn't know about that standard, or we should have such a policy," in this age of extensive written literature and professional specialization, is no excuse.

In the case of a resident who acts out on a pass, program providers will want to be sure that they had in place competent decision-making procedures and policies regarding the granting of passes, and that these were followed. Providers should document reasons why the resident was deemed clinically safe to merit such a pass as well. If the pass was supervised, then the actions of the supervising party may also be questioned. In the end, if we want the community to allow us to send residents on passes, then we need to be sure that we understand what constitutes "pass eligible," and we must consider the safety needs of the community as a higher priority than the treatment needs of the client.

What about the question of clients reoffending after completing a program? The author doubts if any client would be discharged with a guarantee that he will not reoffend, but will program providers be clear in voicing their reservations and concerns? If reasonable care was taken to provide proper and effective treatment, and if providers express their concerns in writing to the funding source and make no promises of safety, then they would be relatively safe from legal action. When a client reoffends after release, one cannot simply conclude that the success or failure of a client is the result of the treatment received in the program. Many other factors are involved, but as treatment providers, clinicians should make every effort to remain free of legitimate blame in such situations.

In cases involving clear negligence on the part of program providers, responsibility also may be shared by the licensing body or state agency in charge of monitoring the program. This fact should put such bodies on notice as to the need for good monitoring and effective enforcement of sound standards of care.

In the final analysis, Yorker (1997) comforts fears a bit when she states, "It is reassuring for professionals to know that they are only expected to act reasonably to protect the children in their care" (p. 15). She continues that if the staff are aware of the potential danger and take adequate precautions, they still may be outwitted by clients and injury may result. However, she states, the courts will "simply hold the institution to the standard of care of a similarly situated institution or professional under the same or similar circumstances" (p. 15).

Chapter 5

The Outpatient Program

Outpatient treatment programs are a vital part of a comprehensive treatment continuum. Although not all clients referred for treatment will require the containment of secure or residential programs, all clients will at some point or other in their course of treatment be serviced by an outpatient treatment provider. In fact, many (if not most) clients will never be placed in a level A or B placement and will receive *all* their treatment from an outpatient provider.

In some cases, the outpatient provider will perform initial evaluations and thus be the client's first contact in the treatment continuum, and *in almost all* cases (regardless of where the client entered the continuum), the client will complete his treatment while in the care of an outpatient treatment provider. Given these facts, it is important to view the outpatient program as a full-fledged treatment program in its own right. Such programs often involve independent treatment for clients from pretreatment through maintenance, as well as treatment of clients stepping down in the continuum.

UNIQUE CHALLENGES FACED
BY OUTPATIENT PROVIDERS

The outpatient provider works with the client when he is living in the community, either in the supervised structure of a level C placement or in the much less structured and less supervised conditions of the home. Clients in outpatient treatment cannot be monitored by staff at all times and enveloped in a twenty-four-hour-a-day treatment milieu, as can their group care counterparts. This limited ability to monitor clients can pose some challenges partly because clinicians have less data to use in therapy sessions than they would able to monitor the clients' behaviors and thoughts more comprehensively. Furthermore, "the [outpatient] treatment provider, in conjunction with the appropriate criminal justice authority, is responsible for setting appropriate external controls in place to allow for the monitoring of high-risk situations and verification of the offender's whereabouts and movements" (Margolin, 1983, as cited in Barbaree and Cortoni, 1993, p. 254). This responsibility to provide quality treatment and the expectation to assist the appropriate authorities in monitoring the client in the community can put the provider in a frustrating bind.

In addition to the challenge of treating the sexually abusive youth with low levels of information regarding his day-to-day behaviors and thought patterns, outpatient providers face many other challenges, such as the following:

- Getting clients who are living in the community to the treatment sessions; includes transportation issues as well as community-related distractions and activities that can interfere with attendance
- Being able to successfully impact the client with fewer hours of contact per week than group care providers have
- Working against the "Hey I'm not locked up; I can't be that bad off" mentality
- Dealing with the possibility of increased family contact, which may bring with it a number of negative influences and unique problems
- Working within the complex network of community influences that can hinder treatment
- Insurance and billing issues—clinicians spending large amounts of time completing paperwork to justify treatment and secure insurance coverage
- Having, at times, to work with clients who may be better served by a more secure program
- Conducting community education efforts
- Ensuring clients complete their treatment
- Coordinating with level C group care providers who refer clients for sex offense-specific treatment, and dealing with secure and residential program providers who refer clients for "aftercare"

Such challenges as these demand a certain level of skill on the part of outpatient providers to ensure effective treatment in the most vibrant, but also the most difficult, program setting—the open community.

PROPOSED OUTPATIENT
SERVICE DELIVERY SYSTEM

An outpatient treatment network should be established in each area to meet the various needs of clients referred for treatment at the outpatient level. Such a community network would contain programs of varying levels of intensity and focus, so that a wide range of clients could be adequately serviced. Outpatient providers in the community would ideally coordinate with one another to ensure the availability of an appropriate diversity of services in their area.

Figure 5.1 provides a representation of this network slightly expanded from Figure 2.1. These options may be seen as a "continuum within the continuum," for it is possible for clients to progress through outpatient treatment in the same way as they progress through different levels in the continuum.

Day and After-School Programs

Day programs can be developed for clients who are in need of more intensive treatment than can be provided by weekly sex offense-specific groups alone. They also are lower-cost alternative to residential placement. Day and after-school programs are appropriate for those clients who have a variety of deficits and who require a greater degree of structure and more services than can be provided by standard outpatient treatment alone. These clients may be living at home, or they could be concurrently placed in a level C program.

Day and after-school program settings are similar to a group care program, but for a given period of the day. Staff can create a milieu, utilize both level and stage systems (to be discussed in Chapter 6), and incorporate a wide variety of treatment components and modes. A well-structured day program will be able to provide, on an outpatient basis, all of the treatment components presented in this book, thus creating a very intensive treatment environment.

Appendix B presents sample schedules for both day and after-school programs for the reader's consideration.

Full-Range Sex Offense-Specific Groups

The traditional backbone of the outpatient program is the outpatient sex offense-specific group (SO group). As noted earlier, the full-range SO group covers the same broad scope of treatment as a resi-

FIGURE 5.1. The Outpatient Treatment Network

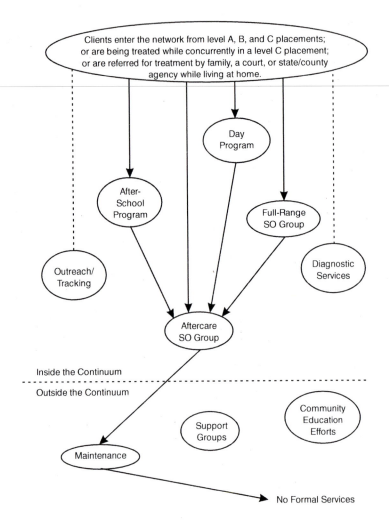

dential or secure program. Full-range groups would be run for all clients who have not had prior intensive SO treatment, whether in day, after-school, or standard treatment.

A full-range group program can easily address the many goals of the treatment phases, even if all possible components of treatment cannot be included. The full-range group services may be supplemented by some of the additional outpatient services mentioned in the next section, as client needs and program resources dictate.

Aftercare Groups

Outpatient treatment centers that can operate aftercare groups will be providing a valuable resource to both their own clients and those of other programs. These groups, which would focus on the finalization and implementation of relapse prevention strategies as well as the day-to-day struggles of applying the work done in the course of intensive treatment, can help clients who have completed a comprehensive treatment program (secure, residential, *or* full-range outpatient) to continue to move forward. Moving from intensive to aftercare treatment can be a sign of positive progress to the client. Furthermore, such groups, which separate those in the early and middle stages of treatment from those in the end stages of treatment, can help clients to fine-tune skills in ways that would be beyond those in less advanced treatment.

Aftercare groups could be designed to mix clients who have completed full-range outpatient programs with those completing secure or residential programs. However, if there are enough clients (and enough clinic resources), one might divide the clients into specific aftercare groups. For example, groups designed to meet the needs of clients reintegrating into the community after out-of-home placements or for those who have been in the community in outpatient treatment and are now entering the last phase of that treatment. Such specialized groups bring together clients who have similar issues and may be particularly helpful to those who are reintegrating into the community.

Maintenance Contacts

After completing an aftercare SO group, clients could be placed on a maintenance schedule. Similar to the contacts advocated as a part of a residential aftercare component in Chapter 14, these maintenance contacts can permit the client to separate more gently from the treatment process and the support that he has received while in treatment. Such contacts may include booster sessions, telephone conversations, visits to the clinic (as deemed appropriate), and a designated person to call if an emergency occurs.

Treatment providers should discuss how to establish maintenance contacts and support services for clients now done with treatment. They must provide some form of safety net and point of reentry for clients who have exited the continuum, for in doing so, they may help to prevent a relapse.

Friedman (1991) discusses the use of other forms of support groups at and beyond the end stages of treatment. Such support groups, which are often based on a twelve-step model, may or may not be helpful for all clients. These groups would be conducted regularly, to be available for clients on an as-needed basis, and the cost could be defrayed by donations from attending members. Regular gatherings of such groups would offer support for remaining offense free and in following relapse prevention plans. They would also provide a setting for discussing ongoing struggles, which could be beneficial for some clients. In addition, they may have potential as pre-treatment interventions for certain clients, as the exposure to other clients who are attending to relapse prevention may set a good example and motivate them to participate in treatment.

For other clients, these groups may be contraindicated due to specific needs and personalities. The process of such groups should be observed by someone who can identify when the group is offering support for healthy behaviors or when it is condoning thinking errors and maladaptive patterns.

ADDITIONAL OUTPATIENT SERVICES

Outreach and Tracking

Tracking and outreach services exist in many communities. *Tracking* refers to monitoring the client's whereabouts and activities through random spot-checking of the client's location, as self-reported via phone calls to an answering service. Tracking has an obvious external supervisory function (cf. Cumming and Buell, 1997), as well as being a source of important information on the client's day-to-day life. *Outreach* involves workers available to assist the client in fulfilling a variety of needs in the community (e.g., school/legal/funding source advocacy, family mediation, 24/7 crisis intervention, employment assistance, conducting recreational activities, informal counseling, etc.).

Outreach/tracking (O/T) programs may vary with respect to the proportion of emphasis that is placed on one or the other of these two services. One O/T program may spend more time tracking than conducting recreational activities or helping families resolve daily conflicts; another program may emphasize the outreach services at the expense of more intensive tracking supervision. Providers should try to balance the two, providing a respectable level of supervision and allowing enough time and resources to do quality outreach.

Such O/T programs have been successfully used with delinquent adolescents released to the community on parole, and with children who require more intensive community intervention than is provided by weekly therapy contacts alone. In addition, the support and supervision that an outreach program can provide on nights and weekends (in terms of worker presence, on-the-spot counseling, and providing recreational activities) can greatly assist those clients who may regress due to frustration, crisis, or boredom.

An O/T program could be run as part of the outpatient clinic, or another agency could be contracted to provide this service. Since the outreach team will be one of the most important sources of information on the client's day-to-day activities and mental status, the former practice is suggested, to maximize data sharing.

Family Treatment and Individual Therapy

These two modes of therapy can be used very effectively in the outpatient program. Developing a family treatment component and providing for individual therapy services can greatly enhance the overall clinical impact of the program.

An interesting option for conducting family (and even individual) therapy in the community is to examine the possibility of providing in-home therapy sessions. Such interventions can be very useful for multiproblem, disorganized families. For more information on home-based therapy services, please see Wood, Barton, and Schroeder (1988); Seelig, Goldman-Hall, and Jerrell (1992); Lundrigan (1994); Halvorson (1992); Bribitzer and Verdieck (1988); and Nelson, Landsman, and Deutelbaum (1990).

Part of the course of treatment, one very often connected with family therapy, is the conducting of victim reconciliation/clarification work. This complex topic has been addressed well by Yokley (1990), O'Connell (1986), and the Association for the Treatment of Sexual Abusers (ATSA, 1997). The outpatient provider is often in a better position to conduct such work, and even if this work has been begun in a previous setting, he or she will likely be providing services to the client and family at one of the most crucial stages of victim reconciliation—the return of the client to the home and community.

Adjunct Treatment Groups

In addition to the SO group, the outpatient program can include other groups as well. Day and after-school programs would likely have an assortment of groups to fill out the treatment regime, such as psychoeducational groups on sex offending and other topics, life skills activity groups, specialized groups (e.g., anger management, substance abuse), and milieu groups (e.g., point/level/stage reviews, activity planning, "call groups," brief transition groups, business meetings, etc.). Programs may also include experiential activity groups on various topics (e.g., trust, self-esteem, teamwork, frustration tolerance, racism), expressive therapy activities (such as art, music, or drama therapy), supervised free time (to help clients learn to structure and use their free time), and recreational activities (organized, informal, or social) that would help clients build skills, improve self-esteem, and increase options for positive and constructive behaviors.

These services can be offered not only to those in a day or after-school program. Consider having closed-ended cycles of a social skills or anger management group as requirements for the standard full-range program. Substance abuse counseling for outpatient clients and the use of support groups are also possibilities. It may be helpful to know what other services are available in your community so that you can help clients address as many life areas as possible, thus providing the most comprehensive treatment.

Diagnostic Services

All programs, regardless of their placement on the continuum, will need to have a mechanism for evaluation and ongoing assessment of clients. Often outpatient clinicians are called upon to perform comprehensive sex offense-specific evaluations both for clients placed in the community and for those who are residing in holding facilities or other group care settings. Since outpatient centers are uniquely poised to handle such evaluations, it can be expected that they will function as diagnostic centers for a variety of programs on the continuum.

A COMPREHENSIVE OUTPATIENT
TREATMENT PROGRAM

Program Content

Having examined a number of elements that can make up an outpatient treatment program, it is possible to consider what a comprehensive outpatient program might be. The proposed program could be run out of a clinic or mental health center and would attempt to provide as many of the various modes of outpatient service delivery as possible. It would provide a day program, an after-school program, outreach/tracking services, and standard outpatient treatment. The program would have both full-range and aftercare treatment tracks available to all clients. Thus, clients could be referred for either full-range or aftercare sex offense-specific treatment in a variety of settings (e.g., standard outpatient, day program, after-school program). The program would also be able to accept clients who need more support and supervision in the community as part of the outreach/tracking program.

A given community would likely only need one of these fully comprehensive programs, with perhaps another after-school program available and other mental health centers providing standard outpatient treatment and diagnostic services.

Clients, Staff, and Structure

The proposed program would be able to accommodate a total of thirty-six clients: eight day program, eight after-school program, and twenty standard outpatient treatment. Twenty-five slots of outreach program services could be made available for any of these clients as needed.

The full-time staff complement for the comprehensive program would number thirteen: one program director, one administrative assistant, one clinical director, three clinicians, three milieu counselors, and four outreach workers. Additional clinical hours can be filled in by fee-for-service or part-time staff if the need arises.

A schedule is provided in Appendix B that illustrates how a day in the combined day/after-school/standard outpatient program could be structured (add to this schedule the night and weekend coverage of the outreach program for those clients involved in that). For more detailed information concerning this schedule, for layouts of staffing patterns, or for salary and cost projection information, please contact the author.

Funding

It would be beneficial to contract with state and county agencies to fund such a program. In this way, referrals from these agencies would have an adequate number of slots in the various outpatient modes of treatment. Other funding can come from insurance company reimbursement for clinical services, especially in the case of diagnostic services. A careful management of resources and working collaboratively with state agencies, courts, charitable groups, area treatment providers, and insurance companies can help to make such comprehensive outpatient programs a reality.

PROGRAM DEVELOPMENT ISSUES

Questions to Consider

One must consider many questions in developing an outpatient treatment program. Many questions presented in the last chapter in relation to group care programs apply to outpatient programs as well. However, some questions, such as the following, are specific to the outpatient setting:

1. How will our services be delivered in an outpatient model?
2. What types of services will be offered (e.g., SO group, family treatment, day treatment, outreach, home-based services, education groups, etc.)?
3. How will we assess which clients are appropriate for our program(s)?
4. How will we establish a network of professionals and others in the community to assist in the work of treatment?
5. How will we interface with providers who will send clients to us for "aftercare"?
6. Will we establish a separate aftercare track or aftercare group?
7. What will be the policies concerning maintenance contacts?
8. What will we do about staff training?

9. What will be the level and type of family involvement?
10. What will be the level and type of victim involvement?

Three Factors That Influence Outcome

Bingham, Turner, and Piotrowski (1995) list three factors that they have determined had the greatest influence on the positive results of their outpatient treatment program: (1) client selection process, (2) networking with the court and supervising case officers, and (3) the use of cognitive-behavioral treatment.

Client Selection Process

Conducting a screening interview is a vital part of overall assessment and treatment planning efforts. Reviewing records, administering psychological testing as needed, and conducting diagnostic interviews with the client and family or significant others will help the interviewer to determine if the client is appropriate for the program. Issues to consider when assessing appropriateness include, but are not limited to, the following:

- Would this client be better served by a program on another level of the continuum (see the previous chapter for specific indicators)?
- Is the client severely retarded? Does he have a profound psychological disorder (e.g., major depression, psychosis) that would preclude treatment in this setting?
- Some authors (such as Bingham, Turner, and Piotrowski, 1995) would exclude violent abusers whose offense resulted in serous physical harm to the victim. What categories of offenders can we treat or are we willing to treat? Who will treat violent offenders who for other reasons do not fit the criteria for another level of care in the continuum? Who will treat them in the community after they complete a residential or secure program?
- Are there sufficient resources, external controls, and networking possibilities to make treatment feasible?
- Is the client likely to benefit from our program?

One must hold as the first priority the safety of the community and potential victims when making a decision to accept a given client for treatment. Accepting a client who stands little chance of benefiting from the outpatient setting or who poses *unreasonable* risks to the community is clearly not a responsible choice. On the other hand, decisions regarding placement must also take into account the safety of the youth who has offended, who may be vulnerable to retaliation from the family of the victim or from other offenders (cf. Groth et al., 1981).

Networking with Courts, State Agencies, and Other Programs

Close contact with the probation officer of a referring court or with state agency caseworkers responsible for the case is of the utmost importance. If the various parties involved with the case mutually share information and support one another through the treatment process, it will, in the long run, better serve the client and community. Regular case conferences on individual clients can help all parties to stay focused and coordinated. Regular meetings between the program providers and referring parties to discuss programmatic issues can both foster a more positive relationship and help refine services to better meet the needs of referring agencies (cf. Bingham, Turner, and Piotrowski, 1995).

Clients who are being referred from other programs require special networking. Level A and B programs will be providing care for the client prior to placement in the outpatient treatment network. It is important to interface with these program providers before the client is interviewed, as the client transitions to the community, during any aftercare efforts by the previous providers, and as needed to consult on the case. Linking as a team with a previous provider can help both to smooth the client's transition and to increase the quality of services provided. Teamwork of a more intensive kind is required when the client is being referred to outpatient treatment at your facility while residing in a level C program. Coordinating services, sharing information, planning treatment together, and trying to view the services provided by both programs as parts of a larger whole will help to make a safer and more effective overall treatment intervention.

Cognitive-Behavioral Treatment

The use of cognitive-behavioral interventions was mentioned already in Chapter 3 and is revisited again in Chapter 7 on the sex offense-specific group. It is generally regarded that such interventions are more successful with this population than some other interventions, and their use is clearly indicated.

Designing Programs That Help Clients Develop a Positive Lifestyle

An important aspect to consider in developing an outpatient treatment program is how the program will help the client to develop a more positive overall lifestyle. Although this aspect should be considered by *all* types of programs, the outpatient provider has a unique ability to promote a positive lifestyle because the client is altering maladaptive patterns and is learning to act in more healthy and adaptive ways *in the community.*

Thompson (1989) discusses three levels in the development of a healthy lifestyle: (1) attending to biological necessities (e.g., eating, sleeping), (2) developing in areas which are not strictly necessary but which promote physical and psychological health (e.g., exercise, stress reduction, meditation/relaxation, prayer), and (3) expanding personal preference activities (e.g., hobbies, social activities, interpersonal relationships). A program that can assist the client in developing more healthy patterns in these three areas will better prepare the client to engage in a healthy lifestyle in future years, which will reduce the risk of relapse (cf. Lundrigan, 1999).

Many behavioral and thought patterns may be targeted in this effort. One must be careful not to consider behaviors themselves as "healthy" or "unhealthy," but one must also take into consideration the ways in which the client thinks about and engages in these behaviors to obtain the fuller picture. As Thompson (1989, p. 220) states, "there are many aspects of a person's lifestyle that can be detrimental or positive depending on the individual's specific level and/or mode of engaging in the behavior." Toward this end, one must help the client not only to engage in healthier behaviors but also to engage in these behaviors in a way that makes them positive in that individual's life.

The individual's physical, mental, and spiritual well-being should be attended to. Frequently clients will not understand the importance of good nutrition and exercise, or they will tend to engage in thinking that makes them unnecessarily anxious and stressed, or they may have neglected their spirituality and lost a sense of the transcendent. Should we not try to help these clients achieve a sense of balanced health, and in so doing empower them to grow out of their maladaptive lifestyles and become the well-rounded individuals they can be?

Constituting Groups

When the program is running more than one SO group (full-range or aftercare), consideration must be given to which clients will be placed in group together. Becker (1996, p. 386) states, "Adolescents should be placed in groups that are appropriate to their age and developmental level . . . it would be inappropriate to place an immature, learning-disabled 13-year-old in a group with mature non-learning-disabled 17-year olds." Adolescents are challenging to work with as a group because they are changing and maturing very rapidly. An age difference of four to five years between peers (while perhaps not significant for an adult population) can mean a tremendous difference in cognitive ability, maturity, and developmental level for adolescents. Different age ranges and different levels of cognitive limitation will require a different approach (e.g., one would present educational material on the dynamics of offending to a twelve-year-old concrete thinker very differently than to a seventeen-year-old with a greater attention span and the ability to think abstractly).

Thought must be given to how clients can be divided by age and developmental level so that groups will be as effective as they can be. Attending to group constitution issues enables the formation of groups that challenge clients without overwhelming them.

Contracts, Conditional Release, and Involuntary Treatment

Sex offense-specific treatment at all levels should be rather structured and may include such tools as written treatment contracts (Barbaree and Cortoni, 1993), agreements with probation or parole officials that make treatment a condition for continued release to the community, and detailed treatment plans. The use of such tools will be discussed in more detail in Chapter 7, but it is important to note that outpatient programs can and ought to make use of tools such as these to aid the client in participating in treatment.

Since most adolescents who have committed a sexual offense do not refer themselves for treatment, and since this is such a difficult topic for clients to discuss, clinicians are often faced with treating involuntary participants. Clients may be under great pressure to show up (which often is formalized in the contracts and grants of conditional release just mentioned), but it still takes some skill to be able to help them to take ownership for their treatment and to make positive gains. Becker (1996) believes that clients should be told in the first session exactly what the conditions of their treatment are (especially if they are involuntary clients). The client, referring source, and program provider must be clear under what stipulations and restrictions the treatment is going to be conducted, what constitutes noncompliance, and what steps the program and referring source will take in the event of such noncompliance (for more information on such contracting please see Green, 1995a).

There is literature that one may review for some guidelines and tips on conducting involuntary outpatient treatment and for information on many other aspects of conducting outpatient treatment with adolescents who have sexually offended (e.g., Meloy, Haroun, and Schiller, 1990; Friedman, 1991; Becker, 1996; Perry and Orchard, 1992).

A COST-SAVING ALTERNATIVE?

Placing a client who might otherwise be placed in group care in an outpatient program would provide a noticeable cost savings. Of course, this should *only* be considered if the client can be adequately and safely treated in an outpatient setting. Funding source and program administrators might well examine how the development of day and after-school programs might serve as an appropriate means of treating offenders effectively in the community, instead of referring them to group care due to a lack of intensive outpatient services in their community. Such a diversion from group care should *not* be considered for clients who are clearly in need of group care, or who have recently been unsuccessful in other outpatient treatment efforts.

A CONTINUUM COMMITTEE

We have thus far discussed the continuum of care and examined in more detail some of the programs that make up that continuum. But how do we ensure that a given geographic area has an adequate diversity of programs? Furthermore, how can we coordinate these programs so that they function as a single system? One solution is a "continuum committee." Such a committee would be composed of representatives of all the programs that treat sexually abusive adolescents in a given area. This group could set common policy, interface with the principal referral sources in the area, work toward establishing a continuity of treatment across programs, and serve as a venue for discussing common cases and for building relationships between programs.

The more that providers in different sex offense-specific programs in a given area know about one another, the more effectively they each can recommend the appropriate program for a given youth. Such a committee meeting on a regular basis can go a long way toward building the ideal of a unified continuum of care presented in Chapter 2, as well as helping to more effectively and efficiently deliver services to the clients referred for treatment.

Chapter 6

Developing the Foundation for Sex Offense-Specific Treatment

INCORPORATING OFFENSE-SPECIFIC TREATMENT INTO THE PROGRAM

Having considered the position of various programs within the continuum of care, and having reviewed aspects of program structure and policies and possible modalities of treatment, we may now consider the foundational issues of putting it all together into a comprehensive treatment program.

The task of incorporating sex offense-specific treatment into a program is somewhat easier if one is beginning a program from scratch. In a new program, the development of program structure and policy and the coordination of different treatment components can be done simultaneously. Thus, the resulting program begins its operations around sex offense-specific principles and functions within a comprehensive treatment model.

More often, however, the need is to take an existing program and adapt it to treat youth who have sexually abused, or to take a program that currently treats sex offense perpetrators and modify and update its services to maximize their effectiveness. In these cases, one begins the task of development with a program that has been operating in a given way. This preexisting sense of identity and the established program operating protocols can be both obstacles and blessings.

The blessing aspect is that one is already past the chaos of setting up and staffing a new program. One hopefully has already established a treatment culture, traditions, stability, as well as a referral and service network, and the day-to-day operational concerns have become routine, leaving the time open to work on more in-depth matters. The obstacles arise when the program has become "set in its ways" and is resistant to the types of changes that need to be made. Incorporating effective sex offense-specific treatment into the program (and/or modifying and upgrading current services) may involve having to think in new ways, deliver treatment in new ways, and somewhat change how other things (e.g., supervising clients, training and scheduling staff, choosing activities) are done. However, on the other side of the coin, it is important that in our efforts to make a good program better, we do not "throw the baby out with the bathwater." To simply perform a wholesale overhaul of the program will likely cause great disruption and harm the effectiveness of a program that is already operating well.

UNIFYING CONCEPTUAL MODEL OF OFFENDING

To ensure a well-coordinated treatment effort, it is necessary to have a common conceptual framework that underlies the services of the various treatment components. Toward this end, it is helpful to adopt a common conceptual model of offending. Several such models may be borrowed from the current literature. Many of these present a diagrammatic representation of the offending process, taking the form of a "cycle" (cf. "The Sexual Assault Cycle," Ryan and Lane, 1998; "The Cycle of Offense," Way and Spieker, 1997), an "offense chain" (cf. Steen, 1993), a scheme for the "dynamics of sexual assault" (cf. Schwartz, 1995b), or some other helpful system (e.g., "The Trauma Outcome Process," Rasmussen, Burton, and Christopherson, 1992; "Four Preconditions: A Model," Finkelhor, 1984). These models provide a means of understanding the complex and often confusing process of sex offending for all who are connected with treatment. Programs need not rely on only one model; many of these models may be successfully integrated and used concurrently to illustrate different parts of the offending and/or recovery process.

The educative value of such models for clients, staff, and parents cannot be overestimated, and the use of common conceptualizations is one of the chief methods of ensuring interconnectedness and overlap among the various components of a program. The use of the same models in SO group, family treatment, staff training, as well as general resident education, and in the explanation of behaviors in the treatment milieu and in the community lends a common language and a common understanding to the two vital questions that all parties must in some ways address: (1) Why do they do it? and (2) What needs to change to prevent future offending?

To this end, these models inform the treatment components by giving direction as to what needs must be addressed and what new skills the client must learn. The reader will note in subsequent chapters that conceptual models play a major role both as a unifying force for the components and as a guide for the more specific work of therapy.

TREATMENT STAGES

In this book, "treatment stages" are specific graduated steps that a client progresses through as he proceeds through sex offense-specific treatment. They help guide treatment by locating for all parties "where we are" in the process, and they also serve as a tangible measure for the client to help him see progress and have a sense of where he needs to go next. Many clients with whom the author has worked have expressed that such predictability and guidance provided them with a level of comfort as they undertook what was often an overwhelming process.

Phases of Treatment and Program Levels

The concept of the treatment stage must be contrasted with the "phases of treatment" presented in Chapter 2. The phases of treatment are overarching divisions of the sex offense-specific treatment that cover pretreatment through termination of all formal therapy. These phases can represent the work done by several programs in the continuum and, as such, are the "big picture" of the client's treatment. The treatment stages discussed here represent a convenient division of that portion of the phases of treatment that will be undertaken by *a given program*. They are therefore specific to the unique structure, goals, and tasks of that program.

It is also helpful to contrast the concept of the treatment stage with the "levels" many programs use to help guide a resident through his stay (note that different programs will refer to their levels by different titles—e.g., levels, phases, stages, steps, etc.). Program levels usually represent advancement in the program and are dependent upon attaining certain goals of treatment and behavior. A client's level status is also typically one of the factors that affects the decision-making process for privileges, passes, and scheduling a discharge date. Levels are a broader category than stages because they take into consideration the whole picture of the client's stay, not just the sex offense-specific treatment. However, since a multi-component model of treatment really involves everything that the client does in the program, it is possible in some programs for stages and levels to be essentially the same thing.

When determining what sort of system a program might employ to guide and mark treatment progress, several model options may be considered. Some of these options are depicted in Figure 6.1.

A. A program level system and a *separate* and unconnected stage system for marking work in SO therapy, or

B. A program level system that is connected to a subordinate stage system via the SO treatment, which is a common criterion for level and stage advancement

C. A coexisting and interconnected level and stage system, or

D. All aspects of the client's advancement covered under the program's level system

If a program is being started from scratch, and especially if it is a sex offense-specific-only program, it may make sense to have one system, such as in model D. However, if the program will have a mixed population and/or if the effort is to modify an existing program that already has a well-functioning level system, one may consider utilizing a dual advancement system. Of these dual systems, model A is the least desirable. This program model involves a sex offense-specific group, operated perhaps by an outside clinician, that is largely unlinked to level advancement and decision making. Such a program would send clients elsewhere for a sex offense-specific group, an arrangement that may afford little opportunity for progress in SO treatment to have a meaningful impact on program level status.

Most programs seem to fall under model B. These have established program level systems, sometimes called "point-level" systems, in which points earned by clients for positive behaviors are reflected in level advancement. In addition, they have a separate series of stages that the client must progress through in sex offense-specific treatment. This allows for the use of guiding stages in the offense-specific work without the destruction of the level system. In such a scheme, the client's stage, in as much as it is an indicator of progress in SO treatment, is one of the factors influencing level advancement. Such

FIGURE 6.1. Four Models of Integration

Model A: Independent Level and Stage Systems (Lowest Integration)

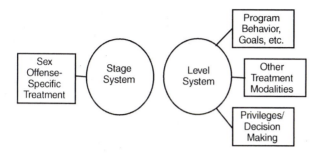

Model B: Stage and Level Systems Linked Through Sex Offense-Specific Treatment

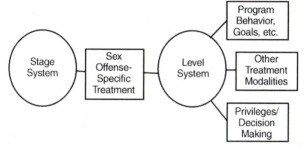

Model C: High Level of Integration Between Systems

Model D: One System for Maximum Integration

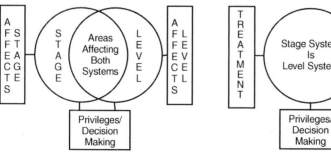

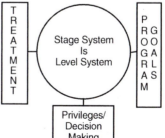

an approach can be utilized in a sex offense-specific only program or in one with a mixed population, in which case the clients in sex offense-specific treatment have an extra set of goals (advancement in the stage system) tied to their advancement in program level.

If a program operates a level system that is less tied to a *point structure* and more geared toward *advancement based upon attainment of defined program goals,* then perhaps it would consider an approach such as model C, in which the attainment of the levels is also closely tied to the attainment of certain stages in the sex offense-specific work. In such a system, many common areas in both the stage and level systems are used to determine advancement. Certain factors affect stage but not level, and other factors which affect level but not stage (e.g., developing relapse prevention strategies may directly affect stage alone, and proper completion of house chores may directly affect level alone). However, in this model, in addition to the particular influences on stage and level advancement, the attainment of level depends *in part* on advancement in stage, and vice versa. Since attaining a stage is partly dependent upon attaining a certain level, and attaining a level is partly dependent upon attaining a certain stage, both systems exert pressure on the client to attend to advancement in the other system. In such a model, stage and level are both taken into consideration in decision making. This model can be used with a sex offense-specific-only program or with a mixed population. In the latter case, the non-sex-offending clients would not have stage advancement requirements for their level advancement, or perhaps they would also have a stage system operating around their primary area of treatment.

A Sample Stage System

The following stage system, which can be adapted and used in the context of any of the four model options presented, was developed by the author for implementation at a long-term residential program where he was employed. It helped to spell out for the client, clinicians, and staff just what the client ought to be doing in his sex offense-specific treatment during each of the defined stages.

1. *Stage 1—Orientation and Assessment.* Tasks include the following (possible time frame of two months):

  • Meet with SO therapist prior to entering group.
  • Disclose offenses to therapist; begin individual therapy.
  • Begin SO group and disclose offenses to group.

- Complete the "orientation packet."
- Finish sex offense-specific assessment.

2. *Stage 2—Exploring, Changing, and Relearning.* Tasks include the following (possible time frame of nine to twelve months):

- Continue in weekly SO group.
- Continue in weekly individual therapy.
- Be able to genuinely take responsibility for offenses.
- Deepen understanding of self and sexual abuse cycle and dynamics.
- Explore family dynamics and role in family.
- Come to grips with own victimization.
- Explore own sexuality, normal sexual behavior, as well as male and female roles.
- Develop a degree of empathy for victims.
- Increase quality of social skills and interactions.
- Learn to recognize, identify, and express feelings.
- Explore the role and function of fantasy, and work to modify deviant fantasy.
- Learn about grooming, maintenance, coercion/force, and pre-offense patterns; apply this understanding to self.
- Develop a background for relapse prevention planning.
- Work on *all* issues through sessions with counselor, daily group therapy, multiple family therapy (MFT), and milieu treatment in the program.

3. *Stage 3—Relapse Prevention Planning.* Tasks include the following (possible time frame of three months):

- Continue with SO group and *all* other treatment.
- Complete "relapse prevention packet."
- Complete preliminary relapse prevention plan.
- Present plan to SO and MFT groups for feedback.
- Complete final plan.
- Participate in aftercare planning; start aftercare follow-up component.
- Establish contact with next therapist.
- Graduate and enter treatment in the community.

4. *Stage 4—After Graduation.* Tasks include the following (possible time frame of three months for active program involvement, at the discretion of the provider):

- Follow up with program by participation in aftercare follow-up component.
- Continue in aftercare treatment with next provider.
- Review and follow relapse prevention plan.

In addition to this general scheme, the client's individualized treatment plan would contain specifics regarding accomplishing the tasks of these stages as well as others more "program-wide." For example, the general goal to increase quality of social skills and interactions may include client-specific subgoals such as the following: "Bring to SO group incidents where I have frustrated others by my behavior and I don't know why"; "Begin to be aware of what feelings I experience when rejected by others"; "Figure out what goes through my mind when I am isolating." More program-wide tasks could include these goals: "Participate in social skills group once per week"; "Participate in at least three recreational activities per week"; "Initiate at least two conversations with peers between supper and bedtime." In this way, the general scheme is individualized to the specific client.

The first three stages of this four-stage system make up the client's active time in the program and take into account two assumptions. The first of these is that assessment and orientation are transitional measures as much as practical concerns. Stage 1 therefore allows the client a "low impact" therapy time while he is adjusting to the program and preparing to do the work of Stage 2. The second assumption is that since clients tend to want to jump to the final work of treatment too quickly at times, they need to have a marker to keep them from moving to this point too soon. Once there, they need motivation to focus on more difficult aspects of this final work. This marker is provided by attainment of Stage 3.

A given program's development or modification of a series of sex offense-specific treatment stages will have great impact on other aspects of the client's stay in the program. In any multi-modal sex offense-specific program, these stages not only will apply to the sex offense-specific group but also will guide the provision of services by other components.

DEFINING A COURSE OF TREATMENT

Once a program has decided upon conceptual models and an overall plan for client treatment and examined how that plan will coordinate with the greater matrix of the program, a course of treatment can be determined. Basically, a course of treatment is a list of steps that outlines the progression of the client through the various interventions and services provided by the program. The more integrated the stage and level systems, the more this course can come to resemble a single line of progression through both systems, not two separate courses of treatment. The program's course of treatment then becomes the framework within which to establish the goals of the treatment plan. An effective course of treatment should attempt as much as possible to outline the provision of services for the client from preadmission screening to aftercare follow-up, incorporating all the varied aspects of the program.

A Sample Course of Treatment

The following course of treatment was successfully used to organize the various components of one treatment program to assign responsibility for different areas of the clients' treatment. Prior to this model of sex offense-specific treatment the program had relied on a four-step level system for almost twenty years. A decision was made to create a sex offense-specific treatment model of type C, described earlier, and to devise a stage system for sex offense-specific treatment that would be linked and coordinated with the highly successful level system.

Preacceptance Screening Interview

Referral material (a complete packet that must be received prior to interviewing a client) is reviewed by the clinical director, education director, and sex offense-specific therapist. Prospective clients who are deemed immediately inappropriate by virtue of this material are screened out and no interviews are scheduled. Those accepted are interviewed by the clinical director, education director, and sex offense-specific therapist. It is also customary to interview the referral source representative, the youth's parents, and the prospective resident—separately. The sex offense-specific therapist uses direct, intense questioning to assess the client's willingness and ability to do work in the program, and to firmly set the tone and expectations for treatment should the resident be accepted. Clients may be rejected for admission for any of the following reasons:

- Denial of offenses for which he has been charged
- Clear intention not to cooperate in treatment
- Determination to be a substantial risk to sexually act out, and hence requiring more supervision that the program is equipped to provide
- Determination that the program cannot adequately provide for the treatment needs of the youth
- Determination that the youth cannot assimilate the group process of either the program or SO groups

Decisions to accept or reject prospective clients are made either at the time of the interview or following consultation with the program director.

Program Intake

Residents* who are accepted for admission complete the program intake and are placed on the "orientation level" of the program. They are assigned an advocate counselor and enter the routine of the milieu (residents do not enter SO group at this time). All residents referred and accepted for sex offense-specific treatment are assigned the sex offense-specific therapist as their individual clinician. Staff are given information via the communication log or face to face with regard to the client and any special concerns that may be present. Supervision is close on the orientation level.

Initial Meeting with the Sex Offense-Specific Therapist

The youth meets with the sex offense-specific therapist in his first week of residency to begin the individual therapy process, become oriented to the SO treatment components, sign the SO group contract, disclose offenses in detail, be assigned a resident "mentor" (to be dis-

---

*For the remainder of this example clients are referred to as "residents." This reflects the fact that this course of treatment was designed for a group care program and does not mean to imply that a course of treatment could not be used by other providers.

cussed later), and begin the assessment stage of treatment (Stage 1). At this time, the resident begins working on his "orientation packet." There may be two or more meetings before the resident is judged ready to enter SO group, but the process of entering group is moved along as quickly as possible. The reasons for this are so that the resident will not be unnecessarily delayed in treatment and so that he will recognize the importance of the group for his treatment. The SO clinician will contact previous service providers throughout the assessment period as all the staff gains an understanding of the youth and his particular treatment needs.

Resident Begins SO Group

Just about all residents are deemed ready to enter the SO group in their second or third week in the program. In his first group meeting, the resident discloses his offenses to the group, a process which has been made easier since he has already done this with the therapist individually. All other residents redisclose prior to the new resident's disclosure. The resident will attend the SO group for the remainder of his stay.

Commit to the Program and Enter Program Level 1

After his first thirty days, the resident makes a commitment to remain in the program and to work on his issues. He presents a request to the full program group to be accepted, and after passing a vote by his peers, he is admitted to Level 1 in the program. He is not pass eligible and does not yet begin family therapy. He is expected to be engaging in all his areas of treatment, and to come to grips with the realities of his situation, including the harshest reality of all—coming face to face with oneself.

Complete Assessment and Advance to Stage 2

After he has attained Level 1, and after he has successfully completed his SO initial assessment and orientation packet, the resident is eligible to apply for advancement to Stage 2. This step (usually accomplished after about sixty days of treatment) means that the resident becomes a voting member of the SO group and can be given additional responsibilities in that group. The resident now begins to focus on the many tasks of Stage 2.

*Begin Multiple Family Therapy and Parent Education
and Involvement Component*

After three months in the program, during which the resident has been focusing on issues of self, he begins multiple family therapy. This creates a bridge to Level 2 by providing intensive feedback on self from the family, while opening up the series of issues that will be the primary focus of Level 2. The parent education and involvement component begins for the family. (Note: Clients who have committed sex offenses and their families are in separate multiple family groups from residents with other issues.) Residents attend the MFT groups and education component regardless of extent of parental attendance.

Attain Level 2 in the Program and Begin Passes

By taking increased responsibility and demonstrating leadership in the program, and by working on his issues in individual therapy, sessions with his counselor, family therapy, peer group therapy, sex offense-specific group, and in the milieu, the resident may advance to Level 2 in the program. This step is taken in the full group after debate and voting. Attainment of Level 2 signals the beginning of greater focus on community and family issues. Level 2 residents are eligible to receive out-of-program passes (provided they meet other clinical conditions). SO residents who have offended a family member are not granted home passes until appropriate family meetings and clinical interventions have been conducted (although they may receive community passes).

Begin Process to Enter Stage 3

Residents who have been engaged in Level 2 and Stage 2 work who feel that they are nearing completion of the Stage 2 tasks (generally after nine to twelve months of treatment) may request to meet with the SO therapist regarding advancement to Stage 3. At this meeting the resident and clinician review the Stage 2 tasks and establish goals to be met in order to advance to Stage 3. The resident then focuses on these areas in addition to continuing work on his other issues.

Advance to Stage 3 and Begin Relapse Prevention Planning

Once the goals have been met, the resident advances to Stage 3. This advancement, similar to Stage 2, takes place formally in the SO group and has its own particular rituals and group voting procedures. He begins to work on his "relapse prevention packet" and is exempt from regular group homework (except assignments directly related to his relapse prevention planning work). The resident makes special presentations to the group to receive feedback and advice to assist in this process.

Attain Level 3 in the Program and Begin Community Reintegration

After progressing in all areas of his treatment, and after displaying to staff and clinicians attainment of relevant goals, the resident may earn Level 3 in the program. Along with other privileges, the Level 3 resident has greater flexibility and freedom on passes (as is deemed clinically prudent). This allows the resident to reintegrate with his home community (or became acquainted with his next living situation) in preparation for his graduation. The resident's general focus of treatment turns to issues of community and life after the program as well as working on issues that still require resolution.

Attend Aftercare Planning Meeting, Begin Step 1 of Aftercare Follow-Up Component, and Meet with Next Therapist

Once graduation can be projected, an aftercare planning meeting is scheduled. After this meeting, the resident is enrolled in the aftercare follow-up component. As part of Step 1 of the aftercare component, the resident will have at least one session with the next therapist, he will work to formulate an aftercare plan, and the SO therapist will begin a dialogue with the next provider to facilitate a smooth transition.

Begin Aftercare Group

The resident then enters the aftercare group (a group consisting of residents preparing to graduate and recent graduates of the program). The resident will continue in this aftercare group following his return to the community, if this is possible and deemed by the next provider to fit into the treatment plan. Placement in an outpatient aftercare group might take the place of the program's aftercare or sex offense-specific group for a client. This would allow the resident to begin work with his next provider while still living at the residential program.

Complete Transition Checklist

This checklist contains the final tasks that the resident must complete prior to graduating. Two important tasks on this list are the completion of a relapse prevention plan and the development of an aftercare plan.

Graduate from the In-House Portion of the Program

A celebration and formal ceremony are held to mark this important step in the client's treatment.

Begin and Continue Step 2 of Aftercare Follow-Up

This involves the client shifting his allegiance to his new service provider and negotiating the very difficult first few months in the community. During this time, the client is in outpatient therapy, maintains contact with the program at mutually determined intervals (to smooth the transition), and continues in multiple family therapy group and residential aftercare group, if this is possible and deemed beneficial.

Complete Transition and Enter Step 3 of Aftercare Component

After approximately three months, the client has successfully transitioned to the community and he and the family have developed a support network apart from the residential program. At a mutually determined time, the family separates from MFT and the client ceases to attend the residential aftercare group. The program remains available to the ex-resident, family, and future service providers to assist as needed.

THE USE OF CLIENT MENTORS

Some programs have experimented with using older clients to mentor younger clients during the early stages of their treatment. This technique, whether official or de facto, has some benefits. The one-to-one assistance of a peer can help to bring a client into the culture of the program and can help to ease his transition. In addition, the mentor benefits, gaining insights through teaching and a sense of competence from positively helping someone. Finally, both new clients and mentors benefit in terms of learning more appropriate interpersonal dynamics. There are, of course, many potential problems with using such a system. These range from clients being able to haze new members under the guise of the mentor-mentoree relationship, clients being given erroneous information regarding program policies, and older adolescents taking advantage of the new clients either for amusement or in an abusive context. One can easily see how the use of this technique with sex abuse perpetrators can be potentially problematic.

This being said, it is possible to use mentoring for client orientation if it is closely monitored and if the program has developed a culture that is supportive of treatment and discourages misuse of power. Some ways in which a client mentor can be useful include the following:

- To help the mentoree by answering questions regarding group procedures and requirements for completing assignments
- To teach the mentoree the basics of the conceptual model
- To guide the mentoree regarding whom he should go to for various needs
- To give input to the group regarding the mentoree's readiness to advance in the stage system
- To serve as a source of information for the clinical staff on the mentoree's behaviors and thoughts

The mentoring relationship needs to be monitored closely by staff. If staff cannot or are not willing to monitor this relationship closely, then perhaps the program should not use mentors. Guidelines must be put into place to maintain an appropriate relationship. These guidelines should be agreed to by both new clients and new mentors, and staff must be trained to know when a mentor-mentoree relationship is moving outside the boundaries marked by these standards. The following are some possible guidelines:

- Mentors do *not* do therapy or counseling with their mentorees; rather, they direct the mentorees to the appropriate counselor or clinician for these needs.
- Mentors do *not* get into the specifics of the mentorees' cycles; rather, they teach the general principles of those cycles.

- Mentors encourage mentorees to form relationships with a variety of staff and residents in the program; they do *not* form exclusive relationships with their mentorees.
- Mentors do not do work for the mentorees; rather, they provide support and reminders to help the mentorees do the work on their own.
- Mentors are not to exchange gifts of any kind with the mentorees nor should they perform special favors for them.
- Mentors *never* help mentorees complete assessment tools given to them; rather, they tell the mentorees that they must honestly complete them on their own.
- Mentors bring *any* concerns they have concerning their mentorees to their clinicians or a member of staff as soon as possible.

Clearly, the decision to use mentors or not needs to be made with due regard for the safety of clients and with consideration of how such a technique would fit (if at all) in the overall treatment structure of the program. It is also important to carefully select which clients would be used as mentors, to train *and monitor* them appropriately, and to match them carefully with incoming clients.

NOTES ON TOLERANCE, RESPONSIBILITY, AND CULTURE

An important foundation for sex offense-specific treatment in the program involves program environment and culture. These concerns center around programs taking steps to create an environment, through education, that is tolerant and understanding of the needs of clients and staff alike. This means that prejudices and myths which would create attitudes counterproductive to treatment have been for the most part removed. In this environment, a strong sense of responsibility on the part of staff and clients helps the clients begin to take increased responsibility for their offending.

Such a program will instill in its clients a sense of investment in treatment and will help clients to feel part of, and responsible for, their treatment. Such a program will work to evaluate its culture and determine (1) what attitudes, positions, behaviors, and policies generate resistance to the development of a healthy treatment culture,

(2) what can be done to positively impact these conditions, and (3) what are we doing well that we need to do more of.

A successful program will produce a setting that encourages clients to work, to have a sense of ownership in their work, and to deal with the issues that got them into treatment. A successful program will make clients feel that they belong. It will make them part of a way of life, tie them to a history, and involve them in ritual that will make them believe they are truly members of this community—that "we're all in this together."

PART III:
THE COMPONENTS OF TREATMENT

Chapter 7

The Sex Offense-Specific Group

WHAT MAKES A GROUP SEX OFFENSE-SPECIFIC?

The staple of a treatment program for sex offenders is the sex of-fense-specific group. Group therapy has long been regarded as the treatment of choice for the work of sex offense-specific therapy (Way and Balthazor, 1990), and it is used in secure, residential, and outpatient settings. Seghorn (1986) has reported that as many as 97 percent of service providers use a peer group as the primary modality of treatment, and most of these recognize that the group, although vital, cannot be the only mode of treatment used. *The 1996 Nationwide Survey of Sexual Abuse Treatment Providers and Programs* by Burton and colleagues (1996) reports that actually 86 percent of the programs surveyed nationwide use a group treatment modality. However, it should be noted that this source also reports that only 2 percent of providers use no group *by choice,* while the others are *not able* to provide groups for one reason or another.

Perhaps the most important benefit of placing a sex offense-specific group in a multi-component setting is that you can do more in-depth work in that group due to the presence of other sex offense-specific components in the program. Unlike a lone SO group, an SO group couched in a larger framework of sex offense-specific treatment modalities may share the burden of addressing a given issue with other components in the program.

Sex offense-specific groups have the benefit of peer interaction, which helps promote self-disclosure through both support and confrontation (Margolin, 1984). Conducting peer groups is more than a matter of saving money compared to the use of individual therapy, as Seghorn (1986) states:

> Group treatment appears to facilitate more direct confrontation of offenses by providing peer support for disclosure and exploration of issues that even the most adaptive adolescent would consider difficult to discuss with adults: sexuality and sexual identity. (p. 18)

In addition to these benefits, the SO group also provides a place for the offender to process thought patterns and behaviors that have occurred in the program milieu or in the community as they relate to his sexual-offending issue. SO groups can use a variety of psycho-educational, cognitive-behavioral, experiential, analytical, and rational-emotive therapy techniques.

Unique and Common Characteristics

Sex offense-specific groups function similar to other groups; they progress through various stages and manifest various problems (Schwartz, 1995a). The sex offense-specific group leader should be well studied and trained in details of general group psychotherapy theory. When dealing with adolescents in a group therapy setting, the many common theoretical positions surrounding group development, culture, and technique will be very applicable. The reader is referred to the vast amount of literature on this subject that is available and in common use (e.g., Yalom, 1985, and later editions; Naar, 1986; Corder, 1994; etc.). SO groups may operate from a variety of different theoretical foundations and formats (e.g., psychodynamic, relapse prevention, cognitive restructuring, behavioral, psychopharmacological, etc.), and most employ a variety of approaches (Schwartz, 1995a). The therapist will want to be well versed in the literature that discusses in detail conducting group therapy for sexually abusive clients (e.g., Ryan and Lane, 1998; Barbaree, Marshall, and Hudson, 1993; Eldridge, 1998b; Ingersoll and Patton, 1990; Maletzky, 1991; Marshall et al., 1983; Perry and Orchard, 1992; Prendergast, 1991; Way and Balthazor, 1990; etc.).

One area that distinguishes SO groups from many other types of groups is the use of cycles, chains, patterns, and clocks* to provide a

---

*"Clocks" are diagrams similar to a clock face which help the client conceptualize his current level of risk. Clients can be asked to state where they are (by reporting "hour" or quadrant) in terms of progressing from safety to warning to danger to offending. For more information please see Cusack, 1999.

framework for the discussion and conceptualization of issues. These cycles (and indeed the basic concepts of relapse prevention) are taken from the substance abuse treatment field (Cusack, 1999) and have been modified for use with sex offenders. One can also find such cycles, chains, patterns, and clocks in use with many substance abuse programs and with male batterers (cf. Pence and Paymar, 1990); however, the sex abuse treatment field has made special use of these tools.

In SO groups, cycles are used principally to identify past and present patterns, to identify future risks, and to develop new and more adaptive responses (Ryan and Lane, 1998). The cycle used in the sex offense-specific group would be drawn from the unifying conceptual model of the program, thus providing a pattern that is theoretically linked to the common model being used by all the interconnected components. An important consideration in the use of cycles in group is the amount of flexibility that the therapist is able to muster in adapting the model to individual clients, without jeopardizing the integrity of the model.

As types of offenders—and individuals—vary, one must try to adapt the presentation, explanation, and specifics of the model to fit the different characteristics of each client (Eldridge, 1998b). It is worthwhile in this effort to have other clients articulate the concepts to their peers in a manner that they can understand (Cusack, 1999). Likewise, it is important to use various examples and to illustrate alternate ways of using the cycle to help the client discover his own pattern. Eldridge (1998b) states:

> When running groups it's important to offer the options of different starting points and different sets of beliefs: the lightbulb visibly goes on in the offenders' heads when they recognize a pattern like their own. (p. 8)

A second area that distinguishes sex offense-specific groups from other groups is the absolute insistence on using a male-female team of coleaders. It is very difficult for one leader alone to tend to the many signs that must be watched and to handle the intense emotional and often aggressive content that may arise in group. The team of leaders also serves as a security measure by minimizing the possibility of group members ganging up on a single leader (emotionally or physically). The presence of a female is a desirable means of correcting members' misconceptions about women (Margolin, 1983), while the male therapist can role model for the clients a male who is assertive without being manipulative or aggressive. In addition, since many of these adolescents may have a difficult time dealing with females, it is good for them to experience an assertive, competent woman in a position of authority. Finally, the interaction between the male and female therapists provides a model of a cooperative, equal male-female relationship (Perry and Orchard, 1992).

The third distinguishing characteristic of SO groups is their relatively small optimal size. Although some strictly psychoeducational curricula indicate that these groups can handle up to twenty clients (cf. Abbott, 1992), most authors advocate for four to ten members at most (cf. Ross, 1994; Perry and Orchard, 1992; Lundrigan, 1996a; Margolin, 1983). The general feeling is that a small number of clients is prudent, given the level of intensity of such groups, the complexity of the material that the leaders must be paying attention to for each client, the need to provide a safe setting for disclosure, and the necessity of coping with the tendency of these clients to try to "blend into the woodwork." This will sometimes mean that a given program may need more than one SO group to accommodate all the clients; however, the benefits of small groups will be worth the effort.

A fourth difference between SO groups and other groups is in the use of certain SO specific counseling techniques and goals of treatment. Many of these techniques are either unique to SO work or have been modified from other fields to be sex offense-specific. These include victim confrontation of offender, restitution, sexual reconditioning techniques, use of anxiety, processing of fantasy and masturbation, study of offense details, and relapse prevention planning. The reader is referred to *The 1996 Nationwide Survey of Sexual Abuse Treatment Providers and Programs* (Burton et al., 1996), which has the most up-to-date and comprehensive information on sex offense-specific programs around the country. This survey also provides information on specifically what treatment methods and models different providers are using in their groups and in their programs as a whole (see Appendix A for more information on this survey).

A fifth area uncommon to some groups but standard with sex offense-specific groups involves active attempts at engagement and "hooking" the client into treatment. By and large, we are dealing with clients who did not choose to seek help for their issues. As with many criminal justice populations (and substance abusers as well), the therapist must actively work to elicit cooperation and participation from the clients, at least until they have been helped to develop a sense of personal responsibility for, and investment in, their treatment.

It is important to note that this does not mean that the client must be bullied, harassed, or threatened into cooperation (for indeed this may increase his level of resistance); rather, the therapist should actively attempt to move the client from a position of being "acted upon" by the treatment to one of working actively himself in treatment toward a common goal.

General Group Format and the SO Group

This section examines four views on group structure. Each of these views will be presented as a comparison between two poles on a continuum, followed by an examination of the most efficacious spot on the spectrum for a sex offense-specific group.

Psychoeducational versus Process Oriented

One may loosely classify groups as "psychoeducational"—that is, oriented more toward education and didactic instruction with the chance for application to self—or "process oriented"—that is, a more intensive and personal group format that allows a focus on various activities more formally called therapy. It is an oversimplification to classify all groups into one of these two orientations, but the tension between the "educational" and the "psychotherapy" groups has played an important part in the development of many sex offense-specific groups.

The earliest therapy groups were largely psychoanalytic and used a process-oriented, open, rather undirected approach (cf. Schwartz, 1995a). Later groups followed this open-process vein, some using more client-centered and humanistic approaches reflecting further developments in the psychotherapy field (cf. Naar, 1986). Certainly, some programs still have groups using these and similar formats with some success. However, it seems that more directive, structured approaches to group therapy are the most effective ones to use with those who sexually abuse (e.g., rational-emotive and cognitive-behavioral approaches); thus, these have become the predominant models used in the past two decades.

Many of the more directive *cognitive* approaches are quite process oriented, while many strictly *behavioral* groups tend to focus more on educational activities. The psychoeducational group is a development of these more cognitive and behaviorally oriented schools, and such groups have been used with great success with sex offenders, especially those in the early stages of treatment, or in cases in which treatment needed to be delivered to a large group of clients.

However, despite the advent and efficacy of the psychoeducational group, the use of even *more* process-oriented cognitive groups has also remained prominent and successful. Some program providers have favored the use of one or the other of these general types of groups in their treatment regimes. Some have even combined both types in one group or have run groups of different formats concurrently within their programs. In fact, it seems that both elements are needed, the relative mix being determined by what other services are being provided to the client. The successful SO group will make use of psychoeducation, on the one hand, and more in-depth, cognitive, emotive, insight-oriented, and group interaction-centered therapy, on the other.

Structured versus Unstructured

Directive, structured approaches to group therapy work better with sex offenders. Often we are dealing with persons who can be highly manipulative, who lack a genuine investment in treatment, who are disorganized and ill prepared to properly interact in group settings, and who would love to avoid discussing some of these very embarrassing and distressing topics. Ross (1994) believes that the groups should be highly structured from the beginning and advocates the use of written contracts and firm rules. He also believes that offending clients are made to feel safe by the imposition of structure, and that they welcome levels of structure that would be unbearable to others. Perry and Orchard (1992) contrast less structured "open psychotherapy" groups with more structured approaches. They discuss the benefits of less structured groups, but they concede that a loose format makes it difficult to gauge progress, plan activities, and encourage client responsibility for treatment.

In addition, a great many topics should be covered in treatment for it to be effective. If one does not have some sort of guiding structure, how will one be sure not to fail to address a pertinent issue? This concern brings us to one of the most important structuring elements that can be employed: a group curriculum. The curriculum is useful whether the group is highly psychoeducational *or* highly process oriented. Other common structuring elements include contracts, firm rules, clear expectations, a directive approach by the therapists, homework assignments, stage systems, visual aids, written handouts/

workbooks, and conceptual models. The purpose is to add structure to the group process without stifling it to the point of ineffectiveness.

Finally, intentional structuring helps those who feel threatened by group therapy (Schwartz 1995a). The structure can lessen the anxiety of attending group by providing a safe setting for the client. Schwartz describes adjusting the amount of structure of the group as needed, advocating a lessening of structure as the group becomes more able to handle emotionally charged material. It is best that such reduction in structure comes in the areas of therapist intensity and directiveness, rather than in the "hard" elements of the group structure (i.e., contracts, curriculum, rules, models, etc.).

Open Ended versus Closed Ended

Another important decision to make with regard to the setup of the group is whether it will be "open ended"—that is, running continuously, taking in new members as they arrive, and terminating individual members as they complete group—or "closed ended"—that is, taking in a specific group of clients all at once, running for a predetermined number of sessions, and then terminating as a group. Both of these familiar formats are commonly used in sex offense-specific treatment programs. The choice to run groups open or closed ended will depend on the setting of the program (secure, residential, outpatient), the theoretical orientation of the program (with more psychoeducational leanings tending to favor closed-ended groups), and the makeup of the services provided by other components of the program.

Many secure, residential, and outpatient groups are closed ended either because it makes more sense to assemble a group of clients due to referral concerns or because such closed-ended groups represent individual "packages" in a planned series of groups. However, most programs opt for the use of open-ended groups (Schwartz, 1995a). Some authors have cited the benefits of an open-ended format because they believe it makes the greatest impact in the long run (Ross, 1994), it helps the client to deal with loss (Schwartz, 1995a), it provides a sense of continuity with fewer gaps in treatment (Lundrigan, 1996a). Other benefits to a continuously running group are the building of a culture over time and the development of a quasi-therapeutic milieu.

It is of course possible to run groups of both types in the same program, but, again, this must be done with due concern for how such an approach will fit into the total treatment package presented by the program. Furthermore, consideration must be paid as to how this coincides with the program's philosophy of group treatment.

One Group versus a Series of Groups

In some programs, the SO group component consists of a single SO group, whereas other programs use several different groups to achieve the same goals. The latter view conceptualizes the sex offense-specific group as not *one* group, but a *series* of groups through which the client must progress prior to termination. An excellent example of such a system is used by the Justice Resource Institute sex offense-specific treatment program at the Massachusetts Treatment Center in Bridgewater, Massachusetts. This program (as explained by Baker et al., 1999) is a well-structured and carefully designed treatment regime that has been used with success and is well worth further exploration.

The author favors the simplicity of a single SO group operating in the program. This group works through a given range of therapeutic interventions while coordinating with other treatment components in the program. The matter is really one of personal preference. The consideration should be, "What type of group setup and format will fit best in our program, will achieve the greatest therapeutic gain, and will be most clear and easy for staff and clients to understand and participate in?"

Several Views on the Goals of the SO Group

Regardless of the format chosen, the SO group (or series of groups) will need to address certain specific goals of treatment. This section examines several opinions on the goals a sex offense-specific group should be working toward. There is, of course, significant overlap between these goals and the general goals of treatment listed elsewhere in this book.

Many resources are available regarding group structure, operation, curricula, exercises, and goals. Appendix C provides a list of group resources. To make sense of the many possible goals for the SO group, and in an attempt to distill these possibilities into one comprehensive list, it is helpful to examine some of the goals proposed by various authors.

Green (1995b) lists the following five goals as the major areas to be covered in treatment:

1. Admitting guilt
2. Accepting responsibility
3. Understanding dynamics
4. Identifying deviant cycle
5. Making restitution

The final goal is not found in all lists but may be an interesting one to consider, as it has been found to be beneficial to victims and offenders alike (cf. Schwartz, 1995a). This list places emphasis on taking responsibility and understanding the dynamics of abuse, but has little to say about personal corrective measures taken by the client, or about the wider context of offending behaviors.

Contrast the previous list with Perry and Orchard (1992), who approach the problem from a slightly different angle. They state that treatment must help the client (1) understand the compulsive nature of his behavior and develop internal and external controls, (2) alter attitudes and beliefs that support offending, (3) become aware that his sexual preference is deviant and that he must learn to develop more appropriate preferences, and (4) find ways of coping with stress and develop behavior management skills to deal with life's demands. The emphasis here is on change as well as understanding. The client is called upon to develop new behaviors to replace those which have been found to be deviant and/or contributory to the offending. There is also an emphasis on some cognitive measures and on the need to alter thoughts (i.e., attitudes and beliefs). This list expands our concept of the group's role, especially in the areas of behavioral modification cognitions.

Another goal list that expands the concept of the group's role is found in Cumming and Buell (1997). They list the six goals for treatment from the Vermont Network of Sex Offender Therapists 1995 guidelines for treatment. This list emphasizes the scope of treatment and mentions posttreatment supervision needs. The six goals are as follows:

1. Accepting responsibility and modifying cognitive distortions
2. Developing victim empathy
3. Controlling sexual arousal
4. Improving social competence
5. Developing relapse prevention skills
6. Establishing supervision conditions and networks

Other lists have placed a greater emphasis on cognitive interventions in more detail than all the preceding have, although sometimes at the expense of some of the more practical behavioral modifications. Consider this list from Eldridge (1998b) which dictates that treatment should address the following areas:

1. Patterns or cycles of offending
2. Cognitive distortions
3. Cognitive empathy
4. Affective empathy
5. Sexuality
6. Social relationships
7. Self

Eldridge expands the role of cognitive interventions and adds the very important area of victim empathy work. In addition, she places some focus on the personal development of the client by looking at sexuality and the self. But what of the more behavioral interventions or the types of skills training and future planning that are included elsewhere?

Becker and Kaplan (1993) emphasize behavioral techniques, planning aspects, as well as cognitive interventions and introduce goals that lend themselves well to psychoeducational interventions:

1. Exposing/modifying cognitive distortions
2. Reconditioning deviant arousal
3. Assertiveness and anger control
4. Handling emotions
5. Enhancing social skills
6. Learning about appropriate romantic relationships
7. Understanding human sexuality
8. Planning to prevent relapse

This increased emphasis on the educational functions of the SO group is also seen in Cellini (1995), whose list of specific goals includes education and training as well as more process-oriented therapeutic activities:

1. Social skills training
2. Assertive skills training
3. Enhancing victim empathy
4. Promotion of nondeviant sexual interests

5. General sex education
6. Cognitive restructuring
7. Understanding deviant cycles
8. Self-monitoring strategies

Here we see a list of goals that begins to address how the goals are to be accomplished, with an emphasis on skills training and the development of strategies for self-management, as well as attention to some of the affective and cognitive elements noted elsewhere.

Having reviewed these various lists of goals for the SO group, we will next consider a model that attempts to incorporate as many of the goals as possible and to provide a framework for achieving these goals.

THE SO GROUP
AS A THREE-DIMENSIONAL PROCESS

Figure 7.1 presents a conceptual model for the SO group. This model presents six primary goal areas under which possible goals may be placed and delineates seven group functions that can account for the many techniques and clinical interventions the group may employ. Each of the seven functions plays some part in achieving the goals. It is important to recognize the fluid nature of the group process and realize that one is often working on more than one goal at a time and using more than one function during the course of a given intervention.

The model is guided by the group curriculum, which provides a structure for the work, and by ongoing assessment, which involves the constant revision of treatment plans and further goal definition for each youth in the SO group.

THE PRINCIPAL GOAL AREAS

Promoting Reality and Responsibility

The sex offender's propensity to fail to accept responsibility for his behavior has already been noted. Even the beginning clinician will have seen many clients engage in "mental gymnastics" such that they are frequently not operating in reality with regard to their situation or clinical needs. This does not mean that the client is psychotic (al-

FIGURE 7.1. The Goal Areas and Functions of the Sex Offense-Specific Group

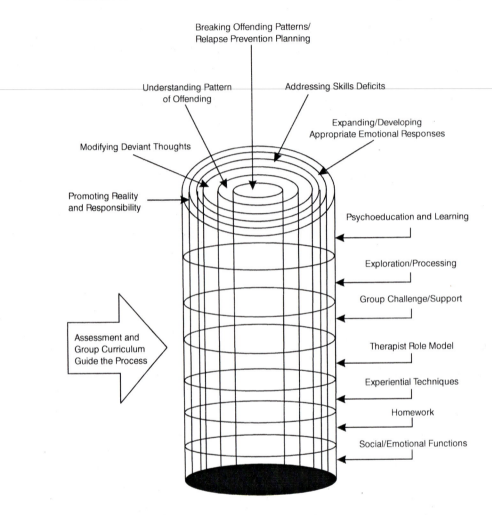

though with some more disturbed persons this may be the case); rather, the client has been hiding from the truth for so long, and covering reality with so many distorted appraisals and judgments, that he may be unable to see the extent and complexity of his problems.

Often this whole process is driven by the client's guilt, shame, and fear of reprisal. Denial and distortion of reality is a defense mechanism the client adopts to lessen the severity of the overwhelming feelings of his own "nastiness," so that on some level he can say to himself, "I didn't really do that. I don't really do that; that's not really me." Often the clinician's part in helping the client to accept reality and responsibility is to show him how to constructively deal with feelings of guilt and shame. The client needs honest self-appraisal and responsibility, not a level of guilt so extreme that it paralyzes.

Acceptance of responsibility is not a one-time event. Once the client has passed the pretreatment phase (usually through an admission to the offense of record and by showing some level of willingness to participate in treatment), he still is not done with the goal of accepting reality and responsibility. As treatment progresses, new issues (and deeper levels of issues) will arise for which the client must accept responsibility and ownership. The client should be encouraged to examine himself, his thoughts and behaviors, his options, and his situation realistically

Finally, the "accepting reality" goal also means that, in some cases, the client *must absolve himself* from responsibility he has assumed *that is not his.* For example, the sex offender who was sexually abused himself must be able to see that the abuse he received was *not* his fault. Accepting responsibility for that can hinder his recovery progress. However, on the other side of the coin, the offenses he committed *are* his to own, and he must absolve his victims of any responsibility that he has placed on them.

Modifying Deviant Thought Patterns

As many of the previous goal lists point out, modifying deviant thought patterns is extremely important to the business of the SO group, and certainly to the entire treatment effort. Deviant thought patterns can take the form of deviant sexual fantasies or beliefs, distorted beliefs about the rightness or appropriateness of certain behaviors, myths concerning sex and sexual offending, mistaken thoughts about victims of sexual abuse and/or specific fantasies of a victim that the offender believes to be real, and deviant thoughts concerning the act of offending.

A second category of deviant thoughts concerns the enabling factors surrounding the offending. These are the many mistaken cognitions, faulty beliefs, irrational thinking, and justifications that allowed the client to engage in thoughts, fantasies, and behaviors that were precursors to the offending behavior. Such patterns of thought justify and enable the early low-risk behaviors that will lead ultimately to an offense. Some examples are failing to believe that future offending is possible; believing deviant thoughts are okay as long as they are not acted upon; "cruising" for potential victims, while denying that is what you are doing; not allowing yourself to see that a situation is risky; mentally "collecting" images for fantasy while looking at others; beginning to have thoughts about potential victims that will enable offending ("I think he really likes me. I bet he would like to have oral sex"—said about a five-year-old); and telling yourself that a relationship is benign when really there is a deviant underpinning.

Finally, the group should address thinking errors that allow the individual to devalue himself and become depressed. Such thinking is damaging to self and can initiate early cycle dynamics. Examples of this type of thinking include putting oneself down, viewing life from a hopeless and negative perspective, rationalizing/justifying substance abuse, and other thoughts that cause one to fail to engage in proper social interactions or to deal with emotions improperly.

Addressing Skills Deficits

Many of the group goals listed previously fall into the category of addressing skills deficits. The client will lack many skills, and a good SO group (along with other treatment components) will address these skills as major goal areas. The client must be assessed for lack of skills in such areas as social and interpersonal interactions, coping, emotion management, conflict resolution, etc. In addition, programs should focus on helping the client to develop skills in practical daily living, financial management, school and vocational pursuits, and treatment participation.

Many of these skills can be worked on in one manner in the SO group while being dealt with differently in other treatment components. The SO group's main tasks in skills building are as follows:

1. Help the client recognize his deficiencies
2. Help him see how these deficits are connected to his offending
3. Direct him to proper resources for developing the needed skills (which includes other program components)
4. Provide him with a venue to practice and refine the newly acquired skills

Expanding/Developing Appropriate Emotional Responses

Sex offenders generally have a rather limited emotional repertoire. This limitation, aside from hampering the development of good social connections and making it difficult for them to express emotions, can also cause them to sexualize relationships (cf. Mayer, 1988). Having a narrow range of emotions means the client may lump emotions into broad categories (e.g., love, closeness, sexual excitement, warm personal feelings, and orgasm are all "love"). This can cause a failure to properly distinguish one emotion, motive, or relationship from another, leading to potentially problematic conflicts. Furthermore, it can be difficult for the client to express in healthy ways the emotions he is experiencing, leaving him to vent them in unhealthy, deviant, aggressive, destructive, and sometimes sex-offending behaviors.

A wide array of benefits can be gained by assisting the client to attend to, understand, and express his emotions in a healthier manner. These benefits range from increased social interaction, to genuine catharsis, to helping build barriers to future offending.

One of the most important foci in this area is the development of victim empathy. A principal factor that has allowed many clients to offend, and may allow them to reoffend, is a lack of appropriate emotional response to the plight of the victim. Development of empathy in offenders is a difficult task, one made more frustrating by the inability of some clients ever to respond fully with empathy for others. Minimally, the client must be able to separate his own feelings from those of the victim (or potential victim). He must realize that the thoughts and feelings of others often differ from those he is experiencing or has experienced. If the client can understand others' uniqueness, he will be less likely to project thoughts, feelings, wants, and desires onto potential victims. This reality, coupled with an ability to authentically empathize with and experience the plight of others, may present a barrier to future offenses.

Understanding the Pattern of Offending

A vital goal area for the group is to help the client uncover his pattern of offending so that this pattern may be understood and broken (cf. Laws, 1989; Marques et al., 1989). This includes discovering what situations (historical, immediate, personal) have led the client to develop sexual offending as a way of coping with his emotions and getting his needs met, how these situations have been engrained into unmanageable patterns, what maintains these patterns, and how they display themselves in everyday behaviors (sexually related or otherwise).

All of the other goal areas are involved with aspects of the sex-offending behavior, but this area examines how the different aspects fit together to produce maladaptive behaviors, including offending. Understanding the overall offending pattern will prepare the client to learn how to intervene in and change these patterns.

Breaking Offending Patterns

The goals in this area represent applying the work done in SO group to the prevention of a return to sex-offending behaviors. Work in this area will generally receive more attention at the end of a residential or secure stay, after other more foundational areas have been addressed at some level. In an outpatient program, the breaking of patterns and the development of relapse prevention plans must take place almost immediately.

Breaking the offending pattern involves developing alternative patterns to replace the more maladaptive patterns to which the client is accustomed. Goals in this area will involve the application of newly learned skills in the development, testing, and attempted use of the new patterns.

Other goals in this area include the development of a comprehensive relapse prevention plan, reconditioning deviant arousal patterns in ways that are more behavioral than those addressed in the "modifying deviant thought patterns" area (e.g., satiation, boredom tapes, pharmacological interventions, masturbatory reconditioning, etc.), and a whole host of practical planning activities to help the client plan for and deal with potentially problematic situations.

THE FUNCTIONS OF THE SO GROUP

Certain aspects of the group advance the client toward the achievement of his goals. These aspects, or "functions," are composed of both techniques that the group may use (see Table 7.1 for examples) and features of the leader and the group itself that are therapeutic and promote growth. Many of the program components use the same functions to achieve their goals. These shared approaches represent areas of overlap between the SO group and the other program components.

TABLE 7.1. Orchard and Perry's Examples of Group Techniques

- **Group Secretary**—A client assumes responsibility for keeping records, recording group topics and homework. Increases sense of involvement and accountability.
- **Journal**—Can be used in many ways, e.g., recording fantasies, journaling emotions, etc.
- **Sexual Issues and Education**—Clients have many gaps and misconceptions to address.
- **Values Clarification Exercises**—Moral reasoning tasks. Can be used for assessment as well as treatment. Helps clients examine beliefs and see other points of view.
- **Video Exercise**—Use of videotapes to stimulate discussions and to teach.
- **Feeling Exercise**—Activities to expand restricted range of emotions (e.g., charades).
- **Psychoeducational Material**—Many curricula available for a variety of purposes.
- **Reenactment of Offenses**—Helping client to understand pattern of offending.
- **Written Assignments**—Homework as well as in-group assignments may be used.
- **Reaching-Out Exercises**—Homework assignments involving trying new behaviors.
- **Skills Training**—Many basic skills deficits that may be addressed by the group.
- **Family Issues**—Examining family relationships as they apply to the abuse. May use such activities as role-plays, discussions, or videotapes.
- **Socialization with Age-Appropriate Peers**—Countering the social isolation that is a contributing factor in offending.
- **Future Planning**—Schooling, employment, dating, marriage, etc.

Source: Revised from *Assessment and Treatment of Adolescent Sex Offenders* (pp. 76-79), by G. P. Perry and J. Orchard, 1992. Sarasota, FL: Professional Resource Exchange. Copyright 1992 by Professional Resource Exchange, Inc. Reprinted by permission.

One will also note that there is some overlap between the functions. This overlap highlights how these functions are used in a combined and fluid way and how the therapist must often employ tactics from different functional orientations almost simultaneously to achieve certain goals.

Psychoeducation and Learning Activities

One of the more important ways in which the group achieves the goals that have been outlined is through educational activities such as discussions, didactic presentations, movies, and other audio and visual aids. The basic theory of the educative functions of treatment is that individuals who are prevented from achieving optimal adjustment due to certain deficits or maladaptive behavior patterns can learn about these patterns and make changes if given alternatives (Green, 1995b).

Green (1995b) lists many benefits of using educational approaches, such as the large number of educational topics that are available, the less threatening nature of didactic presentations when compared to more process-oriented therapy, and the ease with which these methods can help to establish the credibility of the presenter (a definite benefit in pretreatment groups and in the early stages of treatment). Topics of educational interventions include instruction in sexuality issues, sex education, relationships, assertiveness training, offending dynamics, how various deficits and thinking errors relate to offending, techniques and methods that can be used in treatment, and many others.

Another important use of educational functions is to prepare the client for more in-depth therapy work. It is easy to see how teaching the patterns of offending dynamics as well as techniques and methods of treatment on an intellectual level is a preparation for engagement in other more process-oriented clinical activities. More important, many of the noneducational functions discussed in the following material rely on concurrent educational work to achieve their desired effects. For example, cognitive restructuring techniques are often more process-oriented activities, yet as Murphy (1990) reminds us, "As part of cognitive restructuring, offenders need accurate information about sexual abuse and the impact of such abuse on victims" (p. 337).

Many good psychoeducation curricula are available (e.g., Abbot, 1992; Cutler, 1997), or may be developed to suit a program's specific needs. Where appropriate, some of the educational work may be undertaken by other program components, freeing the SO group for other activities.

Therapeutic Exploration and Processing

If the educational functions are responsible for "input" being sent to the client and group, the exploration functions represent the "processing" and "output." These functions involve the eliciting of information from clients in terms of history, present functioning, thought, fantasy, and emotion, and working with these data. These functions ask questions of the client, push him to think and solve problems, and challenge him to apply educational material to himself and make it uniquely his own. These functions take information (verbal, behavioral, written, situational) from the client and pull it apart, explore its meanings, and calculate its implications.

This area also includes many of the cognitive treatment functions. Cognitive modification and cognitive restructuring involve "confronting the adolescent with his maladaptive beliefs about his deviant sexual behavior" and working with him to adapt more reality-based and appropriate cognitions (cf. Becker and Kaplan, 1993, p. 270). An array of techniques available to therapists (see also Becker and Kaplan, 1993; Schwartz, 1995a; and Murphy, 1990) generally involve the dual task of exploration—to determine the current cognitions—and processing—to assess, shed light upon, normalize, and modify the deviant cognitions.

The goals related to understanding and breaking offending patterns are attained partly through therapist exploration and processing. The exploration of client history, thoughts, and present behavior is needed to conceptualize the client's pattern, which is often placed in the context of conceptual models based on educational functions. It is possible to use a variety or combination of cycles (patterns that repeat, with the end stage causing a return to the first stage in the pattern) and chains (linear patterns that culminate in a final condition) in conceptualizing the client's pattern. However the repeating nature of the offending pattern seems to require that a cycle be used, even if a chain is also included (cf. Eldridge, 1998b). The same author also advocates for therapist flexibility in how the cycles are presented and used to maximize their applicability to the client: "Ultimately what is important is that the concepts used relate to what actually happens in real life, and that they make sense to the offender" (Eldridge, 1998b, p. 9).

These exploring and processing functions also work hand in hand with other functions (especially group challenge/support and homework) in helping the client to engage in relapse prevention planning. Eldridge (1998b) summarizes the aim of relapse prevention this way: "The main aim of relapse prevention for a sex offender is to ensure that he knows his own pattern or patterns, recognizes that he is starting to repeat a pattern, and has plans to deal effectively with that situation." Clearly, the essentials of following relapse prevention listed by Pithers (1990) can be addressed by this functional area: (1) identify problematic situations, (2) analyze decisions that set up situations enabling the resumption of problematic behavior, and (3) develop strategies to avoid or cope more effectively with these situations.

The interventions and activities of this functional area help guide the client's exploration of these relapse prevention issues once the group's challenge has pointed out where a pattern exists (in places that the client may or may not want to see it). The group's support helps to encourage the client to engage in the sometimes difficult aspects of the required exploration and processing.

The same combination of exploration and processing is involved as an aspect of victim empathy work. In addition, skills building activities, which are often primarily educational, may be enhanced by processing the feelings surrounding skill levels and successes in advancement.

Group Confrontation, Challenge, and Support

Due to the nature of the offender's issues and defense structure, the group must have confronting functions that work along with the responsibility- and reality-promoting goals. The need for such functions is illustrated by Perry and Orchard (1992): "The adolescent sex offender's motivation is to mislead the clinician so that the offender can appear to cooperate with treatment while not being forced to confront difficult topics such as his offense pattern" (p. 63).

Such confrontation must be done in an atmosphere of support and encouragement to avoid causing the client to "shut down," and to refrain from instigating resistance and denial as defenses. Confronting involves the group (or one of the members of the group, leaders included) essentially saying, "Wait one minute. Look what you are doing; hear what you are saying; attend to what you are thinking," or simply a "That's not true" response. In essence, confrontation stops the client cold during his patterns of deception and self-deception, manipulation, and aggression and calls attention to the process.

Challenging is similar to confronting, except that it involves the group establishing an expectation of performance for the client to make clinical improvements. Becker and Kaplan (1993) list the following possible areas that could be confronted or challenged by the group:

1. Lack of empathy
2. Objectification of females
3. Viewing sex as something one does to another for personal gratification as opposed to a shared consensual experience
4. Lack of remorse
5. Accepting violence as part of life

In the area of relapse prevention planning, confrontation, challenge, and support can also be used when the client needs to be "brought back to earth," or when he begins to adopt unrealistic expectations that can be disastrous:

> As he sees himself gaining therapeutically, he becomes more assured about his ability to handle life's future difficulties without undue distress. Occasionally, his attitude reaches unrealistic super optimism that encourages inattention to behavior maintenance. This assurance increases until the offender encounters a high-risk situation. (Pithers, 1990, p. 346)

Again it must be noted that in this area the support of the group is very important for the client to feel safe to allow himself to be exposed to and analyzed by the group. These functions of confrontation, challenge, and support are well suited to any adolescent group because they capitalize on the peer orientation of adolescents. Confrontation and support by peers is often more powerful than that offered by the therapist (Perry and Orchard, 1992). Confrontation, challenge, and support are also undertaken as part of the milieu treatment component beyond the therapy room.

Homework Assignments

The use of homework assignments in conjunction with many of the other functional areas to achieve a variety of goals is well documented. Homework aids educational efforts, structures exploration efforts, aids in cognitive procedures and empathy training, sets the groundwork for more affective techniques, helps build skills, and is crucial in stages of client aftercare planning (especially relapse prevention planning).

Many homework assignments are written work that introduces a topic, causes the client to think about issues beyond the group setting, structures his presentation of material about himself to group, reinforces learning, teaches responsibility, presses the client to organize thoughts while providing a framework for this activity, and provides needed assessment data. Homework assignments can also be behavioral in orientation and can involve many behavioral techniques for arousal reconditioning, or they can be specific behavioral assignments for trying out and developing new skills.

Clinical work that makes use of fantasy or masturbatory reconditioning is also in the repertoire of many groups, and aspects of this work may be assigned as homework. In the course of this work, aversive stimuli, satiation, intensive journaling, fantasy work, and the making of audiotapes may be used. These activities, which ideally are done in conjunction with individual therapy, can be taught as educational portions in group, and experiences in the use of such techniques can be shared and processed in group. Therapists using such techniques should be aware of what details of these activities are not appropriate for the group setting.

It is also advantageous to integrate activities from other components of the program into group homework. This also helps to reinforce for the client that the work he does in the other treatment components is as much a part of his sex offense-specific treatment as the SO group. Furthermore, it keeps the client focused on treatment issues when not in group or formal counseling.

Experiential Techniques

The functional approaches in group should not be limited to didactic and cognitive-behavioral interventions only. To be most successful, the group must also make use of other approaches. The sex offender has many unresolved emotional difficulties that can be best addressed by expressive or affective techniques. Some groups make use of experiential functions that help the client to "get out of his head" and deal with issues on a less intellectual level. The mind of the offender is fraught with thinking errors and mental manipulations; often the client can get lost in his own self-deceptions and linguistic hiding places. In selecting more expressive and experiential techniques, one may use a considerable amount of creativity and can also follow some fine examples from other providers.

Clinicians may use art therapy approaches (cf. Landgarten, 1981; Oster and Gould, 1987; etc.), music therapy (cf. Skaggs, 1997), and a host of experiential therapies, including psychodrama, role-playing, and therapy "games" (cf. Dayton, 1994). One of the most well-documented experiential approaches for use with sex offenders is "drama therapy," which has evolved techniques of dramatic role-playing and the use of props, and which has been extensively used with this population (cf. Bergman, 1995).

The use of role-play as a technique for discovery and as a forum for expressing previously repressed emotions is perhaps familiar to many therapists. The client in the role-play or psychodrama will frequently experience and express affect that had been previously hidden under layers of cognitive netting. As he loses his defenses and allows the feelings to surface, the client experiences many positive effects, ranging from catharsis to an ability to express deep emotional issues that have been seeking resolution. In addition, if he can become sufficiently involved in the role, we may learn more about what takes place for him mentally, affectively, and behaviorally during daily events and during offense situations. Taking on a more "projective" quality, such techniques as these also allow the therapist a peek into the inner world that the client may have kept hidden under a skillful façade.

At times, clients in the group who are sexual abuse victims can be used to relate information to the group to raise awareness of victim issues and to stimulate affect. Common techniques used to deal with thinking errors include reverse role-plays (in which the therapist plays an offender using thinking errors and the client plays a probation officer, clinician, or other professional), reenacting portions of an offense, role-playing life situations, engaging in activities that call for immediate expression of current thoughts, and any experiential clinical activity that leads to vocalization of cognitions for group feedback (Murphy, 1990).

Using various audiovisual aids, movies, photographs, and pictures is another possibility. The author has had good results using scenes from movies to educate and to evoke emotional response. Visual and auditory material combined with film drama can be very effective, especially if clients are properly prepared and debriefed. Many movies commonly available at video stores depict situations of sexual abuse and/or actors who display various thinking errors and maladaptive patterns of behavior that can be used as examples in group discussion. In addition, using movie examples of clearly prosocial behavior provides examples for adolescents learning new, more adaptive patterns. Several tapes designed for this purpose or for the training of staff are available. For more information on what commercial movies may be used, please contact the author (see Appendix A). For information on ordering training tapes or other tapes made for use with sexual abusers, contact the Safer Society Press in Brandon, Vermont.

Some groups invite the counselors of victims to attend group and to articulate the victim perspective to the group; others use sessions in which an offender is confronted by one or more of his past victims (Schwartz, 1995a). Such an intervention must of course be done in a controlled setting that gives primary place to the physical and psychological safety of the victim. Another possibility is to have recovering offenders speak to the group to role model responsibility and to give a sense of hope to clients who may feel that there is no life or light ahead.

The Therapist Role Model

The therapist being attentive to his or her manner and delivery of services has already been discussed as an aspect of group operation, as has the value of the male-female team as role models of appropriate, cooperative, and equal male-female relationships. To further expand the topic of the importance of therapist behavior, please refer to Table 7.2, which gives some general "dos and don'ts" for which clinicians may want to be on the alert.

The therapist must gain an understanding of his or her own critical behavior areas and be consistent in following through with plans and resolves. Group members will be alert to inconsistencies in the therapist's behavior with regard to delivery of service. They will also notice if the female defers to the male or if one leader consistently takes one or the other role in the group (Perry and Orchard, 1992). This

TABLE 7.2. Prendergast's Group "Musts" and Supervision Errors

Group Leader "Dos and Don'ts"	
• Do direct, but without interfering. • Do keep the focus on the session or topic. • Do refrain from taking sides or becoming judgmental. • Do learn not to give answers. • Do ask indirect questions. • Do prepare for sessions. • Do pay close attention to thinking errors. • Do use BOTH confrontation and support. • Do challenge clients to take increased responsibility for their treatment. • Do adapt approach and specific interventions to the needs of individual offenders. • Do read, study, and attend training to increase skills. • Do make use of individual and group supervision. • Don't begin group with an adversarial role on the part of the therapist.	• Don't be lacking in empathy or genuine interest. • Don't threaten the group or an individual in the group. • Don't fail to educate the group in the concepts of group process or therapy rules and roles. • Don't use force by badgering individuals. • Don't engage in too much interpretation. • Don't ignore lack of readiness and force too soon. • Don't become defensive. • Don't play the victim of the group. • Don't alienate the group through excessive demands, too much control, forced topics, or direction. • Don't talk too much.

Source: Adapted from Prendergast, 1991, pp. 99-100, 102-103.

does not mean that the leaders must try to be superhuman or perfect; mistakes will be made, and inconsistencies will occur—it is then that you are given the chance to role model listening to the feedback of others, self-assessment, taking responsibility for your behavior, and apologizing or making restitution as needed. Some inconsistency in a program is not a bad thing. Remember, the real world is not always consistent. Clients must learn to accept this fact and deal with it accordingly. In the final analysis, it is better if the group helps the client to express frustrations properly and to cope with injustices suffered in the course of life, rather than having the group itself become a place of inconsistency and lack of safety.

An essential aspect of the therapist as a role model is keeping close guard on your speech, and being attentive to the use of the same thinking errors that you are trying to eradicate in the clients. It is a bad double message when a therapist finishes talking about respect for women and then joins in on inappropriate sexist language with the clients to "be one of the guys." You must listen to lessons taught by yourself and then apply them to yourself. This is the core of the therapist role model as a function of the group intervention.

Leaders will want to be "real" and honest, expressing emotions as they would expect clients to do. This does not mean that the therapist must enter into therapy as a client; he or she must remain in the authoritative therapist role. It does mean that the therapist should own his or her feelings and role model how to deal with them appropriately.

For example, a therapist becomes angry at Johnny. Johnny asks, "Are you mad at me?" The therapist would not want to say, "Oh no Johnny, I'm not mad at all." Johnny already knows you are mad or he would not have asked the question. What you have just role modeled is repression of feelings, not telling the truth in group, and not dealing with a conflict. You might even cause Johnny to wonder when (and how) you will express that emotion, making future interactions less safe for him. A response of "Yes I am," followed by an explanation of what made you angry, expressed in a firm yet nonabusive and nonaggressive way, shows him how to express anger appropriately, shows how to settle a conflict fairly, and teaches him a lesson for life. Another valuable lesson is illustrated by your genuine forgiveness of him, not bearing a grudge, and not using your superior power to "get even with him." Remember, you teach more by your actions than by your many words.

Social and Emotional Group Functions

The social aspects of the group and its effectiveness as a kind of treatment milieu (or "minimilieu" if you like) will have an impact on the group's level of effective intervention. One must remember the important functions involved in the interaction of group members, their support and confrontation of one another, and the manner in which they develop and use their leadership to motivate their peers to greater cooperation in therapy. One must also be aware of the negative functions that may be used by the "negative subculture" of the group and develop strategies to manage these without raising a rebellion or causing increased defensiveness.

The social nature of the group as a place where the client belongs, and a place where he feels a purpose, can have a great impact on building social skills, enhancing self-esteem, helping him to trust enough to accept feedback, making him comfortable enough to open up and expose his deepest secret (his deviancy), and helping him invest in treatment. Every effort should be made to develop a positive group culture.

The following aspects of group can help with this endeavor:

1. The use of rituals that clients participate in for the administration of the group or for conducting specific interventions. These rituals are specific behavioral procedures involving client participation, for example, a ceremony to mark the passage of a client into a specific stage of treatment that is done in a similar way each time and with specific roles played by certain members of the group (e.g., senior member of group presents a certificate to the client; all file out to a soda and cookie gathering in the conference room).

2. Developing, maintaining, and passing down group traditions. Some of these traditions may be embodied in the rituals; others may be illustrative stories of past clients, ways of welcoming new members, or special group "lingo" that has evolved over time.

3. Finally, such things as having special jobs in group that are given to members (e.g., setting up, librarian, secretary, etc.), using group voting for stage advancements, having regular feedback groups that allow time for clients to give feedback to one another *and* to the group leaders, and making the successful completion of group a special occasion, etc.

One extremely helpful group ritual is that of disclosure. All clients should be expected to disclose their offenses to the group. Generally this takes the form of the client reporting first names of victims and numbers and types of offending behaviors. These disclosures are frequently placed on poster board and displayed in all group meetings. In open-ended groups, each time a new client is added to the group (or at the start of each cycle of a closed-ended group), the process is repeated (with the newest client going last). This allows for the updating of lists with more accurate information as clients progress in their treatment and accept increased responsibility for their behaviors. Such activities help develop a culture that promotes honesty, emotional openness, and increased responsibility. This type of culture will go a long way toward making the business of treatment smoother and more effective.

The emotional aspects of the relationships that develop in the group provide very important lessons from which the client can learn how to have appropriate caring relationships that do not involve pressure to engage in inappropriate behaviors. Group members making positive and supportive comments to one another, in addition to feeling that they are valued and esteemed when engaging in appropriate behaviors, can help the client to experience nonsexual emotional gains in relationships. Being able to experience and share highs and lows, laughs and tears within the group can bring a feeling of closeness to members previously known only through sexual thoughts and behaviors.

THE CURRICULUM: THE GUIDING PLAN

The group is guided along in its work by two principal sources: the assessment process and the group curriculum. The assessment process and the regularly modified treatment plan created through it helps to set specific goals within the general goal areas. As such, the assessment process refines goals and selects which will be the focus in each goal area for given clients.

The use of a group curriculum with didactic and primarily psychoeducational groups is perhaps most familiar to clinicians. However, such a guide can be used also to direct the areas of focus in more process-oriented group formats. Groups employing a combination of psychoeducational and process elements can benefit from the use of a curriculum as a guide to which educational activity or what therapeutic clinical area will be the topic of group. Such a curriculum also provides for the structuring of homework assignments and helps to ensure that vital goal areas are not being neglected. There are many other reasons why a group curriculum is a positive element. The most relevant of these are summarized in Table 7.3.

The type of group represented in Figure 7.1 would use interventions from all seven of the functional areas and address goals under the six goal areas. A group such as this would employ a wide array of techniques (educational, cognitive, behavioral, experiential, etc.), used at the discretion of the therapists, and would be guided through a series of focus areas by a group curriculum.

The sample curriculum presented in Table 7.4 was designed to be used with an open-ended group but may be used with a closed-ended format as well. It runs through a series of focus topics, taking about three to five months to complete one cycle. There are three different cycles, so clients will be able to revisit each of the topics more than once; each cycle approaches the topic in a different way to avoid repetition. This curriculum requires nine to fifteen months to complete the three cycles. After completing all three cycles, clients returning to the first cycle will hopefully be more invested in the process than they were at the outset, will gain more out of the treatment of the topics than they did the first time through, and should be able to work on a deeper level.

TABLE 7.3. Mandell and Damon's Summary of the Benefits of a Comprehensive Curriculum

Reasons to Guide Group with a Curriculum
• Provides a structure that reinforces an awareness and respect for boundaries, decreases anxiety, and gives clear direction to clients and therapists
• Clarifies the therapist's expectations for the group
• Ensures that all salient issues will be emphasized in a formal way and given appropriate significance
• Allows material to be arranged and introduced in a sequence that corresponds to the client's and the therapist's readiness
• Provides formalized activities that help clients to organize their thoughts, thereby increasing their sense of mastery
• Lends itself well to research endeavors and decreases the time needed to prepare for the group session
• Provides direction for the concurrent parent groups

Source: From Mandell and Damon, 1989, p. 4.

TABLE 7.4. Sample Sex Offense-Specific Group Curriculum

CYCLE A:

SESSION/FOCUS TOPIC	HOMEWORK FOR NEXT GROUP
1. Group rules/expectations, **DISCLOSURES, EP: THE OFFENSE CYCLE**	Cycle Assignment #1 (5)
2. Exploring client victimization, Expressing feelings, Information gathering, Early cycle	Cycle Assignment #2 (5)
3. Exploring coping skills, Looking at improvements made and needed, Review cycle	"Situations That Occur in Families" (1)
4. Family dynamics of offenders' families, Their family relations/dynamics, Link to offending	"What Is Normal Sexual Behavior?" (Reading) (2)
5. **EP: NORMAL SEXUAL BEHAVIOR,** Personalization to self, Consent vs. Coercion	"What Is Normal Sexual Behavior?" (Questions) (2)
6. Relate answers on questions to offending, Fill knowledge gaps, **EP: VICTIM CONCERNS**	Victim Questions Assignment (5)
MIDCYCLE FEEDBACK	
7. Developing emotional connections and expression, Expanding feelings for one another, What a victim feels/what their victims feel, Not adopting a victim stance, for victim it continues	Write Out Offense (5)
8. What happened, Methods, Thinking errors, Feelings, Coercion used, Relate to cycle	Rewrites of Previous Assignment
9. Same as in 8, **EP: PRECONDITIONS** (Clients refer to related material in source 4).	Relapse Questions (Part I) (5)
10. Dynamics of previous offending—choices made, situations, Where were the risks?	Relapse Questions (Part II) (5)
11. Begin to examine what patterns need to be changed, Look at ways to break cycle	Revisions/Expansions of Previous Assignment
12. Same as 11—Elicit group to challenge/help others in the process, **EP: USING NEW PATTERNS**	No Homework

END OF CYCLE FEEDBACK

TABLE 7.4 (continued)

CYCLE B:

SESSION/FOCUS TOPIC	HOMEWORK FOR NEXT GROUP
1. Group rules/expectations, **DISCLOSURES, EP: THE CYCLE AND THINKING ERRORS**	"Thinking of Errors of Sex Offenders" (Reading) (source unknown)
2. **EP: THINKING ERRORS,** Raising awareness of their errors, Real case illustrations	"Steps in the cycle" (1)
3. **FAMILY MAPS,** Sexual patterns in the family, Coping, Family thinking errors/deviant behavior, How offending has affected the family, **EP: DECIDING IF A SEXUAL ACT OR FANTASY IS APPROPRIATE**	Sexual Relationships (5)
4. Appropriate vs. inappropriate relationships, Their relationships, **EP: MYTHS ABOUT VICTIMS**	"Common Reactions of Victims" (2)
5. How personal abuse has affected them, How they affected their victims	Apology Letter to Victim (1)
6. Reading letters to empty chair, Exercises to increase empathy, Feedback as if from victim	Rewrites of the Letters
MIDCYCLE FEEDBACK	
7. Same as in 6	Attempting to Be More Empathic During Week
8. Reports on experience of week, Role-plays, Drama interventions, **EP: FANTASIES**	Fantasy Assignment #1 (5)
9. Relation of nonsexual fantasy to offending, Expressing fantasy life, Examine purpose served by fantasy, **EP: (Review) DECIDING IF A SEXUAL ACT OR FANTASY IS APPROPRIATE**	Fantasy Assignment #2 (5)
10. Content of sexual fantasy, Changes from the past, Placing boundaries around what is fantasized about, Connection of fantasy to offending; **EP: THE PREOFFENSE PATTERN**	Preoffense Pattern Assignment (5)
11. Recognizing their pattern, Thinking about how it may be interrupted	Pattern Interruption Assignment (5)
12. Examining homework and sketching preliminary plans, Preparing for more advanced work	No Homework
END OF CYCLE FEEDBACK	

CYCLE C:

SESSION/FOCUS TOPIC	HOMEWORK FOR NEXT GROUP
1. Group rules/expectations, **DISCLOSURES, EP: THE OFFENSE CYCLE**	Assault Cycle Worksheet (blank cycle to be filled in)
2. **PRESENTATION OF CYCLES,** Understanding cycle, Applying to self	"Legal/Illegal Behaviors" (3)
3. Understanding legalities, Consent vs. coercion, **EP: COURT, EVALUATION, AND INITIAL REACTIONS** (from source 3)	Family Relations and Reactions (5)
4. Exploring current family relationships, Effects of abuse in family, **EP: SEX, LOVE, AND TOUCHING** (from source 4)	"Love and Sex Qualities" (4) "Touching" (4)
5. Difference between sex and love, Implications of touch, Healthy relationships, IN-GROUP ORAL QUIZ: "What Do You Think?" (from source 1), **EP: HOMOSEXUALITY**	"Homosexuality" (4)
6. Addressing stereotypes, Exploring client self-perception, More on dating/sexual relationships	"Victims" (Reading), (4) "Looking at My Own Abuse" (Questions) (4)

MIDCYCLE FEEDBACK

7. Resident history of abuse and its present effects, Connect to offense cycle, **EP: EMPATHY**	"Thinking About What Others Are Feeling" (4)
8. Expressing feelings, Getting into others' shoes, Role-plays, Empathy exercises	"Thinking Errors About Victims" (4)
9. Errors they use, Drama interventions, Movie scene viewing	"Letter from Your Victim" (4)
10. Give letters to others to read, Role reversals, Being placed in their victims' shoes	"Identifying My Grooming and Maintenance Behaviors" (3)
11. Understanding/identifying their preferred grooming and maintenance behaviors, **EP: CONTROLLING THE URGE TO REOFFEND** (from source 3)	Urge Control Questions (5)
12. Review client understanding and application of Urge Control, Escaping the cycle, **EP: CHANGING NEGATIVE TO POSITIVE SELF-TALK**	No Homework

END OF CYCLE FEEDBACK

Notes: EP = Educational presentation. In all three cycles there would be flexibility to add a session to view a movie or documentary and have a discussion. In our groups, we averaged two movies (or selected scenes from movies) per cycle. Added sessions could also be used for speakers, drama or art therapy interventions, and special topics that clinicians think need to be given group time.

The focus topics for the sample curriculum are as follows:

1. The sexual assault cycle (conceptual model and its exploration)
2. Family dynamics and issues
3. Sexuality and appropriate sexual relationships
4. Victim empathy
5. Specifics of own dynamics and offenses
6. Preoffense patterns
7. Relapse prevention planning preparation

Note that other focus areas could be included as well. This list was selected because of the particular needs of the program in which it was implemented and the specific manner in which other components contributed to the treatment effort. The materials used in this curriculum come from several different sources. Complete publication information for these sources can be found in the reference section:

1. *A Manual for Structured Group Treatment with Adolescent Sexual Offenders* (Way and Balthazor, 1990)
2. *Group Therapy for Adult Incest Offenders and Adolescent Child Molesters* (Abbott, 1992)
3. *Pathways: A Guided Workbook for Youth Beginning Treatment* (Kahn, 1990)
4. *The Relapse Prevention Workbook for Youth in Treatment* (Steen, 1993)
5. Original materials developed by the author

An outline of the sample curriculum is presented in Table 7.4 for the reader's consideration. Numbers placed after handouts and assignments correspond to the sources in the previous list. Although not part of this curriculum, the book *Tell It Like It Is: A Resource Guide for Youth in Treatment,* by Alice Tallmadge with Galyn Forster (1998), is also an excellent source for use with groups as well as staff training purposes.

Each cycle in the curriculum begins with disclosures (which are also done each time a new member enters the group). Each group revolves around the homework assignment due that day. The homework review is the central forum for addressing the focus topic areas listed. At the middle and end of each cycle is a "feedback session" during which everyone in the room gives feedback to everyone else, leaders included. The notation "EP" refers to an educational presentation and represents a didactic presentation done by the group leaders.

In Appendix C of this book, the reader will find resources for exploring other group curricula and references to workbooks that may be used for groups. In addition, copies of the handouts and assignments that were developed by the author are included in full and may be reproduced and used by the reader.

GROUP ORIENTATION
AND PRERELEASE PREPARATION

Using an Orientation Packet

Groups may find it helpful to use an orientation packet to smooth the transition for the client from prior treatment (if any) to the current program. Such a packet, while having a standard format, will need to be modified to meet the specific needs and experiences of each incoming client. These packets can include introductions to the conceptual model, group rules/expectations, orientation to the SO regime of the program, disclosure and responsibility-taking exercises, and preliminary assignments the client can complete and present to the group. Such assignments help the new member to share about himself with the group in a minimally threatening way.

Often the completion of such packets is made a condition for advancement in stage, coming off "orientation status," or being formally accepted into the group. These packets, properly used, can be very beneficial transitional measures for use in any SO group.

A Relapse Prevention Planning Packet
As Summary and Link

Ideally, work on a relapse prevention planning packet would begin when the client enters the last stage of treatment, as defined by the program. Relapse prevention planning packets are helpful tools that (1) allow a client to work on more advanced and focused relapse prevention topics that the group as a whole may not be ready for, (2) help to consolidate a client's work and help him in preparing his relapse prevention plan, and (3) serve as a link to the next service provider through a written compilation of much of the work the client has done in treatment. This aids future treatment planning, facilitates disclosure and relationship building, and allows the client to "hit the ground running" with the next provider.

Such packets can include focused work on advanced RPP topics, future planning exercises, plan development aids, and assignments that the client can complete and present to the SO group for feedback. In groups the author has conducted, the movement to this phase of treatment meant that the client no longer was required to complete the regular group homework. Instead, the client would work on assignments from the packet and present to the group those assignments which required group feedback. However, the client was still expected to actively participate in the group for his own growth and to assist others. The formal presentation of the packet and official exemption from regular group homework was a ritual and status symbol that marked advancement to the final stage of treatment. Interestingly, most clients continued to do most of the regular group homework on their own—a great example to the others.

An example of such a packet, presented in Lundrigan (1996a), includes the following topics:

1. Beginning exercises—written exercises that (a) cause the client to evaluate his preparedness to enter this phase of work, (b) require him to list his patterns, and (c) consolidate much of the work done in the pre–relapse prevention planning sections of group
2. Introduction to relapse prevention planning
3. Avoidance strategies
4. Escape strategies
5. Thinking errors related to offending
6. Stopping deviant thoughts
7. Urge control
8. Creating offense prevention plan

While completing this packet, the client explores focused relapse prevention topics built on the foundation of the work he has done, and is continuing to do, in group. This packet is designed to take three months to complete.

Clinicians may want to give consideration to developing a similar transitional measure for their clients. The relapse prevention plan (which in some programs is an extensive document) can be shared with future treatment providers, family, and all others who will aid the client in remaining offense free. The packet itself can be brought to the next clinician to inform him or her of many important facts about the client and his life and patterns that would speed the process of getting therapy underway.

Chapter 8

Parent Education and Family Therapy

A family treatment component plays a crucial role within the scheme of the multi-component program and can be delivered in the form of formal therapy and/or in educational and practical involvement activities. It is beyond the scope of this book to go into all the necessary details in the delivery of family therapy that would be required to fully prepare one to do this work. The information provided presents a framework within which to conduct family treatment, and a starting point from which to do further study in this area.

It is important to recognize that every adolescent enters treatment with a family attached. If the youth is to make real gains, family relationships must change (Pare et al., 1994). Everyone has a basic need for the presence and support of a "family." This need must be fulfilled in the gigantic undertaking of offense-specific therapy by the parents (and/or others) becoming involved with the youth's treatment. The particular developmental needs of the adolescent or child offender make this need even greater.

The involvement of the family is important for other reasons as well (cf. Ehrenberg and Ehrenberg, 1988). The literature has identified the offender's family as a central influence in the development and/or elicitation of offending behavior (Eastman and Carpenter, 1997). In addition, a great stigma is attached to having a "sex offender" in the family, and parents can feel much shame regarding the abuse (especially if they blame themselves for its occurrence). They can experience the same guilt, shame, self-loathing, and despair that the youth experiences. These feelings can impede effective treatment and cause a manifestation of the defense called "denial." Educational efforts can help parents to move past these feelings, and therapy can help them integrate a realistic view of what has occurred and what must be done from now on to prevent a reoccurrence.

THREE PRINCIPAL ASPECTS
OF THE COMPONENT

Although some family treatment activities will differ depending on program setting and client circumstances (e.g., community/home passes as a family treatment activity are vital in residential programs but may not be applicable to an outpatient setting), family treatment in any setting is composed of at least formal family therapy, parent/family education, and individual family meetings. A model for family treatment presented later in this chapter weaves these three aspects of treatment into a "package" that functions as one component of the coordinated treatment effort.

Family Therapy

Some form of family therapy is indispensable in the larger picture of family treatment. This therapy can be delivered as individual family sessions, multiple group therapy, or a combination of the two. Family therapy is especially important if the resident is to return home where a past victim lives, requiring reunification and/or clarification work. Parental involvement in dealing with pertinent family issues, developing the resident's relapse prevention plan, and gaining the tools needed to assist their son and the family system in maintaining the treatment benefits is considered to be of paramount importance (Christensen, 1992).

As important as the need for family therapy is recognizing that the treatment provided to these families must be sex offense-specific. Thomas (1991) reminds us:

> Just as treatment providers agree that a nontraditional therapy approach is necessary to effectively intervene with the adolescent sex offender, treatment of the young offender's family also necessitates an approach that changes the usual concepts of family therapy, therapist, and at times, even the definition of family. (p. 333)

Service providers should be aware of the complexities and specifics of working with these families and develop treatment approaches that will be maximally effective. These approaches will include many common family therapy techniques and interventions used to address issues common to all troubled families in addition to techniques specific to families with a sexually abusive member. The chances of a client's future success may well be reduced if he must return to a home in which significant family problems have been left unaddressed by therapy.

Parent Education and Involvement

Very often in working with sexually abusive youth we are dealing with multi-problem families who require much help and support as they overcome their problems. This is especially the case when the family system itself is partly responsible for the client developing his offending behaviors. Such families (often out of guilt, shame, and stigma—as much as out of disorganization) are notorious for not participating in treatment.

Educational groups present a less threatening way to introduce the difficult concepts that will be explored in therapy. These groups also educate parents who are ignorant of sexual abuse issues and help to answer questions and calm fears that may prove to be obstacles to consistent participation in family treatment.

Educational groups inform parents of the extent to which they can participate in the treatment—how much they are needed and wanted in the efforts. The discussion of topics in this format also promotes the surfacing of "spin-off" issues and opens the door to parents' disclosures of family issues related to the subjects being discussed. Parents learn in these groups the "lingo" of the sex offense-specific group, which facilitates communication between the client and parents as they discuss his treatment and engage in therapeutic activities together.

Individual Family Meetings

Specifically scheduled family meetings can prove to be helpful additions to the family treatment component (especially if therapy is being delivered in multiple family groups). These meetings are important in formal information gathering, in preparation for and engagement in clarification work, and in addressing specific issues that are not appropriate for discussion in a group setting. Individual meetings may be needed concerning structuring specific passes, dealing with legal issues, or working out treatment plan particulars. In addition, such meetings can be used to provide feedback to the family on its level of participation in treatment and to offer suggestions for improvements, if needed.

A MODEL FOR THE FAMILY TREATMENT OF THE SEXUALLY ABUSIVE ADOLESCENT

The model for family treatment that is advocated here conceptualizes the services of the family treatment component as delivered via the three aspects previously discussed and by the three domains of treatment: (1) client-only treatment, (2) parent/family-only treatment, and (3) treatment with family and client together. Figure 8.1 illustrates how the aspects and modes work together within the family treatment component.

The reader will note that some of the work done in the three domains falls outside the boundaries of the three aspects. The client-only family work outside of the treatment aspects relates to family issues worked on by the client in other treatment components, representing an area of overlap between the family treatment component and other program components. The parent/family-only work done outside the treatment aspects involves the parents and other family members working through issues with the support of family friends and, in some cases, mental heath professionals. At the intersection of these two is the work outside the treatment aspects undertaken by the client and his parents/family in their interactions at home, during visits, on passes, while reviewing work, having conflicts, and planning for a safe home environment.

The reader will also note that some of the work in the three domains takes place as part of the activities of one or more aspects of the treatment delivery. The family therapy and educational groups may at times work with parents or the family alone, other times with the client alone, and sometimes with the client and family members together. The individual family meetings, on the other hand, include opportunities for (1) meeting with the family without the client present (since no other program component enables this), and (2) meeting with client and family together. The use of these meetings is discussed in more detail later in this chapter.

FIGURE 8.1. Aspects and Modes in the Family Treatment Component

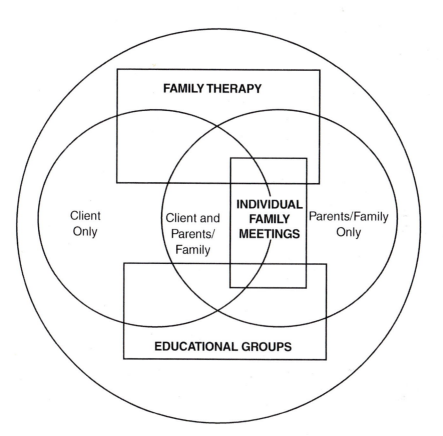

This overlapping combination of psychoeducation, process therapy, individual meetings, parental involvement in decision making, and therapeutic activities creates a more comprehensive intervention. Some of the many general goals of the complete family treatment component are summarized in Table 8.1. Now let us look more specifically at this intervention by examining individual goals for each treatment domain. The work of achieving these goals would take place in family therapy, educational groups, individual meetings, and in other components or as part of other family interventions.

TABLE 8.1. Goals of Family Treatment Interventions and Parent Education Activities

---

- Family members (or at least the parents/caregivers) become more involved in the youth's treatment.
- The parents are somewhat knowledgeable in the specifics of sex offending (especially in their own son's patterns) and can learn to spot signs that their son is on his way to a relapse.
- A working relationship with treatment personnel and the parents has been established to assist the parents in working together with present and future service providers.
- Family members have taken some steps toward engaging in a more healthy pattern of interacting and living together.
- The safety of the family members has been maximized through the effort.
- The family has come to recognize ways in which it might have "enabled" the offending behavior and has taken steps to modify these patterns.
- The family has overcome some of the shame and stigma that the offending has caused and can discuss and address potentially harmful behaviors in a more upfront manner.

Family Work with the Client Alone

This work related to the family is covered in individual and group therapy:

- Engage in individual/peer group work on family issues in preparation for family group
- Learn where he has picked up offending dynamics and thinking errors in the family
- Recognize the patterns in the family that have supported his offending
- Begin to understand his parents shame and denial, and why his parents (similar to himself) struggle with these issues
- Identify individually what things in the family need to change
- Begin to recognize the effects his offending has had on his family and the victim (especially if the victim is a family member)
- Learn how crucial family support is in the process of relapse prevention planning (if the family is to be involved with the offender in the future)
- Work to identify long-standing family issues that could continue to impact the client personally (even if the family will not be involved after treatment)
- Develop the attitude of including parents in his treatment at all steps

- Develop a respect for the need to openly discuss the offending issue in the family (This is not an opportunity for the client to act out offending patterns or to covertly offend members of the family.)

Family Work with the Parents Alone

These areas should be covered with the parents in parents-only education group meetings, family meetings without the client present, and therapist-parent interactions and phone calls:

- Guide parents in how and when to raise certain issues in family therapy
- Initiate discussions of victim issues within the family
- Help parents work through their denial, guilt, and shame
- Absolve parents from unwarranted self-blame for the child's offenses
- Address the feelings the parents have for the offending child and his offenses (some of which they would be unable to discuss if the child were present)
- Help them to recognize that some of their behavior, words, and thinking could have contributed to the offending and/or enabled it
- Help them to see the need to make changes (to work with their son to prevent future offending inside *or* outside the family/home)
- Develop an alliance between the parents and the treatment system

Family Work with the Client and Parents/Family Together

This work is done by the child and parents—and perhaps other family members—during the educational groups and family therapy:

- Engage in family therapy work on various family issues (either directly related to the offense or not).
- Improve family communication and structural patterns.
- Learn to speak of sexual abuse and the offenses in an open yet safe manner.
- Learn why "*a* youth" offends, and learn the basics of the dynamics of sexual abuse.

- Learn why "*this* youth" offends, and explore the specifics of the client's offending dynamics and patterns.
- Learn about victim issues, placing the needs of the victim first, and dispelling many of the "myths" about victims (and sexual offending in general).
- Fill in the gaps in the family's understanding of sexuality, sexual issues, and normal sexual development.
- Recognize that the client could reoffend (he is not "fixed").
- Develop a family atmosphere of continued "vigilance" for the signs that the client is returning to old patterns.
- Place safety of potential victims above the needs of the client and family, and learn not to allow unsafe situations to develop to avoid dealing with feelings or issues.
- Develop a collaboration between the child, parents/family, and therapists to achieve the common goal of stopping future abuse. This involves the following:

  a. The family working together to change patterns of behavior and thought
  b. Parents participating in relapse prevention planning
  c. Child and parents setting aside time to keep up to date on the child's work
  d. Keeping all issues in the open—no secrets (especially from therapists)
  e. The family applying and keeping fresh what was learned
  f. A commitment to participate in ongoing treatment

Center for Family Resource Development Scheme

Figure 8.2 presents a flowchart model for the treatment of adolescent sexual offenders and their families that operates in the three domains discussed. This diagram, which appears in Schladale (1993), gives a good overview of the treatment process under the various domains; other resources provide excellent instruction on the specifics of conducting the therapy involved (cf. Schladale, 1993; Thomas, 1991). This scheme presents another way to conceptualize family treatment taking place within the three domains, and therapists should be able to see how they can employ their skills and knowledge of working with these families to develop treatment approaches that will address the areas noted in this and the preceding section.

FIGURE 8.2. Center for Family Resource Development Scheme

Client-Only Treatment	Family and Client Treatment	Family-Only Treatment

Engagement and attachment

Works on details of committing offense

Works on beginning to understand cycle of abuse; may include discussion of prior trauma

Practices facing up to his or her family without denial and minimization

Assessment of family safety

Family education and support
• Phases of treatment
• Family involvement
• Families as partners

Family prepares for client to begin taking responsibility; makes decisions about hearing details of the offense

Client takes responsibility for abuse with family members by telling details of offense and/or apologizing

Works on influence of past trauma and its role in current situations

Family members work on past trauma and effects on present

Family discusses the impact that past trauma has had on all of their lives

Begins to learn alternative responses to everyday interactions (i.e., learns to intervene early in the cycle)

Family identifies potential areas and situations that could put client at risk to reoffend

Client shares with the family what he is learning about his cycle and how to interrupt it

Client and family identify how the cycle applies to conflictual situations in family life

Client and family develop a relapse prevention plan and begin to practice alternatives to the old cycle

JSOCCP
Center for Family Resource Development
University of Louisville

Client and family invite others into prevention plan and solicit their assistance

Client and family are seen on a periodic basis for an extended time to assist them in monitoring their efforts at preventing relapse

Client receives support and feedback separate from family

Members are seen separately as needed for spin-off issues

Source: Courtesy of Dana Christensen, PhD, University of Louisville, Louisville, KY. Reprinted by permission.

MULTIPLE FAMILY THERAPY GROUPS

There are many reasons why one might consider the use of multiple family therapy groups for the provision of the family therapy aspect of the component. Some of the possible benefits of using this modality are summarized in Table 8.2.

In these groups, the therapist can deliver family therapy in the context of the group setting, which has already been discussed as a positive setting for sex offenders. Some of the areas listed in Thomas (1991) that are targeted by such groups (and any family therapy with this population) include the following:

1. Denial, minimization, and projection of blame
2. Lack of empathy
3. Abuse of power by family members and empowerment of others
4. Intergenerational abuse issues
5. Blurred role boundaries
6. Human sexuality and its healthy expression
7. Divided loyalties in the family
8. Behavior patterns and using behavior contracts
9. Family substance abuse/addictive behaviors

In addition, family communication patterns and methods of conflict resolution may be modified, parental behavior management methods may be bolstered, and issues surrounding interfamilial abuse may be resolved.

Such groups would ideally be co-led (if possible by the same therapists who conduct the sex offense-specific group). Therapists should plan ahead by reviewing the clients' current needs and preparing for the issues the clients (in individual or group therapy) or the parents (in conversations or meetings with one of the therapists) have determined they will explore in the group that day. Likewise, therapists should have a period of debriefing afterward to discuss the gains (or setbacks) from the session, to process the session for clarification, and to deal with their own needs to vent to a colleague after what may have been an emotionally draining session. The ideal number of families in such a group would be four. This means several groups will need to be run weekly in the same program. As with other groups, keeping the same families together will foster the needed group cohesion and facilitate disclosure and receptiveness to feedback.

TABLE 8.2. Multiple Family Therapy Benefits

- It is an ideal environment for conducting family work combined with psychoeducational groups (parents only need to come once per week).
- Families can gain support from one another—"We are not alone."
- More viewpoints mean greater feedback.
- Families can learn from one another and/or do "vicarious" work on issues even if they are unable to raise the issues themselves.
- Parents can serve as "surrogates" for clients without participating families.
- It is an efficient use of the therapists' time, and it is cost-effective.
- Therapists can see clients in the context of their families, and the family systems in the context of society.
- Multiple family groups address the following: rigidity, enmeshment, isolation, poor coping mechanisms, faulty communication patterns, unmet needs for closeness and nurturance, feelings of hopelessness and helplessness, feelings of failure as parents, and the weight of the imagined condemnation of the world for their failure as parents.
- Multiple family therapy decreases the isolation and alienation of the isolated family.
- It gives enmeshed families opportunity to engage in meaningful encounters with other families' members.
- Clients (parents and children) can often listen more openly to members of another family than they can to persons in their own family or to therapists.

Sources: Adapted from Lundrigan, 1996a; Thomas, 1991, pp. 365-368.

Families should be told that although the status of their sons as offenders will be known, disclosure of the specifics of the offense in the group is a family decision. These groups should develop their own rituals and specific practices, as do offense-specific groups (and for the same reasons).

The convenience of bringing families together for education groups and multiple family therapy groups on the same evening is practical, and as an added benefit, the education group may raise some issues that can be processed in more depth in the therapy group. Thus, it is helpful to have one session follow the other (e.g., start with thirty to forty-five minutes of education group, then shifts gears to the therapy group).

Since several adults and children are present, the multiple family group allows for many different viewpoints to be presented to a given person or family. One positive effect of having these multiple viewpoints can be clearly seen when a child or parent is having a difficult time making a point to a member of his or her own family. At these times, it is not uncommon to see the point expressed more clearly by *another* child or parent in the group. Sometimes we grow so used to hearing things from family members and professionals that we tune them out. The author has seen the timid voice of a fifteen-year-old make a point with another client's father—a man who could not listen to his own son. Likewise, in one case, a mother from one family simply restated what the mother of another family was trying unsuccessfully to get through to her son. After agreeing with the other mother that what she said was absolutely reasonable, he looked at his own mother in astonishment and asked, "Is that what you were trying to say?"

Despite these benefits, some may elect not to use multiple family therapy. Some believe that therapy of abuse issues in the family may not be appropriate for a group setting. Other times a given family may need to work for a while in single family therapy to prepare for entering a multiple family group. Finally, as Thomas (1991) notes, some families simply may not benefit from this form of treatment. It is a challenging (and at times emotionally draining) means of conducting family therapy, and some may believe that it does not fit their style and/or abilities. The means of conducting family therapy as part of this component should take into account therapist orientation, program preferences, practical concerns, and the needs of the families involved.

SCHEDULED INDIVIDUAL FAMILY MEETINGS

The following are some of the many uses for individual family meetings, some of which have been stated previously:

- Information gathering, treatment planning, and providing feedback to the family
- As needed individual family therapy sessions
- Preparation for entering multiple family group
- Family treatment orientation
- Clarification/reunification work
- Discussion of specific legal or programmatic concerns
- Examination of conditions before family visits (for adolescents living out of home)
- Processing of results of family visits (for adolescents living out of home)

It may also be helpful to have at least a few regularly scheduled meetings connected to specific points in the treatment. Having these meetings as part of the program may help to reduce anxiety concerning the need to have individual family meetings for other than ordinary, course-of-treatment reasons. Perhaps at least five meetings should be scheduled during the course of a client's treatment.

Assessment Meeting

Meeting with the family (or selected members) very close to the client's intake into the program can be very helpful. This would be a meeting *in addition to* the actual program intake session, which the parents would be asked to attend. During this meeting, the therapist introduces the parents to the sex offense-specific regime that will be the focus of their child's treatment. The therapist lays out specific expectations for the child and the parents as participants in the program and collects valuable assessment data for use in treatment planning. The therapist should use this meeting to clarify, discuss, or otherwise explore information received from previous treatment providers; to introduce parents to relevant portions of the conceptual model of offending; and to begin early education efforts.

One of the goals of this meeting should also be to introduce the therapist to the family and to initiate a relationship that will need to be developed as treatment progresses. Another goal would be to prepare the family to attend the orientation to participation in the family treatment component.

Orientation to Family Treatment Component Meeting

Since it is often the case that we begin work with the youth before we are able to organize family therapy, and/or because we may have determined (in the course of treatment or due to treatment planning concerns) that active family treatment will not begin right away, another meeting will be held to transition the family to the education groups and family therapy. It is helpful to hold such a meeting just prior to the first group that the new family will attend. The parents should come early (a half hour or so), to meet before the group. The group itself should be prepared in the previous session to welcome a new youth member and his family (usually only the parents).

At that time, it is helpful to present the parents with some literature and materials that they can take home. The parents can be more fully introduced to the format of the sessions and provided an opportunity to ask questions and voice their concerns. The literature may be composed of published booklets, pamphlets, or handouts that help families of offenders participate in treatment, or it might include some custom-made materials for the parents to read at their leisure. Examples of such materials are included in Appendix D.

The therapist will also want to explain ground rules for group (probably with the youth present) and outline expectations. It is also helpful to make mention of the next individual family meeting as well as to discuss the possibility for individual family therapy sessions if needed or requested.

Disclosure Meeting

This meeting will need to be held if the youth has not already made a full disclosure of his offenses to his parents. It is best done later in treatment after the youth has done a portion of his work and before he begins relapse prevention planning. This sequence is suggested because the author has found that regardless of how much prior treatment a youth has had, new offenses or new details and clarifications always seem to come up during the course of therapy. This meeting with the parents and youth is a opportunity to bring the parents up to date on the reality of their son's offending so that they may more properly take their place in the treatment and relapse prevention team.

This meeting can also be used as a time to check in with the parents and family to see if they have any questions or something they would like to discuss that they would prefer to talk about in this format, rather than in the group. As with the other meetings, it is good to end with an eye toward the next meeting.

Relapse Prevention Planning Meeting

This meeting can be held just prior to the youth beginning his relapse prevention planning or as he is beginning this work. The purpose of this meeting is to help the parents to become more involved in the relapse prevention planning process and to answer questions as to the parents role in relapse prevention planning. It may also be helpful to provide the parents with some specialized materials concerning this work and to ensure them of the support of the program's treatment team as they move into the final stages of their active involvement with the program.

Once again it may be helpful to check whether they have any questions or concerns that they would like to discuss in the individual family format. The parents can also be prepared for the next (and perhaps final) individual meeting.

Program Discharge Family Meeting

It is prudent to hold a meeting when the program ceases its active involvement with the family. This can be a time for separation, reflection, and encouragement. If the family will be continuing services with the program for a period of time, these can be coordinated and finalized at this meeting. This is also a time to assure the family of the continued support of the program, and to inform them of appropriate ways to use program support in this postdischarge period.

PARENT AND FAMILY EDUCATION GROUPS

This section presents a sample curriculum for conducting educational groups for the families of adolescents who have committed sexual offenses (see Table 8.3). These sessions were designed to be implemented during the first half hour of a weekly two-hour education and multiple family therapy group. After examining the educational topic for the week, the group moves into a more process-oriented therapy group. The group is designed to run open-ended, and attempts were made not to employ too many concepts that build on previous ones so that new arrivals do not feel "behind" the others.

One of the benefits of this education time is that it serves as a means of reinforcing for the youth things he has discussed in SO group. It can also be an introduction to things yet to come. Some of the topics covered are also part of the educational portions of the SO group. Revisiting these some months after discussing them in SO group (or hearing about them in education group months before a more in-depth exploration in SO group) lengthens the topic discussion and permits a deeper integration of learning.

The "Bowl o'Topics" exercise listed under 3b. in Table 8.3 involves jargon terms and concepts of sex offending placed on slips of paper in a bowl. Each youth picks one from the bowl and explains what he knows about it to the group. If he is newer and chooses one he is as yet unfamiliar with, he can draw again. Providing visual aids or props for adolescents can enhance the fun and clarity of the presenta-

TABLE 8.3. Sample Curriculum Outline for a Parent Education Group

SESSION/TOPIC	FULL OR SPLIT GROUP	PARENT READING
1. SEX OFFENSE-SPECIFIC TREATMENT AT THE PROGRAM	***Full Group***	"A Description of SO Treatment at Our Program" (3)
a. Overview of the Treatment		
b. The Sex Offense-Specific Group	***Split Group***	"A Parent's Guide to the Sex Offense-Specific Group" (4)
2. THE STAGES OF LOSS		
a. Common Feelings/Overview of Stages		"Common Feelings Among Parents of Children with Sexual Behavior Problems" (2)
		"Stages of Loss" (diagram based on source 2) (4)
b. Working Through the Stages of Loss	***Full/Split Group***	
3. THE PARENT'S ROLE IN TREATMENT		"The Parent's Role in Treatment" (4)
a. Overview and Explanation of the Parent's Role	*Split*	"Key Concepts You Need to Know to Help Your Teenager" (1)
b. Learning of Definitions and Concepts (Bowl o' Topics Exercise)	*Full*	
c. Continuation of Definitions and Concepts	*Full*	
4. WHY DO CHILDREN ABUSE?	***Full Group***	
a. Some Possible Reasons That Children Sexually Abuse Others		"Why Do Children Abuse?" (2)
b. Overview of Sex-Offending Dynamics		"On the Dynamics of Sexual Offending" (4)
5. HOW DO I FEEL ABOUT WHAT MY SON HAS DONE?	***Split Group***	
a. Exploration of the Feelings Then and Now		"How Do I Feel About What My Son Has Done?" (4)
b. Continuation of 5a./How Have These Feelings Shown Themselves		
6. THE SEXUAL ASSAULT CYCLE (Conceptual Model Exploration)	**Full Group***	
a. Presentation of the Cycle Used in the Treatment Program		"Assault Cycle Diagram/Assault Cycle Handout" (3)
b. Continuation of 6a		
c. Application of the Model (Youth volunteer to describe own cycles)		

SESSION/TOPIC	FULL OR SPLIT GROUP	PARENT READING
7. NORMAL SEXUAL DEVELOPMENT	***Full Group***	"Differentiating Normal from Abnormal Sexual Development" (2)
a. Normal vs. Abnormal Sexual Development (Examine the children's development as well)		
b. Normal Sexual Behavior/Consent vs. Coercion		"What Is Normal Sexual Behavior?" (3)
c. Appropriate vs. Inappropriate Sexual Behaviors		"Deciding If an Act or Fantasy Is Appropriate" (3)
PARENT CHECK-IN SESSION	***Split Group***	
This session is for examining where the parents are in the process of coming to grips with the reality of the abuse. Also a time for feedback and answering questions.		
8. THINKING ERRORS	***Full Group***	
a. What Is a Thinking Error?		"Thinking Errors of Sex Offenders" (3)
b. Thinking Errors and the Sexual Assault Cycle		"Thinking Errors" Diagram (3)
9. ROADBLOCKS TO PROGRESS IN TREATMENT	***Split Group***	"Roadblocks to Progress in Treatment" (2)
a. Parent Roadblocks to Treatment		
b. Removing the Roadblocks		
10. MYTHS ABOUT SEXUALLY ABUSIVE BEHAVIOR	***Full Group***	"Common Myths About Sex-Offending Behavior" (3)
a. Myths Relating to Sexually Abusive Behavior		"Myths and Facts" (2)
b. Myths Relating to the Victims of Sexual Abuse		"Myths About the Victim" (3)
11. THE PREOFFENSE PATTERN	***Full Group***	"Focus: The Preoffense Pattern" Diagram (3)
a. Explanation of the Preoffense Pattern		
b. Examples from the Children's Own Patterns/Relapse Prevention Interventions		
12. CARING FOR YOURSELF	***Split Group***	
a. The Need for Parents to Care for Themselves/ Methods of Self-Care		"Caring for Yourself" (2)
b. Exchanging Experiences/Check-In on Progression Through Stages of Loss		

tions. Allowing young people to "teach" once in a while helps them to learn (as they struggle to articulate the topics they are explaining) and gives them a sense of accomplishment. The parents also gain a sense of pride in their children for this demonstration of learning.

An important part of the education group is the youth and family sharing (voluntarily) how the material being presented applies to them, or how they fit into the patterns described. Skillfully getting families to speak of the topics in a more personal manner can facilitate a culture of disclosure in the group as well as raise topics for processing in family therapy. Also, these discussions can serve as illustrations of the concepts, making them come alive, and thus easier for all to work with and understand. Dividing the group periodically into a "split group" (i.e., parents in one room with one therapist, while the youth are in another room with the other therapist) helps to reinforce the boundaries between the parental and child units of the family system, often a blurred boundary in many of these families. Having time when the parents talk together helps to teach that some things are "adults only" and can help to model appropriate power balances in the family. In addition, the parents will be able to speak freely (without the children present) to their peers regarding what they are experiencing. In this context they are able to draw support and encouragement as well as feedback from other parents.

The education curriculum is built around twelve topics, each of which is covered over a two- or three-week period, meaning seven to nine months to complete the entire series. This should allow all parents to attend the complete cycle during the duration of active treatment.

Materials for the sessions were drawn from four sources:

1. *Pathways Guide for Parents of Youth Beginning Treatment* (Kahn, 1990)
2. *From Trauma to Understanding* (Pithers et al., 1993)
3. Materials excerpted or taken directly from the SO group materials discussed in Chapter 7
4. Custom-designed materials that are reproduced in Appendix D, which the reader may reproduce, modify, and use

In the curriculum outline in Table 8.3, the source of the "Parent Reading" is indicated by a number placed after the name of the reading that corresponds to the respective source in the previous list.

The master outline of the curriculum in Table 8.3 lists all sessions, topics, and parent materials. The second part of the curriculum outline is the "youth split session guide," which gives the focus of the discussion in the split groups during the listed session. Note that the topics are broken into two or three parts. Each of these separate parts takes place during a different week (thus, 1a. "Overview of the Treatment" and 1b. "The Sex Offense-Specific Group" would be discussed on separate weeks).

Youth Split-Session Discussion Topics

The following list of discussion topics and questions was developed to encourage adolescents to think along some of the same lines as the parents with respect to weekly topics. Preparing the adolescents (from their perspective) will allow for easier discussions between children and parents in and out of group. The topics and/or questions are listed here next to the number that corresponds to the session as listed in Table 8.3.

Session	Topic/Discussion Questions for Youth Split Group
2a.	Realizing that parents also have work to do with these SO issues. Recognizing that the abuse has affected the whole family. Exploring how difficult it is for the parents to accept the full reality of the youth's behavior.
2b.	Possible feelings that parents may have about the youth. Has he asked his parents how they feel? Was he sensitive to his parents feelings or was he using them to his own ends? How will he be able to respond with understanding if parents express uncomplimentary feelings about him?
3a.	How the youth can assist parents in being involved in treatment. Explaining the teamwork approach to the family helping the youth to keep from reoffending.
5a.	How did the youth's parents react when they found out? Why? How much more disclosing needs to occur?
5b.	How do the youth's parents feel now about his offending? Do they realize his potential to reoffend? How will

he help them (or not help them) to realize what he did
and could still do?

Check-in   Resident feedback on how the education program is going. Solicit suggestions for improvement. How does the
youth think his family is benefiting? Do his parents have
anything they would like to see changed?

9a.   What gets in the way of the youth and his parents working together on his SO issues? What does he do to make
it difficult for his parents to work on/discuss these issues
with him?

9b.   What gets in the way of the youth and his parents working on their communication? What problematic patterns
are still present in his family? What other issues does he
still need to work on with his parents?

12a.   Recognizing that parents need to take care of themselves. How are the adolescents caring for themselves?
Are they doing all they can in family therapy?

12b.   How is the work on SO issues with the youth's parents
going? What barriers still exist? Where does the youth
think his parents are in recognizing his offending patterns?

GETTING PARENTS TO INVEST
IN TREATMENT AND ATTEND
FAMILY TREATMENT ACTIVITIES

The total family treatment component would ideally seek to involve
parents by means of the family therapy mentioned previously, the educational groups, individual family meetings, regular informal visits of
the parents to the program (if the youth is in an afterschool, day, or
group care setting), and later on, involvement in community passes
with children in residential or secure placements. The parents should
also be involved in the relapse prevention planning process and be inti-
mately connected with the procedure for the client to advance "levels"
in the program and "stages" in his sex offense-specific work.

It seems that if the parents are given clear expectations for participation and are worked with in a caring and noncondemning manner, they may be more receptive to participating in treatment. Linking client advancement in levels and/or stages to specific actions of the parents can lead the youth to help get the parents to the sessions. Involving the parents in decision making and making them feel like a special part of the treatment team are also positive strategies.

At the first meeting, parents should find an environment that entices them to return. Small amenities such as coffee, snacks, and genuine hospitality and attention will make them feel more welcome. Taking the time to make them feel wanted and comfortable will likely go a long way toward increasing their positive perception of the program. Letting them know by word and deed that you are genuinely there to help the family, and that you do not look down on them, will help to overcome some barriers to returning.

The referring agency (be it social service, juvenile corrections, or court) must be enlisted as a partner in working to get the parents to sessions. Some families will never come, but if the program expects participation it may be surprised how many families will rise to that expectation. Another related point is that although a firm expectation must be maintained, program providers should not become so rigid that all flexibility to negotiate with the parents is abandoned. It is better to get the family to agree to attend every other week, than not to have them come at all.

Remember that it is not necessary to have everyone present at the sessions. An effective intervention can occur in the family system with even the client alone in therapy; however, participation by significant persons enhances the effectiveness of these efforts. A past victim should not be included in the sessions until appropriate reunification/clarification work has been done. With enough support and encouragement (and even a little pressure from the client), it is not impossible to have up to 70 percent of SO families attend therapy and an educational component (Lundrigan, 1996b).

THREE FINAL NOTES

This chapter closes with a few final notes regarding the parent education and family therapy component. The three areas highlighted here represent expectations that may established as part of the program, ones that may be very helpful to the total treatment effort.

Parent-Child Private Time

It is helpful to get the families to regard their family work as extending beyond the confines of the formal treatment aspects of the program. This area of work (you may recall) is represented in Figure 8.1 as the overlapping client and parent area that falls outside the bounds of the three treatment aspects. In group care settings, it should be expected that the adolescent and family will set aside time on visits or passes for the child to update the parents on what he is doing in treatment and to discuss issues raised in family treatment. In outpatient settings, the family should be expected to find some time during the week when they can process their work in therapy in a more expanded manner. Some possible benefits of this contact include the following:

- Promoting open communication of offending issues within the family
- Helping the parents to be involved in (as opposed to excluded from) the child's treatment
- Encouraging and training the family to work out problems together
- Providing more material to process in therapy group
- Helping the family to accept more responsibility for treatment and safety

Such conversations should be monitored by therapist-parent contact and in family therapy. Families should be asked in sessions about the outcome of conversations, conflicts, and agreements stemming from these private times outside the therapy setting, and they should be encouraged to accept suggestions regarding things that they need to talk about in the intervening week.

Behavioral and Thought Assignments

The MFT group and/or therapists may expect that the family will work to change behavioral patterns or experiment with new ones in the contacts during the week and report the results in the following family therapy session or MFT group. This is a standard technique in many modes of family therapy, and it is very helpful with these families because they may have a multitude of behavioral patterns that are in need of support and advice to change.

Likewise, they may have thought and/or speech patterns (which would be grouped under the category of behaviors) that can be experimented with to promote healthier patterns. These also should be followed up in family therapy to gauge effectiveness and to gain information that will be helpful in assisting the family to uncover and modify other maladaptive patterns.

Full Population Participation in Family Treatment

It is beneficial to have all offenders in the program involved in the family groups on a weekly basis regardless of the level of parental involvement. The following are some reasons to support mandatory group attendance:

- Such a mandate will likely increase attendance and participation in the groups. If a child and family discover they can avoid the pain of family treatment by simply not showing up, they may opt out.
- The youth will at least receive an exposure to working on the family issues involved in sexual offending (and other family issues in general).
- The educational modules reinforce for the youth things learned in the sex offense-specific group.
- It is possible to systemically impact the family system working with the youth alone. Such changes may prompt absent families to begin attending treatment.
- Family therapy can be an indispensable means of working on trauma or abuse inflicted by parents, looking at issues of family abandonment, and receiving family support from others.
- Participating in the work of other families helps the client to feel less isolated and alone in his family issues and struggles. Also, it can give the client a sense of hope for future resolution of his own family's issues.
- Assisting others to achieve success with their families can instill a sense of mastery and competence (in a positive and healthy sense).
- The groups provide a place for the youth to work on family issues in more detail than he could in other settings.
- Therapeutic work can be accomplished vicariously through the work of others. Also, seeing the patterns in other families may make the patterns in the client's own family more clear to him.

The author has found that if such mandatory attendance is simply an expectation of the program (and everybody does it), clients show little resistance. In fact, some clients hope that their attendance will motivate their parents to come. Those whose parents do not attend can at least be part of *some form* of family activity with their peers.

Chapter 9

Individual Therapy

THE PLACE OF INDIVIDUAL THERAPY
IN THE TREATMENT
OF THE SEXUALLY ABUSIVE ADOLESCENT

Individual therapy as an adjunct to SO group and other interventions can be a very helpful and important mode of treatment (Ryan and Lane, 1998). Furthermore, in a multi-component model, which requires a high level of coordination, individual therapy can serve as the linchpin that helps the client to organize and coordinate his work in the various components. If the individual therapist is also one of the SO group facilitators, is present in the program's other therapy groups, and is the SO family therapist, the ability for individual therapy to be a unifying force is greatly increased.

However, the use of individual therapy with sex offenders has not gone without some criticism (Perry and Orchard, 1992). The primary criticisms arise from the use of individual therapy *alone* for sex offense-specific treatment and also with the potential treatment pitfalls that accompany use of this therapy mode with this population. The individual therapy relationship with sex offenders can be difficult to negotiate. The one-to-one nature of the individual therapy relationship can be easily confused, it can allow the client to reinforce dysfunctional interpersonal styles, and it can provide the client an opportunity to play seduction games (Schwartz, 1995a). Individual therapy, Schwartz (1995a, p. 14-3) believes, "can be useful as an adjunct; however, it should be recognized that individual therapy may undermine group participation" if it is not properly used.

If individual therapy is properly utilized in careful coordination with the other components, and if monitored with adequate clinical supervision, this mode can potentially be one of the most significant components of the program.

Table 9.1 presents a list of the "pros and cons" of individual therapy for the reader's consideration. The reader is referred to Schwartz (1995a) for a more in-depth discussion of these pros and cons; however, a few of her points will be highlighted here. She believes that "certain traits of the sex offender [i.e., denial, guilt, and secrecy] make them especially difficult to treat in individual therapy [for] it is quite a task for a lone therapist to muster the strength or evidence to confront their defenses" (p. 14-2). She also notes that the individual therapy relationship alone is not a realistic representation of relationships in the "real world," and that the confidential nature of this relationship may serve to propagate the "sexual secret." A dangerous message is sent when an offender is in a relationship that involves a shared sexual secret (with an expectation of confidentiality), and

TABLE 9.1. Schwartz's Pros and Cons of Individual Therapy

Pros	Cons
• Provides more individual attention	• Therapist more easily manipulated
• May provide more confidentiality	• Denial may be more easily maintained
• May be used to develop trust and basic interpersonal relationship skills	• Therapeutic diad perpetuates the social skills for extremely withdrawn relationships that seem to perpetuate the "sexual secret"
• May be provided in a variety of physical settings	
• May be used on a short-term basis to overcome initial reticence and anxiety	• More opportunity for attempts at seduction on the part of the client
• May be used when crime is extreme, unusual, or stigmatized, e.g., sadism, coprophilia, and necrophilia	• Less opportunity to practice and develop social skills
• May be used when offender is mentally retarded or mentally ill and has trouble cognitively functioning in a group or is disruptive	• Less opportunity to learn empathy or help others
	• Less therapeutic confrontation by peers
	• Creates unrealistic social expectations
	• May be dangerous for the therapist
	• Is more costly
	• Undermines the power of the therapeutic community

Source: Copyright 1995 by Civic Research Institute, Inc. Reprinted with permission from Schwartz, Barbra K. (1995), Group Therapy. In B. K. Schwartz and H. R. Cellini (Eds.), *The Sex Offender: Corrections, Treatment, and Legal Practice* (14-4). Kingston, NJ: Civic Research Institute, Inc.

wherein the therapist is accepting of and consistent with the offender during the therapy process (Schwartz, 1995a). This is not to mention the fact that therapists reward a client (by signals of approval and statements of doing well in treatment) for discussing shocking sexual matters individually. It is partly because of the possibility of giving these mixed signals to the client in individual therapy that the concurrent use of a sex offense-specific group is a must when conducting individual therapy with a sexually abusive youth. Even though the necessity of group treatment is clear, in some cases, a client may be clinically unable to attend group, and individual therapy is all that can be feasibly provided.

Although it may be the case that an offender can only be treated individually, this decision should be made with caution. The author has made this decision in isolated cases (usually due to extreme disintegration or mental illness/retardation). However, the reader is warned that most any client (even one who could be able to attend groups with a little extra effort) will be able to come up with reasons why he *cannot* attend group. The reality is that he would likely do well in group. In almost all cases, except the isolated ones mentioned previously, the exclusive use of individual therapy will be a preparation measure and not an end in itself.

Although the group is the primary place to conduct the business of sex offense-specific therapy, there simply are some things that the group setting is unable to provide. The key to integration seems to be to use individual therapy to fill the gaps that the group cannot effectively cover, to provide the opportunity to have one-to-one time for discussing difficult issues, to provide support for discussing issues in group, and to coordinate the whole treatment package.

THE SCOPE OF INDIVIDUAL THERAPY

Individual therapy is the place to work on all presenting issues, not just sex offending. It is also the place where the client may be able to discuss topics that are too embarrassing or threatening to bring to the group at that time.

Some additional uses of individual therapy are as follows:

- Conducting SO assessment interviews
- Doing specific and detailed work on offending (e.g., fantasy work, reconditioning techniques, discussing difficult sexuality issues)

- Connecting SO work with other issues
- Providing a place for the client to make initial disclosures of offending behavior that will later be brought to group
- Reviewing work being done on orientation and relapse prevention planning packets
- Discussing the resident's progress in treatment, and doing treatment planning with him
- Assisting the resident with day-to-day issues being experienced
- Conducting psychotherapy of other mental health issues that can appropriately be treated in an individual therapy situation

COORDINATING WITH THE OTHER COMPONENTS

Therapists can ensure good coordination between the individual therapy component and the other program components in at least five ways. The first four equally apply to this or any other component: (1) sameness of staff, (2) good team communication, (3) consistency, and (4) continuity.

Having worked as a therapist conducting one or two program components while other clinicians conducted the remaining components, and then as a therapist involved at some level in conducting all of the components, I believe the latter to be preferable. Above all, a team approach is important. We would not expect that one therapist could "do it all" and/or that all clients would be able to respond to a single person equally as well as to a team. It seems that having the same *team* involved in all the components with a given youth maximizes consistency, continuity, communication, and coordination. This also provides a better way to link the work done by the youth in various components. The same team present in the delivery of all components also promotes this flexibility and blending of one component into another, so as to produce a more seamless unified treatment effort.

This team effort breaks down with individual therapy because it is perhaps the only component that does not directly involve the whole team. However, the team must be included at some level. Team meetings, during which the sex offense-specific treatment team reviews clients, are needed to (1) bridge the gap between the team and the individual work being done by members of that team, and (2) serve as a place to discuss treatment planning and to develop intervention strategies for each youth. The weekly team meeting is a good standard.

A final way that individual therapy can be coordinated with the other components is the "linchpin concept." Basically, since the therapist and youth are meeting one-on-one, it is an ideal time to discuss the progress of work in all the components, and to brainstorm with the youth how he can better utilize his treatment. The less threatening ground of the individual session provides a place for the youth to try out ideas before taking the plunge of bringing them up in group. It prepares the youth to initiate group discussions and provides a basis for the individual therapist to gently guide the youth to areas that he needs to address, which have been identified in team meetings. In this way the work from group filters to individual therapy, and from individual therapy back to group. The client has in the SO group, family groups, adjunct treatment groups, in the milieu, etc., a single person who provides consistency and linkage across all components. This can be a source of stability for the youth, and, furthermore, it is an effective means of ensuring accountability, especially for the youth who has not begun to take proper responsibility for his treatment.

THE THERAPIST AND THE YOUTH IN THERAPY

The individual therapist is in a precarious position while in a room alone with a sex offender. Although some of these adolescents may be soft-spoken and outwardly compliant, they have perpetrated serious, self-centered crimes against other persons. Schwartz (1995a) warns the therapist to be vigilant during interactions with the client by making known this shocking truth: "many sex offenders have covertly sexually assaulted their individual therapist" (p. 14-2). The therapist should always be aware of the process taking place during the therapy time. Many offenders are tantalized and tempted by having the therapist in a position where he or she will likely not leave the room. The therapist must remain apparently free from being shocked and confront the behavior if a client attempts to use this situation to shock or intimidate the therapist. Many clients would like to practice their "techniques" and get all the possible "benefits" that their manipulative and at times highly sexualized behaviors can provide.

The individual therapy session, which lacks the benefits of a cotherapist for help, support, and vigilance, can be one of the more powerful tests in meeting the challenge of dealing with the sexually abusive youth. The reader is directed to three resources that will be helpful in forming a productive, safe, and therapeutically challenging individual therapy relationship: (1) *Treating Perpetrators of Sexual Abuse,* by Ingersoll and Patton (1990); (2) *The Sexually Abused Male,* by Hunter (1990); and (3) *The Difficult Connection: The Therapeutic Relationship In Sex Offender Treatment,* by Geral Blanchard (1998).

The Firmness of Compassion

Nowhere are the dynamics of the "tough and tender" balance of being warm enough to elicit a positive response and foster acceptance while being firm enough to address behaviors that need to be confronted more evident than in the individual therapy relationship. Therapists must pay special attention to the quality of their relationship with the client, for, as Blanchard (1998) has stated, "the quality of the therapist-patient relationship is equally important, if not more so, than any technique or instrument in restoring sex offenders to safe and healthy relationships within society" (p. 36).

Part of the function of the individual therapy relationship is to help the client learn to interact in a one-to-one situation in an appropriate and healthy way. We have already noted how difficult this is to do in a professional relationship due to the "unnatural" quality of such a relationship, which is characterized by regularly scheduled and time-limited individual interactions with a professional who is part of a system of caregivers and often too consistent for a real relationship. Teaching interpersonal skills for relationships becomes even more difficult if the therapist, on top of all these "drawbacks," is *also* sterile, cold, and emotionally distant. "When the fundamentals of relationship-building are not applied to sex offenders, little movement or growth will take place in counseling" (Blanchard, 1998, p. 32). One must develop a compassionate stance that allows for as much emotional openness and connection as is appropriate and prudent, while providing the needed boundaries to prevent the therapist from being sucked into the offender's often twisted and manipulative emotional world.

This leads us to the "firmness of compassion." Many are misguided to think that a firm stance is not loving or caring. Offenders will want to push the therapist to draw this conclusion, as will most any adolescent. In reality, a certain degree of firmness is an important part of a loving and caring relationship. It is *vital* that the relationship have limits and firmness, and that the therapist be in a position of authority (although it is not necessary to "rub it in" or "make your power felt"). The client may feel victimized by anyone taking a firm stance to confront behaviors, to address difficult and uncomfortable subjects, and to deny inappropriate requests. To him, it may seem as if he is being victimized, for the challenging or confronting actions may trigger old feelings from times when a tyrannical, unfair, and abusive adult degraded him or was overly punitive. However, if the therapist is keeping his or her emotions in check and not becoming overly involved with the client, then his or her actions, although bringing cries of "You don't really care about me," etc., are most likely in the right.

In times of conflict, the key is for the therapist to step back from the interaction and assume a more neutral stance, evaluating himself or herself, his or her techniques and methods, the client, and the reality of the situation. It may be that this interaction has provided valuable information on how the client misinterprets people's behavior in light of his own past trauma, and the therapist can help him to view things more realistically in the "here and now." It may be in fact that the therapist was being too severe or unfair, in which case he or she is provided with an opportunity for personal growth, a chance to role model apologizing and taking responsibility for errors, and an opportunity to help the client realize that in the real world people are not always fair—and he must learn to cope with this fact without acting out. The therapist may even discover that despite the youth's protestations and cries, he knows that the therapist is right, realizes his error, and truly appreciates the therapist for helping to keep him in line (if you expect a thank-you in these situations, chances are you will be waiting a long time).

Transference and Countertransference

A personal awareness by the therapist of his or her own vulnerabilities is important. The author has worked with clients who developed a strong transference, often experiencing similar feelings and playing out similar relationship dynamics with the therapist as were part of other significant relationships. These relationships may have been with parents, other authority figures, perpetrators of abuse they received, or even some of their own victims. These clients often became lost in the confusion of their feelings and urges and became what we might call "perplexing," "irrational," or "difficult." In the group setting, more people are present to help the client ground himself in the reality of the present experience, but in individual therapy, there is only you and the client.

Transference can cause sudden outbreaks in what seems to be a calm situation. The author recalls a young man with whom he worked in a residential treatment program. This youth had developed a warm relationship with the author and had responded with gratitude to many firm confrontations during the course of his residential stay. One day in the sex offense-specific group he was getting in touch with some particularly intense emotions, and the author made a statement that challenged his pattern of thinking. He suddenly turned to the author and responded in a hostile and aggressive manner, which surprised everyone in the room. The group questioned him about what he was doing, and the cotherapist was able to get him to engage her in a calmer manner as he continued to shoot angry glances at the author. When he began to think about the incident and why he had felt such hostile feelings toward the author (which he began to see were out of proportion to the situation), he realized that the author had used an expression of speech that his father frequently used in argumentative preludes to physical abuse.

This incident provided material to process the continued level of anger and hostility he felt toward his father. He learned to separate these feelings from those he experienced toward the author. The author could not help wonder how the situation would have played out in an individual therapy setting. One must be prepared to deal with such intense transference from clients in individual therapy (which a careful therapist can successfully manage) and view them not as personal attacks but as manifestations of the same patterns of externalization of anger and blame that are part of the sexual or physical assault. Transference in this sense is positive because it demonstrates to the client how his emotions can be acted out upon a person who is not the actual cause of the pain he is experiencing.

Such experiences as those just mentioned can escalate disastrously if the therapist is unaware of his or her own countertransference issues. Some clients get to us either because they remind us of people from our past (even past abusers) or because they touch some of the sensitive areas that cause us to experience intense emotions. In individual therapy, the one-to-one dynamic of the relationship can cause feelings to be elicited toward the client that the therapist may not know how to handle. These may be good or bad feelings, anger, disgust, sexual excitement, confusion, or a generalized anxiety. It is important for the therapist to attend to these feelings (without becoming overly worried about them) so that they do not play out in a diminishment of his or her effectiveness. In this effort, the therapist will need to have a sounding board to guard against the individual therapy relationship becoming "isolated" from other professional contacts in the program (i.e., individual supervisor and team members). Once again the reader is referred to Blanchard (1998) for more advice in the management of countertransference and related issues.

The Danger of Isolation

One of the chief dangers in working one-on-one with a sex client is the danger of isolation. Sex-offending clients are often skillful in gradually moving persons into greater levels of secrecy and exclusiveness in interpersonal relationships. The prelude to an offense is the development of a secret. Grooming their potential victims to maintain a secret level of intimacy in the relationship makes the offense possible. This dynamic plays out in the individual therapy relationship as well.

The therapist must be aware of the client's attempts to draw him or her into a relationship that promotes secrecy or that allows emotional ties to the client to strengthen. It is easy to be drawn in, to be inclined to set aside professional norms (such as communicating relevant clinical information to members of the team) to strengthen the relationship with the client.

The first guard against such isolation is individual supervision. It is easier to share information in individual therapy with one person than it is to bring it to a group of colleagues. The author would customarily tell the youth in the first session that he (the therapist) will feel free to discuss anything that the client says with his supervisor. This has not proved an impediment to disclosure; even with this disclaimer in effect, clients still open up and share even the most embarrassing and difficult issues. With this ground rule laid out, the therapist can freely discuss in supervision information that could be part of a "secretive bond" with the client. Furthermore, the therapist can share with the supervisor his or her feelings surrounding work with the client so that the supervisor can help to keep track of the status of the relationship.

Once the author was supervising an intern working at a sex offense-specific treatment program. The intern was doing quite well working with some very serious offenders. She had been given instruction by the author never to meet with a certain client alone but to counsel him in the dining room in sight, but out of earshot, of the staff. One day in her supervision session, she related that she had been faithful in keeping to this directive but wanted to try to meet with the client in a particular classroom in one corner of the building. After questioning her on her reasons for wanting to do this, the author became suspicious and discussed with her the development of her relationship with the client. She began to question the wisdom of meeting alone with the client, seeing that perhaps she was letting herself get too close to this young man. The author offered to speak with the client to see what he could learn.

During this conversation, the young man stated that he had been having frequent rape fantasies concerning this intern and had been working to convince her that it would be a good idea to meet alone in order to carry them out. He explained in detail why this classroom had been selected: it was isolated, the door opened into the room and could be barricaded to trap her, and it had only one other door (opening to the outside), so he could escape if she screamed. If this intern had not been so diligent in discussing her thoughts in supervision, he might well have succeeded in his plan to rape her.

One final note regarding isolation. The therapist must be sure that the work in individual therapy does not become isolated from the other work the client is doing in the program. It is easy for this component to become disconnected from the coordinated treatment effort if it is not well linked to the other components (as mentioned previously), and if the individual therapist does not keep his or her team updated on the progress of individual therapy. In the previous example of the intern, her being open in supervision and with her team achieved more than ensuring her personal safety; her coordination of individual work allowed a previously unknown continuation of rape fantasies to come to the attention of the team, and this would not have been known otherwise.

Developing a Comfort Zone, Collaboration, and Supportive Partnership

As much as therapists need to avoid isolation, we also need to provide enough security in the individual therapy relationship that we create a "comfort zone" where the client can feel able to raise and discuss some very difficult topics. We need to have him feel that he can bring in his past and current triumphs, failures, concerns, joys, and endeavors so that he can learn from them. He needs to feel that he can initiate discussions of ways in which he is failing to follow through with his treatment, or of times when he is slipping back. This calls for the kind of supportive, firm compassion that has already been discussed as well as the construction of a level of confidentiality that is reasonable, therapeutically indicated, and safe.

We should be working in this relationship to form a collaboration, a supportive partnership if you will, with both parties (individual therapist and client) striving for common goals. The successful individual therapist will be able to start by forming this collaboration with the client and then help him to extend the partnership to the other members of the team as well. This therapist will also be able to use his or her relationship with the client to widen the client's circle of support, for this truly serves his needs and best interests.

Chapter 10

Adjunctive Treatments and Therapies

THE RANGE AND SCOPE
OF ADJUNCTIVE TREATMENTS

Adjunctive treatments are those services and therapies provided by the program as part of its regime that are not strictly sex offense-specific interventions. This chapter examines all such services as a component unto itself. This component supports the sex offense-specific treatment, assists the client in personal growth, and targets the many other maladaptive/delinquent patterns in the client's life that are contributing to the offending.

It is important to remember that since sex offending can also be part of a larger pattern of maladaptive and/or delinquent behavior (Blackburn, 1993), failure to address these patterns can reduce the effectiveness of sex offense-specific treatment. Programs must treat the whole person, using adjunctive treatments that target the larger range of issues that, although perhaps not directly part of the offending, are part of the total clinical picture and can affect the probability of reoffense.

Development of an adjunctive treatment component should not be difficult because many programs already employ many of these treatments in the care of their clients. Within the framework of the multi-component model, all non-interventions and services can be seen as an adjunct to the offense-specific treatments. This is not to diminish the value of any of the treatments themselves; however, since many of these treatments impact the offending issue in an indirect way, from the *perspective* of the sex offense-specific treatment team, they are adjunctive.

Taken from other vantage points, the case may be quite different: the program's substance abuse treatment team may regard the sex offense-specific group as an adjunct to *their* treatment, or the recreational activities coordinator may not see the sex offense-specific treatment as connected to his area at all—it is all a matter of perspective. The point is to use all available means to assist the client in resolving the issues that have led to him needing treatment, and to help him to live a healthier life after he leaves the formal treatment arena.

Through assessment and treatment planning, clinicians must decide what combination of such treatments is most beneficial to the client to help him overcome deficits and to grow as a person in all areas of his life. Some examples of adjunctive treatments are presented in Table 10.1. This list draws on the author's experience with helpful interventions and also on material from Maletzky (1991) and Thompson (1989).

USING VARIOUS PROGRAM SERVICES AS ADJUNCTS

Using these services as adjuncts to the sex offense-specific treatment simply means that they are conceptualized as fitting with the other components in the multi-component model and are seen as playing a part in the achievement of the goals of the sex offense-specific treatment regime. Once again, this is not to limit what these treatments can accomplish individually for the client apart from their connection to the sex offense-specific treatment, but it does mean that clinicians in sex offense-specific components will delegate work to this component and receive work from this component in a collaborative relationship.

A better-functioning client in all areas stands a better chance of remaining offense free. The offender in treatment must be prepared for a positive adjustment to the community (cf. Lundrigan, 1999). It has been found that boredom (often from the client's inability to structure his time and to engage in appropriate social activities) and substance use or abuse significantly increase offense risk (cf. Ryan and Lane, 1998). Furthermore, clients with unstable employment (perhaps due to a lack of vocational training and poorly developed work habits) are at a higher risk to reoffend (Maletzky, 1991). Clinicians should recognize this and will want to see the client develop in all areas possible, using whatever means are at their disposal. Program activity groups, rec-

TABLE 10.1. Examples of Treatment Interventions Used As Adjuncts to Sex Offense-Specific Therapy

• Substance abuse groups and/or attendance at AA/NA/Al-Anon, etc.
• Team-building activities (e.g., ropes course, wilderness trips)
• Discussion and activity groups on various topics related to the development of prosocial thinking and behavior
• Anger management groups
• Informal counseling with direct care staff
• Participation in an aftercare group (such as a skills for independent living program)
• Vocational exploration/training
• Open psychotherapy groups that afford an opportunity to work on a variety of issues and needs for growth
• Engaging in new types of recreation and hobbies to expand possible range of leisure skills and activities in the future
• Activities that help develop new coping patterns and a positive, healthy lifestyle to replace the gap left by the removal of offending patterns and behaviors
• Training in social and dating skills
• Impulse control and assertiveness versus aggressiveness training
• Anxiety reduction and relaxation techniques training
• Activities that promote the development of a positive spirituality

reational activities, informal educational groups, and groups focused on specific topics are helpful and serve to round out the treatment provided by the program.

Other program therapy groups are one of the most important adjuncts. These groups give the client opportunities to process and work on areas opened up in SO treatment that need further attention. In addition, they give him a place to work on other important issues that the SO group in a multi-component model would consider only in passing (e.g., substance abuse, anger management, etc.). This sharing of work allows the SO group to remain more focused and helps the client to become accustomed to using a variety of services in the maintenance of offense-free behavior.

Passes, visits, and client contact with the community are useful and extremely important adjuncts, and they are an integral part of preparing clients in group care for transition to a less secure setting. Also important in this preparation effort is the use of community support groups, services, and institutions. Efforts at helping the client to use these services while in formal treatment will benefit him when he must seek services on his own.

A SOMETIMES NEGLECTED ADJUNCT

One area of adjunctive treatment listed in Table 10.1 that many programs seem to neglect is attention to clients' spiritual needs. Treating the whole person involves giving equal attention to this very important aspect of the human person. In addition to providing opportunities for clients to attend church services and to engage in reasonable spiritual practices, staff should be sensitive to and respectful of a client's spirituality and supportive of efforts aimed at increased personal integration.

It is also important to take religious beliefs into consideration in assessment and treatment. Many clients may misunderstand, distort, or improperly use religious beliefs to justify unhealthy behavior or to burden themselves with unwarranted guilt. Clients having accurate information regarding religious beliefs from appropriate persons can minimize potential problems in this area. Also, it is important for clients to have a sense of the divine and transcendent in their lives, so that they may find one more place from which to draw strength during the difficult process of treatment and ongoing recovery.

Chapter 11

Milieu Treatment

When we speak of a "milieu" in a clinical context, we typically refer to the whole living environment surrounding a client in a group
care program or the daily environment set up in a day program. For
some time, the milieu has been regarded as an avenue for clinical
work. Austrian August Aichorn has been regarded as the "father" of
milieu therapy and was perhaps one of the earliest (1907) to conceptualize the construction of a living environment to produce therapeutic effect (McCord, 1982).

The approach was popularized in the late 1950s by Fritz Redl, who
advanced the concept of a "therapeutic milieu" and examined what
composes a so-called "therapeutic community." Such communities
work to generate an environment that exerts a therapeutic influence
on the client and thus perform a mode of therapy known as "milieu
therapy" (Redl, 1959). Many today steadfastly defend milieu therapy
as an important intervention, stating the premise that "only a total
transformation of the child's environment over an extended period of
time can lead to a lasting change" (McCord, 1982, p. 10).

THE MILIEU AS A VENUE FOR TREATMENT

Today it would be hard to find a group care setting in which the milieu is not seen as part of the program's treatment effort. In fact, in
some programs, almost the entire treatment effort is seen to come
from the milieu and formal therapy, if it exists at all, is viewed as a
secondary component (Durrant, 1993). Although the concept of milieu treatment has been around for a long time, and despite many pro-

grams employing a milieu treatment approach, it still sometimes does not receive the focus it should. It is very common for clinical staff and administrators to focus on the formal therapy components and downplay the importance of the milieu in the treatment effort.

The following quote reflects one clinician's growing understanding of the importance and impact of the program's milieu on the client:

> I well remember . . . my growing suspicion that what I did in the "therapy room". . . was ultimately not nearly as effective as the "therapeutic" interactions that occurred around the pool table, the trampoline, and the dining room. (Durrant, 1993, p. 159)

Unfortunately, many clinicians do not come to a fullness of this realization, and as a result, they do not allow the milieu to be used to its potential.

The Milieu As a Clinical Intervention

Clients exposed to the controlled environment of a treatment milieu have greater opportunities to modify their range of behaviors and responses. To properly manage the milieu, direct care staff must have a sense of treatment approaches in general, but especially the approaches used in milieu treatment. It is also important that they have some knowledge of the issues the clients are dealing with and that they are regarded as part of the treatment team.

The direct care staff should be aware of all the client's goals and treatment areas so that they can address these as they present themselves in the milieu. Their viewpoint should be taken into consideration and properly respected in the selection and refinement of treatment goals. Staff who are aware of the total treatment picture will be able to make milieu interventions related to a client's goals, and they also will be able to give feedback to other members of the team when an issue appears to require further attention in one or more of the other components.

Recognition of the milieu's value in treatment and active efforts to create a clinically challenging milieu will determine whether the milieu is a place to "hang out" or a place that encourages client growth and enhances the impact of the other treatment components. A good program will create a therapeutic community that does the following:

- Enhances self-esteem
- Teaches appropriate social skills
- Reflects behavior back to clients to raise their awareness so that they can process these behaviors in group therapy
- Stresses empathic responses to others
- Makes extensive use of peer feedback to help residents to modify maladaptive patterns of behavior
- Teaches new skills and introduces the resident to new recreational activities
- Develops leadership skills (and the all-important skills needed to follow directions when someone else is the leader)
- Emphasizes taking responsibility for actions and words and making appropriate restitution of wrongs
- Teaches prosocial values and ways of dealing with others
- Helps clients to learn different ways of meeting their needs that do not involve aggressive and/or abusive behaviors

Since these treatment goals are very important for sex offense-specific therapy (as they are many of the nonsexual areas of *paramount* importance in treatment but often overlooked), they are perfectly suited to be part of the treatment package.

Some Key Factors Involved in Milieu Treatment

Much literature has been amassed regarding the conducting of milieu treatment, and the reader is encouraged to do further reading in this area (e.g., Berlin, 1997; Crenshaw, 1988; Durrant, 1993; Goyette, Marr, and Lewicki, 1995; Schaefer and Swanson, 1988; Knopp, 1982; Roush, 1984; Schneider and Cohen, 1998). This section highlights some of the more important factors in milieu treatment.

One important factor is the staff's ability to manipulate environmental variables. This ability allows them to set up reinforcement contingencies for behavioral interventions by designing program setup, rules, rewards, and consequences in such a way that positive behaviors are reinforced. Manipulation of the environment also includes program scheduling, activity planning, meals, and special events added to the ordinary routine. Such manipulations of the environment represent one of the ways that staff in group care, day, and after-school programs can influence the development of the program's peer culture. How staff deal with problem behaviors and the extent to which they allow such behaviors to affect the environment of the program also affects the level of safety, the degree of client comfort, and the level of "positivity" of the peer culture.

The peer culture concept merits mention here as well. A child's self-concept is partly formed in peer relationships, as are self-esteem, views on one's strengths and weaknesses, and many behavioral manifestations of emotional states (Gwynn, Meyer, and Schaefer, 1988). The peer group can have a positive or negative influence on the client as he resides in the milieu. This great ability of the peer culture to influence the client is one of the reasons that staff must be vigilant in their use of environmental manipulation, personal interaction, and groups to help shape this culture. One must not be too overt in culture-shaping efforts, or the clients may subtly revolt by establishing cultural norms for the community that are at odds with those the staff are "pushing." Staff who enter into community with the clients and gently guide them to establish norms conducive to treatment that are positive and hopeful regarding the program, "community building," and safe will be most successful in helping to shape this most important aspect of milieu treatment.

Recreational activities are an important part of the treatment. Clients can benefit from learning more appropriate ways to spend their leisure time and can be greatly enriched by having their horizons broadened. Learning a sense of fair play (not to mention the concept of "playing by the rules") and equitable treatment of others are important impacts that may result. Social skills enhancement and a sense of increasing skills level and mastery can be positive effects that will help to enrich relationships and raise self-esteem. In addition, recreation provides an outing, a change of scenery, a chance to "kick back," and an opportunity to healthfully "blow off some steam." Such releases may be needed, especially for clients who are engaged much of the time in a somewhat rigorous clinical program.

Formal milieu educational activities provide opportunities to teach in a more organized manner, perhaps by setting up educational groups or classes aimed at helping clients acquire new skills. Informal education occurs in day-to-day interactions between staff and clients and also through staff role modeling.

Allowing clients to have some input into the running of the milieu can enhance their sense of ownership and help them to engage more fully in the program. Some ways of doing this include holding "community" or "business" meetings during which clients discuss and vote on programmatic decisions, forming client committees responsible for certain decisions and day-to-day concerns, and placing residents in positions of "authority" over certain projects, chores, or activities. The author has seen these efforts taken to an extreme, with the staff compromising their control over the program and thereby losing some of their ability to form culture and keep clients safe. Putting the wrong client in charge of supervising other clients can have disastrous results (e.g., a well-trusted client who sexually abused other clients under his supervision when out of the staff's sight).

A balance must be struck between giving clients a chance to enhance leadership skills and develop a sense of ownership in the program and letting them have too much say and thus having staff spend inordinate amounts of time finding solutions of which all clients approve. Remember, part of what these kids need to learn is that they cannot have their way all the time (as they did with their victims), they do not have all the answers (neither does anyone else), they are there for treatment and not to set up a milieu that will reduce the impact of treatment, and *responsibility* must guide decisions. Staff must set parameters for the clients to operate within and, in the author's opinion, retain the right to veto irresponsible decisions.

Influences from outside the program, although not part of the milieu, do affect the client and hence are "carried" into the milieu by the client. The impact of these influences should not be discounted. Staff will want to stay up to date on what is going on in the client's outside world, as well as in formal therapy sessions that take place (strictly speaking) outside the milieu. By attending to the timing of clients' emotional reactions and behavior patterns related to external events, by keeping abreast of information received by the program regarding the family and friends of the clients, and by asking clients questions in informal conversations, the staff will come to learn how clients are being affected by influences outside the confines of the milieu. By helping clients to process thoughts and feelings; by offering suggestions, advice, and a listening ear; and by assessing what issues have been raised that may be addressed in other areas of treatment, the staff may help clients to learn from these experiences, formulate appropriate plans of action, and lessen the negative impact on the milieu as a whole.

Groups: The Core and Foundation of the Milieu

Groups are indispensable in the delivery of milieu treatment and vital in helping to create the essential positive peer culture. Apart from formal psychotherapy groups (facilitated principally by the clinical staff), programs should also have milieu groups (more often facilitated by the direct care staff). Such groups can range from simple gatherings of clients in one room to transition in an orderly manner to the next activity to very organized educational or activity-based groups.

"Goal review groups" provide a structured setting for giving clients feedback on their progress on their milieu goals, whereas "call groups" (i.e., unplanned groups assembled in response to a specific situation) permit staff to address immediately a prominent concern. "Focus groups" on specific topics may be scheduled to discuss a pertinent issue, provide a chance for learning, and help to open clients' minds to other ways of thinking and possibilities for acting.

Groups may be used for planning special activities, organizing program work assignments, and providing the formal setting to review progress and advancement in program levels. Special groups may be used to introduce new clients or staff and to say good-bye to those who are leaving. Groups may be held at the beginning of the day, to set the tone for the day and to help clients identify goals to work on that day, and at the end, to recap and review the day, assess progress on the goal(s) set in the morning group, and provide a chance to air grievances before bedtime or to express hope for a positive tomorrow.

EXTENDING AND ENHANCING
THE IMPACT OF FORMAL THERAPY

The Connections of Milieu Treatment to the Program As a Whole

Staff members are central to the effort of coordinating milieu treatment, if the work done in formal therapy is to be expanded, reinforced, strengthened, and more deeply integrated by the client. Figure 11.1 presents a conceptualization of the role the direct care staff play in the milieu treatment of the youth. The milieu is a vibrant place with many connections to entities both inside and outside the milieu space. Tables 11.1 and 11.2 list the nature of the inputs and outputs (represented by arrows in Figure 11.1) from the perspectives of the direct care staff and the client. The inputs are what the staff and client receive from a given source during milieu treatment; the out-

FIGURE 11.1. The Direct Care Staff Engaged in Milieu Treatment

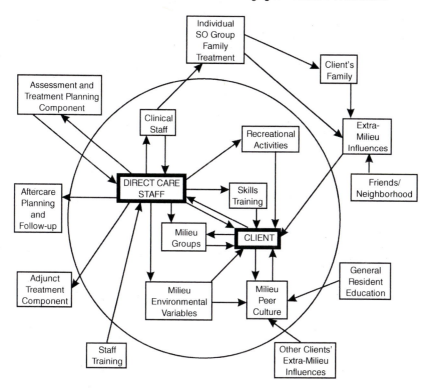

puts are the contributions by the staff and client to various parties while conducting milieu treatment.

Assessment in the Milieu

Assessment is discussed in more detail in the next chapter; however, it is important to note here the milieu's importance as a place of assessment. The milieu is uniquely suited to information gathering. In the milieu, clients act and react to various situations, they have endless opportunities to engage in old or practice new behaviors, and, more important, they are under the potentially constant observation of staff. The information gained by observing clients is tremendously important for gauging their progress, determining what areas still need attention, and directing future treatment efforts.

TABLE 11.1. Milieu Treatment Functions from a Staff Perspective

Input and Output Functions of Direct Care Staff
INPUT TO THE STAFF MEMBER FROM: • **Clinical staff**—supervision (individual and/or group) and sharing of data • **Staff training**—education, tools, and methodology • **Assessment and treatment planning**—goals for the client in the milieu and goals from other components that can be treated via milieu intervention • **Client**—behavior, speech/thought, feedback, and information from conversation **OUTPUT FROM THE STAFF MEMBER TO:** • **Clinical staff**—ideas, insights, concerns that need to be addressed in other treatment components, advocacy, requests for information, and sharing of data • **Recreational activities**—planning, involving clients, and clinical conceptualization • **Skills training**—assessment of client needs, planning, and implementation • **Client**—feedback, discipline, guidance, support, limits, education, and mentoring • **Milieu groups**—cofacilitation, structure, initiating needed discussions, active participation, and using group to further influence the culture of the milieu • **Milieu environment**—clinical manipulation of variables and conditions • **Adjunct treatment**—data, coordination, facilitation, engaging clients, and participation • **Aftercare planning**—data, concerns, suggestions, aid in planning, and client support • **Assessment and treatment planning**—data, goal setting, and helping client in process

TABLE 11.2. Milieu Treatment Functions from a Client Perspective

Input and Output Functions of Clients
INPUT TO THE CLIENT FROM: • **Staff**—feedback, discipline, guidance, support, limits, education, and mentoring • **Milieu groups**—feedback, peer support, ideas, time to talk and work through issues, sense of belonging and mastery, and education • **Milieu environment**—arousal of various thought/affect states to be processed, pressure to use appropriate patterns, safety, and opportunities to experiment with new behaviors • **Peer culture**—encouragement of positive and negative change, sense of belonging, ability to work on interpersonal skills, and uncovering of relationship issues • **Extra-milieu influences**—distractions, issues to take to groups, preparation for discharge, and learning from peers how to cope with these issues • **Recreational**—new ways to use free time, sense of accomplishment, and socialization • **Skills training**—education to improve deficit areas **OUTPUT FROM THE CLIENT TO:** • **Staff**—behavior, speech/thought, feedback, and information from conversation • **Peer culture**—influence, leadership, helping others, and working to build a positive peer culture • **Milieu groups**—helping others, supporting, sharing insights, challenging, confronting, and active participation

Staff should trust their gut feelings and convey their observations to other members of the treatment team. Sometimes a failure to relate observations that may or may not be important can have drastic consequences (see the story of Kevin at the end of the next chapter). Every piece of data is potentially significant. The client who is trying to hide maladaptive patterns may be able to do so in some situations or with some people, but a coordinated team of observers should be able to uncover the truth sooner or later—"You can fool some of the people all of the time, or all of the people some of the time, but you can't fool all of the people all of the time."

A "Perfect" Milieu Is Not Necessarily Better

A milieu cannot be just like negative environments in the outside world and should not be a place where treatment and personal growth are not valued. The impact of formal therapy will be counteracted to a degree if this is the case. Clients will inevitably be exposed to negative and contradictory messages in the milieu (from other clients and also from some staff). This is nothing other than a preparation for having to stand tall in the face of even more severe influences in real life. A degree of this negative influence provides opportunities to learn how to defend against it, yet too much will cause the more fragile client to cave in to the pressure and, in the end, will create a culture that is hostile to treatment and potentially unsafe for clients and staff alike.

As with a vaccine, a bit of the pathogen helps to build resistance, and too much causes illness. The staff and culture of the milieu should not deliberately present negative messages, but they should ensure those messages which inevitably arise are properly processed so that a positive clinical effect can be drawn from the client's experience.

THE MILIEU AS IN VIVO EXPERIENTIAL APPLICATION OF THERAPY

The "Laboratory" of the Milieu

Practice is needed throughout the course of treatment. Skills are being taught to clients, maladaptive patterns are being identified and alternatives charted, latent strengths are being observed, and ideas and suggestions for relating differently to people are being suggested. The milieu, passes (in group care settings), and out-of-program recreation are good settings for practicing, exploring, and experimenting. The upside of using the milieu to experiment is that clients are kept safe and usually gain feedback on how well their experiment is going. The downside is that the milieu is, in reality, an artificial environment. Learning to use a new skill or exercising a newfound strength in the milieu may be very different from doing so in the real world.

The outpatient client has a greater ability to work on new ways of thinking and behaving in the real world, since (even in the case of an intensive day program) the client will be in the community every day; however, there are more uncontrolled variables and less observation and feedback in the outside world than in the milieu. The client will need to self-report much of what occurs outside for the staff to help him stay on the right track. The informational and control aspects may be lower in an outpatient setting, but the possibilities for learning are greater. In a group care setting, the milieu provides, at a minimum, a controlled transitional environment in which the early experimental work can be done in preparation for less restrictive placement. When the client earns passes, he will begin to experience some of the reality of the outside world. At this time, he will need to do the same type of self-reporting and intensive processing that is a significant part of outpatient treatment.

The key in this effort is to help the client productively experiment in the "laboratory" of the milieu when he is there, and then to help him apply the gains he has made and the lessons learned to the outside world in the times that he is in the community.

Teaching Skills in the Milieu

With clients experimenting, succeeding, and failing, the staff are uniquely poised to do a great deal of educational work with these adolescents. Highlighting successes, noting failures, disciplining, mentoring, teaching, guiding, encouraging, and supporting are all part of this effort. Many of the educational activities that staff will do with clients will be formal, but it is the informal feedback and guidance slipped in between the scenes that makes the difference. At the point of a success or failure, or confusion or hurt or joy, the client is often very receptive to the advice and direction presented by a caring adult who happens to be there.

Education in the milieu by the staff is really threefold: (1) staff teach when they group the clients together in a formal educational activity or a structured experiential group activity; (2) they teach when they discipline, support, encourage, admonish, listen, and talk to the clients outside of structured activities; and, most significant, (3) they teach by what they do. Attending to these areas of education will allow the staff to be more effective educators of their clients and to enhance the adolescents' lives by presenting sound counsel, guidance, and example.

Chapter 12

Assessment and Treatment Planning

Current authoritative opinion is that assessment of the sexually abusive adolescent is necessary to inform a variety of decisions regarding his management (Barbaree and Cortoni, 1993). Comprehensive assessment must be viewed as ongoing. The knowledge base concerning the client is constantly changing, requiring reevaluation of treatment goals (Ross and Loss, 1991). This process of assessment (and reassessment) helps to drive the whole business of placement and treatment (Northeastern Family Institute, 1994). Each program will therefore need to establish a process to assess clients and to plan treatment accordingly.

The assessment and treatment planning component is assigned these tasks. It is the "foreman," if you will, of the various components—always watching to observe progress and directing the efforts of the various entities so that they function more smoothly as a unified whole. Without such constant monitoring and adjustment, the program could easily go astray, having different components (and persons) working at conflicting goals.

The assessment of those who commit sexual offenses (as noted earlier) is a highly specialized process requiring a great deal of training and supervised experience to master. Given a number of factors, the task of assessing the client to ascertain the actual level of deviancy and treatment need is a difficult task. However, beneficial and useful assessment can be done on a variety of levels. These levels range from informal behavioral observations to full-scale formal assessments done by a trained specialist. In this chapter, "assessment" refers to the information gathering, observation, monitoring, and other functions performed by the program staff during the course of treatment. More formal assessment, such as would be done by a sex offense-specific assessment specialist (which might involve batteries of psychological tests and other more formal SO assessment measures), is referred to as an "evaluation."

The following proposed protocol is one possible conceptualization of program set up, with assessment and treatment planning functions that are a combination of program "assessment" and formal "evaluation." This scheme is organized chronologically and attempts to illustrate what assessments could be done as a client progresses through the program.

A PROPOSED ASSESSMENT
AND TREATMENT PLANNING PROTOCOL

The Offense Evaluation

A juvenile who has been suspected of and/or adjudicated for the commission of a sexual offense is customarily referred for a comprehensive sex offense-specific evaluation. This evaluation (often ordered by the courts or requested by the child protection agency) constitutes the first step in a youth's entering the continuum of care for sexual offenders (cf. Chapter 2, p. 20). The reasons for this evaluation are to gain information on various factors that will be helpful to future treatment providers, to determine risk to the community, to assess the ability of the client to do clinical work, and to recommend an appropriate placement or treatment option (Wenhold et al., 1994). This evaluation is crucial. Perry and Orchard (1992) list the following goals of such an assessment:

1. Provide information to the court
2. Design an intervention strategy
3. Make recommendations for placement of the youth
4. Begin orienting the youth (and family) to treatment

The information gathering and orientation functions of this intervention will have the greatest impact on the youth's future treatment.

Program Admission Assessment

Programs with control of who they accept for treatment will conduct an assessment of the appropriateness of a given client for their setting. Such an assessment should not take place until a comprehensive evaluation done by a sex offense-specific specialist is on file. The information gathered by this evaluation, the court and police records, school and previous placement reports, and an interview with the youth and his family will help to determine whether *this* program will accept *this* youth for treatment.

If he is deemed appropriate for the program's style of treatment, if it seems that (given the program's complement of services) this client can be successful and reach his goals, and if it is judged safe to permit him to participate in the program, then he will likely be accepted for intake. If the client is deemed inappropriate, the program providers will generally explain their reasons to the referring agent and might make recommendations of what setting or program may be more suitable for this client.

Initial Program Assessment and Treatment Plan

If the client is accepted, the program providers should conduct their own assessment of the specific treatment needs of the youth to prepare a comprehensive treatment plan. Such an assessment would include the following actions:

1. Synthesize all the data available on the client (gained from offense evaluation, admission assessment, conversations with family and collateral sources, and current behavioral observations of the youth)
2. Assess treatment needs
3. Determine specific clinical interventions that will be used
4. Set goals for the youth in all the various components of treatment
5. Determine how the attainment of goals will be assessed (cf. Green, 1995d)

This assessment would also take into account the delineating risk factors, including those which are "static" (i.e., the risk factors always present for the client due to his makeup) and those which are "dynamic" (i.e., changes in the environment that increase or decrease his risk of offense) (cf. Proulx et al., 1997).

These assessments would make use of record reviews, behavioral observations, structured interviews, and perhaps the administration of informal assessment tools to the client. The product is an initial treatment plan, a set of baseline measures that will be used later to gauge client progress, and an idea of the level of client offense risk and what factors can influence his risk to offend at any given time.

Family Assessment

As mentioned in Chapter 8, a family assessment should be conducted. This gives an opportunity to ask specific questions of family members, gain additional information on the behavior of the client, and clarify information passed on by prior treatment providers. Such an assessment aids treatment planning for family therapy as well as client individual therapy.

This assessment is a chance for the therapist to become acquainted with the family members and for them to have the opportunity to share information that may be crucial to the case, but that has not been made known. Sometimes people are just waiting to be asked. More important, such sessions allow the therapist to educate family members, orient them to treatment, and begin preliminary clinical interventions. This assessment may be one of the first times the parents are placed face-to-face with the reality of their son's offending. It is important as a time to begin the process of accepting that the abuse occurred and to begin engaging in treatment.

Periodic and Ongoing Assessment

After the initial assessment period, the client should be monitored in an ongoing manner and progress should be discussed in regular (ideally weekly) meetings of the treatment staff, who will plan adjustments to interventions accordingly. In addition, the case should be reviewed in a more formal manner every few months to determine progress on attainment of goals; to give feedback to the client, family, and funding source; and to generate the development of a modified treatment plan that more accurately reflects current needs.

An important part of this process is a review and reworking of the treatment plan with the client. This gives him feedback on how the team views his progress, helps to refocus him on the relevant goals, and allows him to comment on how he would assess his own progress. These invitations for the client to assess his own progress can be both informative for the clinician and beneficial to the client. Sometimes one discovers that "something is missing" in the client's thinking, or one area is in need of more attention. On the other hand, the client's assessment may indicate progress and increased responsibility. Some negative examples are the client in treatment for twelve months who is having deviant fantasies but does *not* identify this as a goal for treatment, or the youth who is engaging in quasi-offending behaviors who wants a pass to see his victim as a goal of treatment. More positive indicators would be a client adding a goal regarding an issue that he had not previously discussed, or the youth who admits that he really has not been putting enough effort into one area and needs a goal to focus his work. Sometimes this regular forum for meeting to assess goals and progress is the opening the client needs to disclose additional issues or difficulties to the therapist.

Reevaluation

If significant time has been spent in one placement (i.e., a year or more), or if the client is being considered for a change of placement, a comprehensive sex offense-specific evaluation should be done by an *outside* specialist. An outside opinion is needed because evaluations conducted by the same persons who provide treatment can be colored significantly by the day-to-day exposure to the client and, therefore, be less accurate (Northeastern Family Institute, 1994). Reevaluations will inform decision making regarding the appropriateness of the current placement and will help to determine what the next step in the continuum should be.

At the year point, the program may want to perform its own major reassessment as well. Such an assessment would be essentially a repeat of the more intense initial assessment process performed just after intake. The program's internal reassessment affords the opportunity to compare the client's current clinical presentation with the initial baseline to determine effectiveness of treatment to date, to guide treatment plan modifications, and to plan program improvements (cf. Marques et al., 1994; Marshall and Barbaree, 1988; Marshall and Barbaree, 1990; Steele, 1995a).

Final Assessment

The final assessment and data collection is done just prior to the client leaving the program for his next setting. If a reevaluation was recently performed, then this would form part of this assessment. The purposes of this assessment are as follows:

1. Summarize the work done by the client in the current setting
2. Provide detailed material to be transmitted to the next treatment provider (if there is to be one) to smooth transition
3. Offer suggestions and recommendations that might be helpful to future providers
4. Take final stock of how the program was able to meet the treatment needs of the youth and look for ways in which to improve the program in the future
5. Offer a prognosis and revised risk assessment that takes into account dynamic risk factors

CONNECTIONS AMONG AND WITHIN PROGRAMS

Assessment Links Providers on the Continuum

The person writing a final assessment and compiling a packet of information for the next provider should ask himself or herself: "If this client was coming to my program, what would I want to know?" Since many staff and clinicians tend to want to know as much as possible, such an approach will likely prompt us to be a bit liberal in our sharing of information. This is good. The well-being of the client and teamwork with other providers should be placed above the need to retain information.

One may also consider, as continua become more connected and defined, whether it makes sense to standardize the assessment process among various programs on the continuum. Certainly interprogram consistency will more accurately allow us to gauge client progress over time and across various providers. The better our efforts in accurately assessing and providing smooth passage through the continuum, the better able we will be to prepare the client for life after formal treatment.

Planning for All Areas of Treatment Within the Program

The assessment process helps to guide *all* areas of treatment within the program. The general goals listed in the treatment plan would be ideally broken down into specific goals relevant to one or more of the program components. Thus, the distribution of tasks across components is more clearly defined. The ongoing assessment process helps each of the components refine its part in the achievement of the client's major goals and helps to connect the components by codifying their many overlapping interests and common goals.

The treatment plans produced are master guides that not only tell staff what goals are being addressed and what methods will be used but also provide the criteria for determining progress. These plans must be flexible and open to modification as needed so that all parts of the program work to ensure that treatment is tailored to the needs of individual clients (cf. Dougher, 1995).

NOTES ON THE ASSESSMENT PROCESS

Performing Assessments

Since assessing sex offenders is such a detailed process and has been written about extensively elsewhere, the reader is referred to the many excellent resources in this area, such as the following: Abel and colleagues (1988); Association for the Treatment of Sexual Abusers (1997); Barbaree and Seto (1997); Becker and Hunter (1992); Doughter (1995); Green (1995b); Hunter and Figueredo (1999); Knight and Prentky (1993); McGrath (1993); McGovern (1991); Monto, Zgourides, and Keenan (1998); Murphy (1990); Perry and Orchard (1992); Quinsey and colleagues (1995); Ross and Loss (1991); Saunders and Awad (1988); Stickrod Gray and Wallace (1992); and Ward and colleagues (1997). More information on these resources can be found in the reference section.

These resources can help the clinician to determine what information is important to gather at initial assessment and reassessment, what areas to explore and pay attention to in determining treatment plans, and what all these data mean in terms of the client's functioning, pathology, and his amenability to treatment. Resources of the type mentioned previously can also provide help in negotiating the ethical issues that arise out of the involuntary nature of the treatment, or out of the criminal nature of some of the disclosures the client may make in assessment and treatment (Ward et al., 1997).

All clinicians in treatment should have a degree of training in formal assessment techniques, especially if the clinician is to administer assessment tools. Such training will be helpful in assisting the clinician in knowing how to interpret data and what those data mean in terms of treatment planning. This training will also help to make the clinician more sensitive to his or her personal opinions and biases, and it will educate the individual regarding what predictions should or should not be made based upon the data present (McGovern, 1991).

Assessment As a Clinical Intervention

Many clinicians will agree that the assessment process (and ongoing reassessment) is a clinical intervention in itself, especially in the area of client consciousness raising (cf. Prochaska, 1984). The use of the assessment time to provide a space for further disclosure and for conducting psychoeducational work have already been discussed, but the possibilities do not stop there. The interviews in the assessment process cause questions to be asked that would not normally be asked and draw attention to behaviors that would perhaps not yield clinically relevant material otherwise. If these behaviors were not looked for, were not interpreted as indicators of other more covert processes, and were not reflected back to the client, they would likely not be available for use as part of clinical intervention. Assessment is also a means of confronting the client in tangible ways with the reality of his continuing use of sex-offending dynamics (even if manifested in nonsexual behavioral patterns), and it directs him to other components of the program where he can constructively work on these dynamics.

The assessment process, in addition to yielding information relevant to treatment, helps to support the group goals of promoting reality and responsibility and serves as another forum in which to discuss and explore the offending issue.

Behavior and Clinical Performance

In the process of ongoing assessment, the clinician will want to remain attentive to two major factors of this assessment: clinical performance and observable behavior. The client's clinical performance will be measured by his attainment of goals, cooperation in therapy, change in problematic thought patterns and values, skill level augmentation, and increased responsibility for remaining offense free. However, observable behavior is also a crucial assessment indicator and may be monitored *within* therapy sessions and *outside* formal sessions. All staff will want to be aware of which behaviors are indicators of progress and which point to potential problems. For a list of behavioral changes that denote client progress, please refer to *Sexual Abuse in America*, by Freeman-Longo and Blanchard (1998).

Outside formal therapy sessions, it is important to rely not on a single person's observations but to enlist a "supervision network" to gain information (Cumming and Buell, 1997). The members of such a team would include, first of all, other staff in your program (from janitors to secretaries to teachers to child care workers to administrators) and others who have contact with the client (parents, friends, siblings, teachers, employer, etc).

It is amazing how often clinical staff will fail to gain information on clients from other staff in their program or from others in the community. This author recalls several times (when going to a program to perform an outside evaluation) that line staff were astonished when asked for their opinions, impressions, and observations. One child care worker even remarked that none of the clinicians ever asked him for such input. He then proceeded to tell me of a client's behaviors that he observed on recent recreations, which he thought were relevant but did not bring up because he was not sure if they were. Indeed they were quite relevant, and this information exposed something important of which the clinical staff were unaware.

Assessing sex offenders is like putting together a puzzle (Cumming and Buell, 1997). The difference with this puzzle is that *no* one person has all the pieces (even if he or she believes so). To gain a complete picture you must gather all the information you can. Isolated behavioral observations are often dismissed by the observer and not communicated because, without corroborating data or a broader context, they seem to mean nothing. Frequently, when all these scattered pieces of information are collected, a picture begins to take shape; all the little behaviors that drew attention but were not brought up to the team officially begin to mean something when placed together. Staff should be taught to trust their gut feelings and to communicate any behavior that makes them look twice—even if they are not sure if it means anything. Clinicians must also ask for such information through informal conversations and staff meetings. Remember that there are many reasons why a person may feel reluctant to initiate a conversation about something he or she has observed. As with parents and clients, sometimes staff need to be asked.

Outside sessions, information from staff, parents, and teachers can be very helpful. One young man seemed to the clinicians to be a model client. He was respectful, polite, always had his group homework done in detail, and consistently participated in therapy. Informally, a clinician remarked to a teacher about how polite the young man was. The teacher proceeded to inform the clinician how disruptive and disrespectful he was in class, how he neglected his assignments, and how he was cruel to less powerful clients. Such observations were also made by staff regarding weekend recreations. This young man was trying to present the appearances of progressing in treatment to the clinician (who wrote the progress reports), but the reality of his continued problems were showing themselves elsewhere. The clinician saw the client's "other side" when he questioned him on his classroom and recreational behavior, and the young man (angered and frustrated because he would now have to address the issues he was avoiding) displayed the disrespect and aggressiveness that the teacher had described. A supervision network can make an endless array of behavioral observations that will yield information relevant to client treatment needs and will show how well the client is integrating treatment and learning new patterns of thought and behavior.

Within formal sessions, clinicians should be observant of the body language and the tone and manner in which the client speaks. One should also note when the client is acting in an abusive or aggressive manner and also when he is demonstrating a greater ability to negotiate interpersonal situations. Often one will note the subtle operation of maladaptive patterns, and these observations may be reflected back to the client for his benefit. On the other hand, one may observe that a client is putting in an especially good effort or is using new skills appropriately. These observations should also be shared with the client. Attend to what he does at least as much as to what he says in therapy.

Behavioral observations give as much assessment information as more goal-based indicators of progress in treatment. One should pay special attention to the behavior of the client when he is not "in the spotlight." Often we find important information can be gleaned by observing reactions of passive clients to other clients who are talking. Their expressions may reveal when they are relating to what another is saying and may indicate where they might be invited to share with the group. It is a good idea in group sessions to have the group leaders get into the habit of dividing their attention as a team, with one focusing attention on a client "in the spotlight" and the other watching the reactions and behaviors of the other clients.

A story that may illustrate the way in which observable behavior in and out of the therapy sessions can be used for ongoing assessment comes from the author's experience as a clinician in a residential treatment program. A young man in the program, let us call him Kevin, had perpetrated some especially horrific sexual offenses. His therapy, while seeming to go well, was failing to progress as the treatment team would have liked (with respect to goal attainment). We wondered what we were missing. He was a great actor in therapy and had been known to produce "crocodile tears" on occasion, though it was difficult to tell when he was being genuine or when he was displaying bogus emotions for dramatic effect.

At this time, he had been engaged in doing some empathy work in SO group and was able to produce heartfelt and tearful accounts of how he had hurt the children he had abused. His behavioral displays in group seemed to indicate that he was serious, and that he was making progress in this area. He claimed to be filled with remorse and empathy for the children. Certainly he believed he understood how bad they felt, and he stated that he could never abuse again.

One afternoon a few weeks later, another resident at the program returned after having dental surgery. He was still groggy from anesthetic and clearly in some degree of pain and discomfort. I stood out of sight to observe the reactions of the adolescents in the room. One by one the residents who saw him visibly winced at the sight of his swollen face and offered him a seat, a glass of water, or simply a word of sympathy. Kevin, glancing up from a newspaper he was reading, looked at this boy, said "Hi," smiled, and looked back at the paper. I was immediately struck by the expression on his face—not even a pretended empathic response.

A few months later, Kevin was discovered to have abused another youth in the program. In a discussion before he was removed from the program, he related to the author that he really never did feel anything for the kids he had abused. In fact, he not only felt nothing for the young man he had just recently abused but had been planning and offending for weeks while pretending to make great strides in modifying his deviant patterns.

After the abuse was disclosed to the entire program, staff and residents revealed one by one little pieces of information that they had not shared. The typical lead-in was, "I didn't think it was that important at the time but . . ." In fact, each piece of information in and of itself was not much to go on; however, when placed together they clearly pointed to a young man losing control and escalating in his maladaptive patterns. This information would have helped the team to fill in the gaps in their knowledge and would have confirmed that this young man was in need of a program with a higher level of supervision and security.

Another example comes from Mullen (1998), who relates an experience of entering a PO's office to conduct a sex offense-specific group. He was surprised to see one of the pedophile offenders in the waiting room talking to a young child. After he had brought this to the attention of persons in the office, the two were immediately separated. The man stated that he liked to talk to children because they were accepting, understanding, and nonjudgmental. It certainly says a lot about how poorly this client is managing his thoughts and behavior when, as a convicted and paroled pedophilic sex offender who is supposed to be staying away from children, he cannot refrain from doing so *at the parole office!* Also, his statement about why he likes to talk to children reveals his continued use of children in roles that more properly should be filled by peer supports. Such behavioral observations, and the discussions that follow them, can be very helpful in gaining information about where the client *really* is in his treatment, as well as providing further avenues to explore in therapy.

PART IV:
PRETREATMENT
AND AFTERCARE

Chapter 13

Pretreatment

THE DEFENSE KNOWN AS "DENIAL"

In recent years, much has been written about treatment approaches for sex offenders yet unable to enter into therapy due to a high level of "denial" or "resistance to treatment" (e.g., Blanchard, 1997; Cotter, 1996; Kennedy and Grubin, 1992; Maletzky, 1996; Marshall, 1994; Mayer, 1995; Northey, 1997; Sefarbi, 1990; Stevenson, Castillo, and Sefarbi, 1989; Winn, 1996). Although most offenders are in some degree of denial regarding their sexually abusive behaviors (Rogers and Dickey, 1991; ATSA, 1997; Happel and Auffrey, 1995; etc.), for some, the level of denial is so extreme that sex offense-specific treatment cannot be done effectively.

Three principal reasons that conventional sex offense-specific treatment is not considered feasible for this group are as follows: (1) a high level of denial is fundamentally incompatible with the basic prerequisites of a therapeutic relationship, (2) denial rejects the basic premise of therapy, i.e., the person is coming to the therapist seeking help, and (3) denial creates hostility and obstacles to the therapy process. Furthermore, denial does not allow for the emergence of information that is essential for the successful therapy of sexual offenders (O'Donohue and Letourneau, 1993). It also must not be forgotten that clinicians often do not like to work with this group of individuals because they are difficult to treat, their presentation is inconsistent with what we have been trained to work with, or they often simply do not like clinicians (Murphy, 1996). These factors taken together can influence a clinician's decision that a resistant or denying client cannot be treated at all.

Some clinicians, frustrated at how to manage cases that they could not "treat" with the methods with which they were accustomed, refuse to admit clients in denial to treatment (Murphy, 1996). This practice, still employed in many programs, has come under fire from clinical as well as correctional and social service groups, for many believe that allowing a high level of denial to prevent a person from entering treatment (or, as some would say, "getting them off the hook" of going through the pain and embarrassment of therapy efforts) was not productive and did not serve the best interests of the client or the community at large. Although it is important to continue to refuse to admit highly uncooperative and/or denying clients to a group or program *that is designed* to work with clients ready to do treatment, the wholesale elimination of this group from all treatment (or pretreatment) efforts seems to be an excessive measure.

The Search for an Intervention

Since refusing all manner of treatment is seen as an inappropriate option, many clinicians have accepted the challenge of working with this group and have experimented with various approaches, including group exclusion, coercion and bullying, special "deniers groups," or integration of these clients into a well-functioning group in the hopes of achieving success (i.e., to "break" them). Unfortunately, some of these efforts have been less than successful and have resulted in denying and difficult clients "digging in their heels" in defiance and influencing others to do the same.

In the past several years, we have become more sophisticated in understanding the dynamics and rationale of the defense we call denial; we began to understand denial in its function as a means of protection, as opposed to viewing it as simply a defiant or antisocial behavior. Furthermore, Blanchard (1997) and others were able to conceptualize resistance as potentially being as much the responsibility of the therapist as it was of the client, a realization that broadened our understanding of the role of the therapist in the denial process. We were then able to see that fighting denial and resistance might be counterproductive, and, in fact, that some denial-breaking strategies can actually increase the need for the psychological protection that caused the response of denial to be manifested initially. We needed to develop even more innovative approaches to working with this population.

Types of Denial

Denial is not only a failure to admit to the commission of the recorded offenses; denial, broadly understood, represents a continuum of minimization concerning the offense, its precursors, and its consequences. At one extreme lies minor minimization and failure to accept full responsibility for some aspect of the offending behavior, and at the other, what is sometimes called "total" or "absolute" denial, with the client staunchly denying that the offense occurred at all. Happel and Auffrey (1995) list twelve types of denial:

1. Denial of the crime itself
2. Denial of responsibility for the crime
3. Denial of intent and premeditation
4. Denial of deviant arousal and fantasies
5. Denial of the frequency of the deviant acts
6. Denial of the intrusiveness of the offense behavior
7. Denial of injury to victims
8. Denial of sexual gratification from the offense
9. Denial of various types of grooming behavior
10. Denial of risk management activities
11. Denial of the difficulty of change and the need for help
12. Denial of relapse potential and possible recidivism

One can expect that as many as 98 percent of offenders will initially present with *some form* of denial and/or minimization (Schlank and Shaw, 1997), and most of these will carry much of their minimization into treatment, where it will be addressed. The operative questions are, "At what level of denial or minimization is standard treatment considered not feasible?" and "What level of denial indicates the need for pretreatment?"

Levels of Denial

Brake and Shannon (1997) have proposed a four-level scale for defining the severity of denial: *Level 1* represents a weak avoidance of responsibility. At this level, the client admits that the offense occurred yet does not accept full responsibility for many of the areas listed in the previous twelve points. Clients at this level often are not considered "deniers." *Level 2* represents a moderate avoidance of responsibility. At this level, offenders admit to some of the behaviors involved in the abuse, but they justify its occurrence and minimize its significance. They may or may not be considered "deniers," depending on the level of avoidance. *Level 3* represents strong avoidance of responsibility. Offenders at this level do not admit that the offense occurred but may admit to "less harmful" behaviors (e.g., "I hit her. I didn't rape her"). *Level 4* represents severe avoidance of responsibility. Offenders at this level deny committing the offense and may even deny responsibility for remotely similar behaviors.

In their complete scheme (which is well worth reviewing), Brake and Shannon (1997) twelve types of denial that are grouped under these levels. The dividing line for those who are not ready to enter standard treatment would likely be drawn between levels 2 and 3. This means that clients in levels 3 and 4 denial would be those most needing a pretreatment intervention.

WHAT IS PRETREATMENT?

A pretreatment intervention addresses the clients who, due to their level of denial and/or resistance, cannot yet productively participate in standard SO treatment. Such interventions may be run in preplacement detention or shelter settings or in functioning treatment programs. These preparatory interventions are designed to be only a time-limited approach that enables the client to enter into formal sex offense-specific therapy—they do not take the place of formal therapy.

> [I]t would be misleading to assume that offenders who participate in deniers groups which offer only didactic training have completed offense-specific treatment. . . . Graduation from pretreatment means that a client is ready to begin the hard work of therapy, not that he has finished it. (Brake, 1996, p. 3)

Many successful psychoeducational group models have been designed to prepare and pretreat clients not yet ready for treatment (cf. O'Donohue and Letourneau, 1993; Schlank and Shaw, 1996; Lundrigan and Breault, 1999), one of which is reviewed in more depth later in the chapter. In addition to group interventions, it is possible to conduct pretreatment on an individual basis. Brake and Shannon's (1997) pretreatment program is delivered to clients individually to maximize the tailoring of the intervention to the client. They use a six-stage process—containment, symptom relief, reframe denial, reframe accountability, enhance empathy, successive approximations of confrontation—to help the client move to a lower level of denial. Please refer to Brake and Shannon (1997) for more detailed information on this program.

Effective pretreatment interventions will recognize that denial is a defense mechanism and that it serves a purpose for the client. The pretreatment efforts "open the door" to the offending issue by helping the client to overcome the barriers that have blocked his ability to accept and admit the reality of his thoughts and behaviors (Jenkins, 1990). Total acceptance of responsibility is more than can be expected from pretreatment and will likely only come (if it ever does) after some significant time in therapy.

Pretreatment interventions may make use of some of the successful techniques from the substance abuse field, such as "motivational interviewing" (Miller and Rollnick, 1991), recognizing that the manifestation of denial is also a prominent treatment obstacle with substance abusers. They may also use techniques to "invite responsibility" (Jenkins, 1990) and thus attempt to defuse denial. The clinician will want to have studied some of the more recent articles concerning denial processes in sex offenders (e.g., Rogers and Dickey, 1991; Schlank and Shaw, 1997; Marshall, 1994) and articles that give helpful information regarding treatment approaches with this group (e.g., Happel and Auffrey, 1995; Schlank and Shaw, 1996; Stevenson, Castillo, and Sefarbi, 1989; Winn, 1996).

In addition to such study, the clinician undertaking this work must be well versed in the reasons why sex offenders deny or minimize their offenses and resist treatment. This information is best gained by talking to the clients themselves, learning what their fears are and why they are unable to take responsibility. Speaking to clients who have begun to participate in treatment will help one to gain valuable insight into why some clients resist treatment and deceive others (including themselves) about their thoughts and behaviors. It is only through understanding these reasons and attempting to empathize with the client that the clinician can join with him and lead him out of the dark cave of deception and secrecy into which he has retreated for protection and comfort.

In the final analysis, a successful pretreatment intervention will help the client to admit to the occurrence of *at least* one of his offenses, and hopefully some of the related deviancy. In addition, it will help to explain the process of the ensuing therapy, calming fears about what will be required in treatment. Finally, pretreatment will begin some of the educational work and conceptual model introduction and will raise issues for reflection that the client may not have considered up to that time, but which he will have to look at in great depth in subsequent treatment. The therapists who will then treat the youth will have a foothold from which to draw the client into accepting an increased amount of responsibility, a good starting place for treatment.

WHEN AND WHERE
IS PRETREATMENT INDICATED?

Clients in Need of Pretreatment

Clients who are in complete, total, or absolute denial or who are so hostile to the treatment process that they will do virtually anything to keep from being treated are a challenging population, to say the least. Pretreatment interventions are best suited to these clients as well as all those with level 3 or 4 denial. Such clients try to avoid the pain, embarrassment, consequences, reprisals, rejection, punishment, shame, and intrapsychic conflicts connected with their offending by (1) working to convince themselves and others that it did not happen (or that if it did, then it was not really sex offending but something else, something quite normal and natural—so what is the problem?), or (2) engaging in behaviors designed to get the staff and clinicians simply to throw up their hands and give up (in which case, they are "off the hook"). Most engage in *both* of these strategies, much to the frustration of those contracted to provide them with treatment.

It is important to note that some of these clients will *never* respond to any interventions. Although some advocate continuing to try indefinitely, others believe that if a youth has not responded after six months of pretreatment, then he should be considered not amenable to treatment (Brake and Shannon, 1997). Some adolescents, due to psychopathy or severely entrenched antisocial personality traits, will not make progress in accepting increased responsibility. In the author's experience in evaluation and in conducting pretreatment groups, such individuals are the exception—but they do exist. Since working with a psychopathic offender will likely yield little result and, in fact, since empirical evidence shows that treatment may increase a psychopath's risk for reoffense (cf. Rice, 1997; Seto and Barbaree, 1999), these offenders should perhaps not be treated.

This being said, clinicians must not be *too willing* to give up and simply place persons into this category, for they might be facing a particularly entrenched "denier" whom they have failed to reach. Schlank and Shaw (1997) relate evidence suggesting that those who complete a treatment program yet remain in denial are *more* successful than those who admit but do not complete treatment. A potentially treatable offender whom clinicians dismiss as untreatable and do not expose to treatment interventions may go on to damage the lives of many others. Clinicians owe it to those potential victims not to give up too soon.

Determining What Your Program Is Designed to Handle

Program administrators must consider carefully whether they will be able to deal with clients who are in total denial and/or very resistant or hostile to treatment. Most treatment providers will likely determine that the negative effects on the treatment culture of the program will preclude the acceptance of such clients, whereas other providers may decide that they can offer this service. The following are some considerations:

1. *Temporal:* If we only have a limited amount of time to work with the youth in our care, will we be able to devote the few months it may take to do pretreatment work?
2. *Clinical:* How will the introduction of clients in heavy denial and resistance affect the operation of the SO treatment? Furthermore, how will they impact the other clients in treatment? What techniques will need to be employed?
3. *Programmatic:* Does this mode of treatment fit with the program treatment scheme?
4. *Practical:* Who will do it? Who will want to or be able to do it?

If a program's funding source does not grant right of refusal, then providers may have little option but to accept whomever is sent. However, if able to select clients, then they should establish clear guidelines about what conditions will make a denying client acceptable for treatment at that program.

Intensive residential treatment programs and full-range outpatient groups have a great deal to work on clinically and may be unable to devote time to the pretreatment effort. In addition, the presence of these youth in the treatment program can have very negative effects on the other clients and will certainly hold back the progress of the group as a whole. Holding facilities conducting pretreatment to prepare clients for a future treatment setting and secure treatment centers, where many of the more difficult offenders will likely begin their treatment, seem to be the optimal locations for such interventions.

If a youth at this level of denial and resistance is placed in the community, outpatient centers need to focus on organizing local pretreatment groups. The reality is that many of these adolescents may be very reluctant to advance in treatment and take responsibility (since being placed in the community is often an indicator for the youth and family that he "is not so bad off"). However, one should still require an adequate clinical presentation before accepting such a youth for community treatment and recommend or provide pretreatment to those clients who cannot be accepted into the regular SO treatment program. Perhaps an outpatient provider can team up with a local detention center, shelter, or other program that runs a pretreatment group and obtain services for the client there. Perhaps the youth can be placed in a more restrictive setting where pretreatment is conducted. This also lets him know that his offending is serious business. Some localities would even make release to the community contingent upon admitting to the offense. Although this is often an effective strategy, it must be used with caution to avoid false confessions to gain release.

Pretreatment Is a Time-Limited Intervention

Sometimes pretreatment can be done in evaluation and individual therapy sessions; other times it will need a coordinated group intervention. If the youth is not making progress toward increased responsibility during an intensive evaluation process (as many are able to do), then he should be placed in a pretreatment group. Whatever the available and appropriate way to pretreat a given youth, it must be remembered that such efforts are time limited. Lundrigan and Breault (1999) found in their pretreatment group that clients made their most significant progress in the first month, leveling off by the third month with no further significant progress. It was concluded that the design of the group (as a psychoeducational pretreatment effort) and the continual introduction of clients in denial into the group kept the group at a superficial level.

Those clients who were at this point in pretreatment, who were far enough past their difficulties that they were appropriate for intensive treatment, were sent to the clients' programs (some to a lower level of security than was originally thought necessary). Those who were unable to enter treatment were generally sent to secure treatment centers where the work of pretreatment could be continued (hopefully being completed in a shorter time due to the first pretreatment effort).

A MODEL INTERVENTION FOR PRETREATMENT

The pretreatment intervention presented here is from Lundrigan and Breault (1999), who explain a collaborative effort between a secure detention center and an outpatient clinic that made use of both individual and group pretreatment interventions. The sessions were facilitated by a male-female team and conducted in the detention center. The clients participating in this intervention were all scheduled to be placed in long-term secure or residential treatment, and all were in a significant degree of denial or were resistant to the idea of future sex offense-specific treatment. The intervention was designed to do the following:

1. Help those youth in high levels of denial to begin to accept some responsibility for their offenses and treatment
2. Help those clients who had begun admitting to a small portion of their offending to take increased responsibility and develop habits needed to productively engage in treatment
3. Give both of these groups a headstart on their future treatment in order to make the best possible use of their preplacement detention

The hope was that this effort, in addition to moving clients to a position amenable to treatment, would buy some time for the future provider by laying foundational work to build on. Services were designed for a period of one to three months and were delivered in two distinct phases of intervention.

Phase 1: The Interviews

Once referred to the group, each youth was scheduled for an initial interview session. This initial interview and often a few other private interviews constituted the first phase of the intervention. These intensive sessions were conducted by both group leaders and consisted of information gathering, extensive use of techniques designed to reduce denial, and efforts to reduce anxiety surrounding entering the group (see Happel and Auffrey, 1995, for a description of a similar intervention, and Brake and Shannon, 1997, for specific tactics to use in such sessions). After one or two such sessions, the youth knew the expectations for group, had often begun to take at least some degree of responsibility for his offenses, and was less resistant to the idea of participating in the group. A client would only be excluded from entering the pretreatment group after the first interview due to clinical determination that he was not ready to enter the group process and required further preparation. Remaining in complete denial was not a reason to be excluded from group, yet those with high levels of denial could continue to attend individual sessions concurrent with group. Clients who refused to enter the group were seen to need more preparation. In fact, only one youth in six months vehemently refused to cooperate in this group at first, yet he was able to enter group after a month of individual meetings.

Phase 2: The Pretreatment Group

The second phase of the intervention was participation in the sex offense-specific pretreatment group. This group was facilitated by the same two clinicians mentioned previously, and consisted of a fourteen-module psychoeducational curriculum designed to reduce denial surrounding the offending behavior *and* to prepare subjects to enter long-term sex offense-specific treatment. The group met once per week for ninety minutes. The curriculum of the group was delivered on a rotating basis, with the group remaining open-ended. Each member was required to disclose his offenses in his first group and each time a new member was added to group. Clients in complete denial were required to disclose the offense of record as reported by their victims. It is important to note that denial was not the only focus of this intervention, and that efforts throughout were geared toward preparing the clients for the real work of sex offense-specific therapy.

At each group session, a psychoeducational topic related to sex offending and/or sex offense-specific treatment was presented and discussed. Presentations were didactic and made use of movie segments, videotapes, and the testimony of offenders who had moved past their denial and were productively engaged in treatment. The outline of the

group curriculum is provided in Table 13.1. One may note the similarities between this curriculum and the one presented in Chapter 7
for the sex offense-specific group. Although several topics are shared
(to provide an overlap between the pretreatment and formal treatment
groups), there are a couple important differences: (1) the focus of the
pretreatment group is on preparation for future treatment and on
teaching habits that would increase the clients' success in that treatment, and (2) it is almost exclusively educational and not designed to
engage in much of the more in-depth clinical processing and exploration that is required in treatment.

At the close of each session, clients were assigned homework to be
completed for the following week. These assignments reinforced
what had been discussed and/or prepared subjects for upcoming sessions, while getting the client accustomed to the concept of doing
group homework. Subjects who refused to enter group sat in the hall
during group time and worked on written work that would be reviewed in the next "preparation" meeting. In addition, they would be
given the same homework that the group received, if this was feasible.

Clients who were either more advanced than others (most often
due to prior sex offense-specific treatment or less significant pathology) or lagged behind (most often due to cognitive limitations or discomfort in speaking in a group setting) attended collateral individual
sessions provided by one of the group leaders. In addition, clients
who were delayed in their transfer and perhaps were entering their
second cycle of group received a packet of more advanced assignments, coupled with individual work, along with an expectation that
they go deeper into the issues this time and assume more of a positive
leadership role in group.

The performance, presentation, and general progress of each client
was summarized by the group leaders with a customized assessment
tool (see Appendix E) at the initial encounter and at one month intervals thereafter. These assessment tools were placed in the clients' personal files and were forwarded to their treatment programs upon their
discharge from group.

This model represents one example of a pretreatment intervention
that can be included in a continuum of care both in detention or shelter
settings and also some treatment programs. The more continuity between providers on the continuum (in terms of models used and
method of treatment delivery), the more effective a generic pretreatment intervention will be in providing clients with adequate preparation for their next stop on the continuum, wherever that may be.

TABLE 13.1. Sample Curriculum for a Pretreatment Group

SESSION/TOPIC	HOMEWORK
1. Group rules/expectations, **DISCLOSURES, EP: GOALS OF SO TREATMENT**	Review Questions
2. Review goals and nature of treatment, Explain how SO groups work, **EP: NORMAL SEXUAL BEHAVIOR**	What Is Normal Sexual Behavior?
3. Normal sex behavior, Definitions from SO groups, Consent versus coercion, **EP: WHAT IS OFFENDING BEHAVIOR?**	Legal and Illegal Behavior
4. Types of offending behavior and their consequences, Definition of what is legal and illegal behavior, **V: VIDEO CLIPS (VARIOUS MOVIES)**	Audio Assignment #1
5. Same as 4, with examples from video, range of possible behaviors, reading nonverbal cues, **EP: APPROPRIATE SEXUAL RELATIONSHIPS**	Sexual Relationships Assignment
6. Client ideas of sexual relationships, M/F roles, **V: *WHEN HE ISN'T A STRANGER* (SELECTED SCENES)**	Audio Assignment #2
7. Same as 6, with video examples, Not only "weird" people offend, **EP: MYTHS OF SO BEHAVIOR**	Myths of SO Behavior
8. Exploring/correcting faulty assumptions, Intro to the cognitive work of treatment, **EP: MYTHS ABOUT VICTIMS**	Myths About Victims
9. Victims of sexual assault and how they are affected, **V: *THE ACCUSED* (SELECTED SCENES)**	Audio Assignment #3
10. Same as 9, with examples from the video, **EP: INTRODUCTION TO EMPATHY**	Empathy Assignment
11. Assessing their level of empathy, Why is empathy important? **EP: THE TRAUMA OUTCOME PROCESS**	TOP Assignment
12. Exploring how they cope/express past trauma and feelings. Helping them to understand the nonsexual aspects of offending. How treatment focuses a lot on nonsexual things, **V: *SCARED SILENT* (DOCUMENTARY)**	Read SA Cycle Handout
13. Intro to concept of patterns and cycles, **EP: THE SEXUAL ASSAULT CYCLE**	SA Cycle Worksheet
14. Beginning to see how such a cycle/pattern can apply to them, **EP: FUTURE TREATMENT**	Review Assignment

Key to Abbreviations:
EP = educational presentation, V = video presentation/discussion, Audio Assignment = taped testimonials from offending youth engaged in treatment.

Note: For additional information on the assignments, tapes, and videos used, please contact the author (see Appendix A).

Chapter 14

Aftercare Component Development and Implementation

GOOD AFTERCARE PLANNING IS VITAL

What Is Aftercare?

Most every secure treatment, hospital, and residential program is careful to provide aftercare for clients who have been released to the community. In the case of group care programs, this aftercare generally consists of the client being referred to an outpatient therapy group for continued sex offense-specific work. Greer (1991) defines aftercare as "that portion of comprehensive adolescent sexual perpetrator treatment intervention that takes place in the community after the offender is released from an institutional treatment program" (p. 377). Furthermore, he states that the essential functions of such aftercare services are to monitor the offender and to "facilitate the transfer of the therapeutic process to the community" (p. 377).

Some outpatient providers may take exception to this definition, believing that they, too, provide aftercare (for their clients who were never placed in group care) in the form of an aftercare group and maintenance contacts. As stated earlier, it is best if a specialized outpatient aftercare group is used with adolescents who have completed an extensive stay in group care *or* full-range outpatient treatment. This is to be preferred to simply placing these clients in groups with adolescents in the beginning or middle stages of treatment. Outpatient providers should consider clients who have transitioned from their full-range program to the aftercare group as in "aftercare" as much as those who were previously in a group care setting.

In a somewhat different vein, others question whether aftercare exists at all in the continuum of care. After all, are we not providing "care" at all levels in the continuum? How can we say that one type of care is *after*care?* Perhaps this term is best understood relative to each treatment environment (i.e., *after*care for one program may be *present* care for another for the same series of interventions).

Although these questions raise valid concerns, the common use of the term seems to align with Greer's definition, and the remainder of this chapter was written from that perspective. The term as it is currently used seems to imply that the treatment (care) takes place in the institutional (i.e., group care) setting, and that future outpatient treatment is a follow-up to this treatment. This chapter considers outpatient programs and their possibilities for setting up an aftercare component; however, the increased complexity and necessity of residential aftercare demand it receives primary attention.

Outpatient providers may benefit from the following discussion in at least two ways: (1) As they will likely be considered aftercare providers by a variety of institutional programs, it is helpful for them to understand how the services that they will provide can be best delivered to adolescents leaving a group care setting. (2) The information presented can easily be adapted by outpatient providers as they work to develop aftercare for their full-range, comprehensive treatment programs.

Three Aspects of an Aftercare Component

Three aspects of aftercare should be kept in mind. First, aftercare has a supervisory function. An offender in the community must have some level of supervision if he is to negotiate the return to a setting filled with potential pitfalls and successfully apply his relapse prevention plan. Relapse prevention efforts (such as aftercare services) have at least three supervisory functions:

1. Fostering the development of a collaborative relationship between the mental health professionals treating the client, probation/state agency supervisors, and the family members who witness the client's day-to-day behaviors
2. Increasing the efficiency of supervision by creating an informed network of collateral contacts who monitor the client

---

*Special thanks to William (Bill) Ballantyne of West Central Services, Claremont, New Hampshire, for raising these questions.

3. Enhancing the efficacy of supervision by specifying distinct precursors that can be monitored by professional and collateral contacts (Stickrod Gray and Pithers, 1993)

Second, aftercare has a treatment function. Rather than viewing group care treatment as concluding at the end of the institutional stay, treatment should be seen as continuing in the real world of the community (cf. Perry and Paquin, 1987). Steele (1995a) reminds us that "conducting treatment only in a controlled institution is like teaching someone to swim in a bathtub" (p. 19-2). Continued treatment for the sex-offending issue and other collateral issues will need to be taken up in the community, especially given the trend in some areas toward shortening the stays of adolescents in residential programs. Some things simply cannot be dealt with until the client is in the community. Follow-up therapy should be in place as long as needed for new skills and behaviors to be used successfully in the noninstitutional environment (ATSA, 1997). For outpatient clients, the move to the aftercare group should be viewed as a transition to a different treatment context in which treatment continues (albeit with some changes in foci).

Finally, it is important to distinguish between ensuring that the client has adequate aftercare and client participation in an aftercare component. For a group care setting, the former case implies that the program provider has discharged the resident to a community treatment provider, whereas the latter implies that the group care program is still involved in the aftercare treatment of the youth. For outpatient settings, the difference is between setting in place a support system after full-range treatment has ended (in the former case) and operating an aftercare group and related services (in the later case). For both types of settings, the more intensive nature of a program aftercare component, and the greater support it provides, makes the use of such a component an important consideration.

Why Should Group Care Programs Provide Aftercare?

Aftercare is perhaps the most crucial part of the treatment of sex offenders (Steele, 1995a). Staff and clinicians should not begin preparing aftercare services only when the youth is nearing release from the current program. Planning for aftercare must begin in the early stages of treatment and be part of the work thereafter (cf. Freeman, 1979).

It is easy to recall cases of clients who appeared fine upon release from a secure or residential program but soon experienced significant regressions and even reoffended. If the lessons that were taught and the gains that were made in the group care program are to transfer to the community, aftercare and/or follow-up in the community is essential (Steele, 1995a). Greer (1991) proposes three primary reasons that aftercare is a significant conjunct to offense-specific treatment. These reasons are summarized in Table 14.1.

Programs with aftercare components have been lauded as providing an important adjunct to treatment, and also for providing a service that can substantially reduce the risk of reoffense (Steele, 1995a; Cellini, 1995; Lundrigan, 1997; Beck, 1989). In addition to the important clinical benefits, such a component makes it possible to collect important data necessary for effective program evaluation (cf. Green, 1995d).

TABLE 14.1. Three Reasons for Aftercare

1. An aftercare program assists the offender with acknowledging that he still continues to be at risk of offending.
   - The staff help him to realize that his behavior problem is still part of him and has not "magically vanished."
   - They encourage the youth to use the tools he has acquired to prevent reoffense.
   - They strengthen continuous behavior management and provide a therapeutic link.
   - Transition to the community is difficult after experiencing the structure and support of the residential program. Treatment for the offending issue is even more needed.

2. An aftercare program provides a method for monitoring the client's behavior after release/discharge/graduation.
   - Aftercare team can monitor client behaviors and thinking patterns that could prove dangerous and make appropriate interventions.
     —Behaviors may indicate the need for a return to a higher level of structure.
   - Client can be monitored for "high-risk" behaviors.
     —Team members need to know what is "high risk" for *this* youth.
   - Aftercare supervisor will need to maintain close contact with the offender, family, school, probation officer, clinicians, and the client's previous treatment provider.

3. An aftercare program helps the offender establish a community-based "locus pairing."
   - Aftercare helps to establish an association of the therapeutic messages received in prior treatment with the new "locus" of the community.
   - Change of setting may precipitate new denial and/or regressions that can be addressed.
   - Treatment helps client to recognize and interrupt signs of a potential reoffense.

Source: Adapted from Greer, 1991, pp. 377-378.

DEVELOPING AN AFTERCARE COMPONENT

Aftercare As a Component of the Group Care Program

An aftercare component is a functioning portion of the group care program that begins to work with the youth during his institutional stay and continues to work with the youth after he has moved to the community or outpatient level of care. These aftercare services are meant to supplement, not replace, the services of the outpatient provider. The new provider would ideally be seen as the head of the treatment team and would direct the total treatment picture.

The continuation of the institutional program in the treatment efforts with the youth after graduation means that the old and new clinical services overlap and coexist for a period of time to facilitate a smooth "passing of the torch," while still providing the support that is so critical in the early months after release. Such a continuation of the former program in aftercare efforts has been beneficial as attested to by Prendergast (1991): "For offenders who are released from an institutional setting, whether private clinic, hospital, or correctional facility, *aftercare by that facility* is essential" (p. 119). Given the potential benefits of the institutional program providing coordinated aftercare services with a community provider, one should give serious consideration to including such an aftercare component in the treatment regime.

In the case of out-of-state clients who are being treated at the program, it may not be feasible to continue providing aftercare services as with other clients. However, the ability to provide aftercare services is not eliminated by the lack of face-to-face meetings with the client. The previous program can be a part of the next treatment effort in many ways.

For example, a young man, whom we shall call Mark, graduated from his residential program and within hours was on a plane to live with a relative 1,500 miles away. Prior to his graduation, the next treatment provider had been identified, conversations had occurred between the old and new providers, and both providers had spoken with the family in the new state. Information packets were sent, the client had a couple phone conversations with his new therapist, and after he moved, he engaged in aftercare services with the old program via telephone for three months while he transitioned to the new program. During this time, both programs collaboratively worked with the client and family to provide an overlapping service that helped the client to make the necessary adjustments and to have a successful transition.

Elements of a Successful Component Design

Many tools and interventions can be employed when designing an aftercare follow-up component. The following tools, strategies, and interventions have been used by some of the successful programs currently in operation.

- Establishment of a network of aftercare service providers with whom to interface when setting up aftercare plans
- Obtaining consent forms from client and family in order to freely communicate with future service providers
- Having clients begin therapy with the next provider while still in the group care or intensive outpatient program
- Having clients attend outpatient aftercare groups prior to discharge from current program
- Having clients return to a residential program for a "transition to aftercare" group following discharge to help process successes and failures on the outside (This is helpful to both the discharged youth and those still in the program who also could attend the group in preparation for their transition to aftercare.)
- Time-limited, scheduled contact between the client and the old program
- Regular contact between the therapists (outpatient and group care) involved
- Ability to contact old program twenty-four hours a day, at least until trust is transferred and comfort level is established with new program
- Going on passes to the community prior to release from group care
- Processing in group and individual therapy the thoughts, feelings, behaviors, situations, urges, problems, struggles, joys, and old memories that surfaced during passes
- Client involvement in developing aftercare plans
- Use of special graduation rituals to mark transitions
- Processing the inevitable prerelease regressions
- Old program providing advocacy for client to ensure that appropriate aftercare services have been put into place and are operative
- Availability of contact with most recent therapist
- Clear establishment of boundaries and support of the new therapist by the old therapist

- Therapist willingness to talk to the client who failed in the community after release to aid in the learning process (for the client *and* the therapist)
- Using one or two joint sessions between client, old therapist, and new therapist (This can help the client to relinquish dependence on the old therapist, and it sanctions the transferral of the therapeutic alliance and loyalties to the new therapist.)
- Ongoing AA-style support groups run by the program that discharged clients can attend if needed
- Availability of "booster" sessions held with agreement of the treatment team
- Early education of client and family that treatment must continue after release from the group care setting or completion of the intensive outpatient program
- Family therapy and ongoing family involvement in treatment at the aftercare level
- Victim involvement in the planning for the offender's aftercare

AN AFTERCARE COMPONENT MODEL

Description of the Model Component

This model component was developed for use in a long-term residential program to smooth the resident's transition to the community. Recognizing that the first few months after return to the community are a particularly difficult time for the client, and since this may be a time when the client is at a higher risk to reoffend, this component was put in place to supplement existing aftercare services.

Through involvement with the component, the resident prepares for outpatient therapy, connects with community services, and begins to set up the support network that will help to sustain him during this difficult time. For three months after graduation, the client is required to make follow-up contact with the program, and program staff maintain at least monthly contact with the client's next service provider. The residential program provider remains a part of the treatment team and works with the outpatient provider to provide services to the client (which may include the client receiving some clinical services from the residential program). The outpatient provider is recognized as the primary provider throughout. Gradually, the residential program provider reduces the program's involvement and eventually becomes, at most, a support resource that the client can contact in times of crisis.

Some of the materials used in this model component are included in Appendix F and may be reproduced, modified, and used by the reader.

Goals of the Aftercare Component

This component was established to accomplish some specific goals:

1. Insure that the resident has *in place* a comprehensive aftercare plan prior to graduation
2. Provide maximum continuity of services with the next treatment provider through communication, information sharing, and mutual consultation
3. Provide a comfortable and safe way for the resident to transition to his next service provider by allowing him to build new relationships while gradually withdrawing from relationships at the program
4. Provide added support through the critical first three months of community placement
5. Help to fill the gaps that inevitably arise during such a transition
6. Collect statistical data as to the progress of clients after they leave the program for the purpose of improving our services
7. Interface with community service providers to establish a close network of providers along the continuum, and to receive feedback from them on how to better prepare clients for return to the community

The Three Steps of the Model Component

Services in this model aftercare component were delivered in three distinct steps of intervention. Each of these represented a one-step advance in the client's transition to the community from residential treatment.

1. *Step 1—Pregraduation Services.* Services include the following (time frame is from first aftercare planning meeting to graduation):

   • Program provider assists the resident and funding source in developing an aftercare plan that will best meet the resident's needs and the community's needs for safety.

- Releases are obtained so the program provider and the future service provider can communicate and share information.
- Verbal contact between the program provider and the future service provider occurs to establish a line of communication and to share preliminary information.
- Resident develops a written aftercare plan.
- Resident meets with next therapist at least once prior to graduation.
- Sex offense-specific treatment team prepares a detailed "final statement" on the resident that includes outlining the resident's course of treatment and a final written progress assessment.

2. *Step 2—Transition Services.* Services include the following (time frame is from graduation to three months in aftercare):

- Program provider sends materials to the next service provider.
- Client makes agreed-upon follow-up contacts with the old program.
- Program provider maintains at least monthly telephone contact with the new provider.
- Client follows relapse prevention and aftercare plans as contracted.
- Program provider helps the client to separate from relationships in the residential setting and to develop a strong relationship with the new provider.
- Program provider is available to provide assistance to the future service provider and client as requested and appropriate.
- Program provider informs the next provider of content and frequency of the client's contact with the old program and modifies that approach as the new provider feels is clinically indicated.

3. *Step 3—Ongoing Availability.* Services include the following (time frame is indefinite):

- The program provider remains available to the future service provider as needed for assistance and consultation.
- Any calls that the client makes to the old program provider are accepted and recorded in writing. Future providers may request to be informed of such contacts.

- Special care is taken to see that the client does not attempt to maintain a clinical relationship with the old program provider or to use the previous provider to interfere with current treatment.
- The program provider attempts to make six-, nine-, and twelve-month follow-up contacts with the client and future service provider (for data collection purposes), unless requested not to do so.

These three transition steps of an aftercare component are graphically displayed in Figure 14.1. This diagram visually depicts how the client and family are transitioned from one provider to the next in a way that provides the maximum support during the most crucial part of the transition (Step 2).

One may initially note the changing relationship of the client and family to the two providers over time, represented by the proximity of the client/family oval to the two programs. The client (and his family) moves from being integrally connected to Program 1, to a transition during which he separates from Program 1 yet has not yet established an integration with Program 2, to finally being integrally connected to Program 2.

A CASE EXAMPLE

To illustrate this component in action, let us consider the case of Rick, a young man in the final stage of residential sex offense-specific treatment. Rick entered the program from a secure treatment center where he had spent eighteen months in treatment. For the first four of those months, he had been in complete denial of his offenses. Through pretreatment work done at the center, he was able to admit to the staff and his parents that he had committed not only the offense for which he was charged but also some previously unknown offending behaviors. He did a considerable amount of work in that setting but had a great deal more work to do, especially in the areas of exploring the wider context of offending, improving social skills and coping strategies, and planning to reenter the community.

He worked hard at the residential program and truly showed some remarkable growth. He was approaching the end of his stay, and as a sixteen-year-old who had been in secure or residential settings since he was thirteen, he was a bit concerned for the future. On the other

FIGURE 14.1. Use of an Aftercare Component for Client and Family Transition

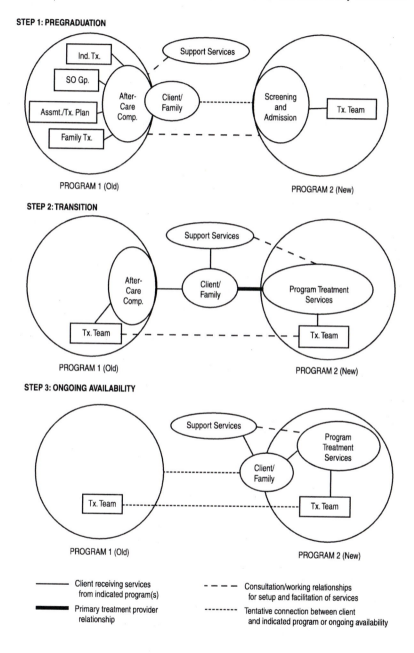

hand, however, he also had a degree of confidence; sure he would face difficulties, but he had just completed nearly three years of intensive treatment and was in great shape. He had earnestly participated in all forms of treatment, including individual, group, and family therapy, and had gone on a few weekend-long home passes that had left him and his mother very hopeful. He thought that he could negotiate the transition without too much difficulty.

He met his next therapist (Kerry), and the two hit it off well. Kerry knew his old therapist (Ben), and the two had worked together on other cases before. The familiarity between Kerry and Ben only added to his security; he was sure he could (in time) trust Kerry as he had trusted Ben. He also hoped that Ben would inform Kerry of some of the things that Ben and others had learned about how to approach and get through to him. The plan was for Rick to have individual and SO group therapy at the outpatient clinic, and to continue in multiple family therapy, parent education group, and an aftercare group periodically at the residential program.

Rick spent some time working with his mother, Ben, other staff, clients, and support people in writing up his aftercare plan. He decided that he wanted to make follow-up contact to the program by phone three times per week. Although Ben thought that this might be a bit much, he recognized Rick's level of anxiety and agreed, reminding Rick that they could alter that portion of the plan when Rick was ready. Rick had learned about the aftercare contacts in his orientation, and he knew that they were supposed to become spaced further apart as time went on. He was ready for this.

Following his graduation dinner and ceremony at the residential program, Rick went home with his mother. The next day he made his first follow-up contact by phone to say that all was well and to discuss some anxiousness concerning his therapy session in a few days with the new therapist. Ben helped to calm his anxieties and reminded him of how well he had gotten along with Kerry, and he assured Rick of Kerry's abilities as a therapist (after all, other kids coming back for the aftercare group at the program had said so). At Rick's request, Ben said hello to a few of the staff and residents at the program, and he passed on to Rick a message from one of the other kids in the group that they were all supporting him.

The first few weeks went well. School was set up, sessions with Kerry went fine, and Rick entered an outpatient sex offense-specific group at Kerry's clinic. He was a bit concerned that he was mixed in with clients who were just starting treatment and even felt that he was taking a step back. He spoke about this with Ben and Kerry, and both reassured him. Over the phone, Ben and Kerry discussed this concern and how to approach this topic when Rick raised it again. Family therapy was going well. In the MFT groups, Rick and his mother shared many of their struggles with the families who would soon be experiencing transition and reunification, and they received support and guidance from the group. Rick enjoyed the every-other-week visit to the program for MFT (as per his treatment plan) and would give positive examples to the adolescents who were soon to follow in his steps.

Soon, Rick asked about lowering his number of follow-up calls to twice per week. Ben thought that was fine and asked what days he would like to call. As time went on, Rick initiated more such changes (once increasing calls during a tough time), as he made expanded use of the support network that he had set in place. After two and a half months, he alternated between a call one week and a few minutes to check in on his biweekly family therapy night.

The transition did not go without its problems. One night, about a month after discharge, Rick and his mother came to family therapy as usual. They stated that they had been having some problems and had brought them to the group. What became evident is that many conflicts had been suppressed, and that they had built up to a major conflict. The two had a loud argument in group and Rick left the room (presumably to sit in the hall to calm down). After ten minutes or so, the other parents had helped the therapists to reason with Rick's mother, who had high expectations and had a difficult time coping when real life did not live up to those expectations. She wanted Rick taken out of her house that night and placed in foster care. One of the therapists left the room to check on Rick and found that he was not in sight. He had taken off into the streets.

Ben found Rick walking up the road about a half mile from the program. Rick got into Ben's car and talked about how things were a lot harder than he thought they were going to be. Ben reminded Rick that he had committed his most serious offense following an argument with his mother. Rick realized that this was a particularly dangerous time and that he should not have been walking around the streets in that condition. After an individual family session with Rick and his mom (after the group was over), the two were able to return home, having made plans to deal with this situation. The next morning Ben called Kerry and related all the previous evenings incidents. Kerry said that she would meet with the two of them that evening. That session and other interventions during the week enabled mother and son to live together, and to deal more openly with conflicts. After two months, Kerry assumed the family work, and Rick and his mom were able to separate positively from the family group that they had attended at the program for over a year.

On another occasion, Rick told Ben about a date he had had with a girl a few days previously. Ben picked up in Rick's account of this date that Rick was engaging in old grooming behaviors and employing some of his thinking errors. Ben reflected this back to Rick. Rick was silent on the phone for a minute and then said, "Oh my God, you're right! I didn't even notice it!" Rick asked Ben to tell Kerry about it so that they could discuss it in SO group (he was too nervous to tell her himself). Ben told Rick that he needed to tell Kerry on his own. Ben stressed the importance of discussing these things with Kerry so that the two of them could work together. Rick agreed. The next day, Ben called Kerry (without Rick knowing he was going to) to see if Rick had followed through. Rick had, and in the process, had been able to strengthen his relationship with Kerry.

As time passed, Rick called to speak with Ben less and less, while becoming a leader in his outpatient group and building a strong relationship with Kerry and the other members of his support network. In later months (after he had completed his outpatient treatment), he would call Kerry to check in or to ask for a booster session. Currently, Rick remains in the community and is not known to have reoffended. His case might not have been as successful if during the crisis periods of the first three months he had not had the coordinated support of both programs.

PART V:
TRAINING AND EDUCATION

Chapter 15

Staff Training

THE IMPORTANCE OF SPECIALIZED TRAINING
FOR ALL STAFF WORKING IN THE PROGRAM

Training Is Not Just for Clinicians

Staff training is a crucially important component in a comprehensive sex offense-specific treatment program. Much has been written regarding the qualifications of *clinical staff* working with sex offenders (e.g., Perry and Orchard, 1992; Jensen and Jewell-Jensen, 1998; ATSA, 1997; Smith, 1995; Prendergast, 1991). Less has been written, however, regarding training for child care workers, teachers, outreach workers, milieu counselors, support and janitorial staff, administrators, etc. Most programs try to provide opportunities for clinical staff and administrators to engage in continuing education training, perhaps regarding these persons as most in need of such training. However, it can be forgotten that the direct care staff, who have the greatest amount of contact with the clients, also require specialized training.

The Association for the Treatment of Sexual Abusers (1997) has stated, "Providers at every level must have a combination of education, training and experience in the evaluation of sexual deviance" (p. 9). It is not enough for clinical staff alone to receive specific training. Siding with this belief, some groups have advocated for providing mandatory sex offense-specific training for the direct care and educational staff who will work with clients who sexually abuse (cf. Northeastern Family Institute, 1994). It is interesting (and perhaps distressing) to note that the mandatory training required of direct care staff in some programs *does not* include specific training in sex offense-specific issues, although these programs treat primarily clients who have been sexually abusive (cf. Heinz, Gargaro, and Kelly, 1987).

Issues Pointing to the Need for Staff Training

Many issues highlight the need for specialized training and ongoing supervision for all those who work with sexually abusive clients. First of all, the staff as a whole needs to "increase its sensitivity and awareness of what are sex offenders' behaviors vis-à-vis typical adolescent behavior and vis-à-vis sexual mores and traditions that may be influenced by geography, culture and race" (Northeastern Family Institute, 1994, p. 4). Staff must be educated regarding the common traits of the those who commit sexual offenses (cf. Prendergast, 1991; Farrenkopf, 1992), they must learn about the myths that they hold regarding "sex offenders" and offending, and they must become sensitive to their comfort level with issues of sexuality (Prendergast, 1991). Perry and Orchard (1992) remind us that rigid stereotyped attitudes toward sexuality, maintenance and support of myths regarding sexual offending and offenders, and responding with shock and revulsion to sexual material can be detrimental to therapy and treatment efforts, when direct care staff, teachers, occupational therapists, interns, and others are involved as much as when clinicians are involved. Staff who hold rigid views of sexuality, who believe and support false concepts concerning sex offending, and who do not understand sex offense-specific treatment and the requirements and rationale thereof can seriously undermine treatment. Staff need to be "on the same page" to provide a coordinated treatment effort.

SPECIAL ISSUES ADDRESSED BY STAFF TRAINING

Staff Self-Awareness

In addition to the previous concerns, it is important for staff to have a degree of self-awareness regarding their own sexuality issues. Ingersoll and Patton (1990) have correctly stated:

> Unless you have worked through the issues around your own experiences, they will undoubtedly color, and probably interfere

with, your work. Self-awareness is the key to planning and delivering client-focused intervention; it is difficult to keep the focus on the needs of the client and the client-system if your own needs interfere. (p. 6)

One of the greatest challenges for staff working with sexually abusive clients is to be aware of how the client and his behaviors affect them personally. Staff who hold erroneous or rigid views, as mentioned previously, or who are dominated by homosexual fears regarding sex offenders (cf. Prendergast, 1991) are likely to react to clients with a history of sexual offending in antagonistic and/or rejecting ways. In addition, staff who were themselves victims of sexual abuse may experience many feelings toward their clients who have sexually offended, ranging from fear and timidity to anger, revulsion, and hostility (cf. Perry and Orchard, 1992).

Staff need to be aware of the effects that working with sexually abusive clients can have on them. They must assess in an ongoing manner how they are being affected and what impact this is having on their personal and professional lives. Farrenkopf (1992) warns that those who treat this population can become cynical, fearful, and carry their work home in the form of hypervigilance regarding members of their own families. Furthermore, such stress can lead to staff trying to protect themselves from uncomfortable feelings by failing to address needed issues or to recognize potential dangers and problems. The reader is referred to *Impact: Working with Sexual Abusers,* edited by Stacey Bird Edmunds (1997), for a more complete treatment of this topic.

Staff As Maintainers of Program Safety

Connected to this last point is that staff training is needed to maintain the safety of the clients, staff, and visitors from sex-offending clients. Staff with a high level of discomfort in dealing with sexually charged matters may be more inclined to "look the other way," rather than address issues that make them anxious or uncomfortable. This situation can lead to unsafe conditions in the program and cause clients to believe that they cannot approach staff with their concerns regarding sexualized behaviors. Staff training and support are needed if the staff are to address what they need to address, both in the interest of treatment and in the interest of safety.

Staff As Conductors of Milieu Treatment

As part of the milieu treatment team, staff need to know what they are required to do to maximize the program's treatment effectiveness and to conduct quality milieu treatment.

- Staff members need to increase their skills in working with offenders in order to know what to say, where to go, and how to bring up certain topics in informal counseling sessions.
- Staff members need to know what types of thought patterns and actions are clinically significant and should be brought to the attention of the clinical staff.
- Staff members must understand the program's conceptual models and the ways in which treatment is done in the program so that they can intelligently guide residents and appropriately advocate for them.
- Staff members need to understand concepts of milieu treatment so that they can create a therapeutically challenging milieu that extends treatment beyond formal therapy and allows them to work with the resident on the many related issues that can be effectively dealt with in the milieu.
- Staff members need to understand and have some information about incestuous families so that they can recognize the degree to which family contact at the program should be monitored and appropriately deal with family conflicts.

THE DELIVERY OF TRAINING TO THE STAFF

Methods of Training Delivery

Training for staff can be provided in a variety of ways:

1. Program administrators can provide funding for staff to attend trainings and educational programs conducted in their area or nationally by recognized experts in the field.
2. Specialists can be brought in from the outside on a consulting basis to conduct sex offense-specific training.
3. The program can conduct its own training.

An in-house training program presupposes that the persons who will conduct the training are themselves specialists in the field and knowledgeable in the areas they will present. Also, any in-house training program must address the needs and structure of the program's particular model of sex offense-specific treatment.

Perhaps the best approach is to consider a combination of the aforementioned three ways of providing training to staff. Administrators should be on the lookout for training opportunities offered in their areas and should make the effort to free up staff to attend them. In-house training programs can be augmented by the addition of expert guest lecturers who can provide supplementary or advanced training sessions.

Planning for a Staff Training Program

The range of topics that may be planned for staff training programs is extensive. Regardless of its setting, a program will require some level of training for all new staff. It is likely that one will have to select certain training and educational programs as mandatory, while offering other training on a periodic basis. The mandatory training must be completed at the very start of employment for the good of client and staff safety, order, and program operation. In addition, failing to properly train and educate staff early on sets them up for many conflicts with their peers and clients as well as being very discouraging and frustrating for staff members. It can also open the door to potential liabilities if an incident occurs. Staff should be encouraged to get as much training as possible beyond the mandatory training to keep current on important topics and also to refresh their memory on things that inevitably are forgotten over the course of time.

Programs that treat clients who have sexually offended should also have sex offense-specific training, to acquaint the staff with the particulars of this population and to teach skills needed for them to do effective milieu treatment (if applicable). It is likely that outpatient programs will employ fewer paraprofessional staff than group care settings. However, the persons in need of training include *all persons* working in the program (from the program director down to the part-time relief staff). Programs should provide training for *each and every employee.*

Training programs may be set up quite easily. Once it has been determined what training will be offered, and which of these programs will be mandatory, a training schedule may be established. Mandatory training, as noted earlier, should be made part of the orientation program for new staff, while other training opportunities (offered either by the program or elsewhere) can be noted on a regular calendar. Staff should be given every opportunity to attend training and should not be regularly impeded because they "cannot be spared" from their work duties. It is also possible to set up training in different levels and to present certificates of completion to staff who have attended all the training levels in a given series.

Ongoing Supervision

An indispensable part of any training regime is ongoing supervision. Clinical staff will certainly receive supervision (and well they should) from a knowledgeable specialist in the field, but line staff, teachers, administrators, secretaries, and others working in the program also benefit from supervision. Frontline staff who attend regular supervision meetings (even if this is just for one hour every other week) will be able to better apply what they have learned in training, gain valuable insight from their supervisor and peers, and continue education by receiving information on the many subjects not covered in formal training programs. Supervision is also important for planning to address situations and client issues as they arise, attending to personal and professional growth, and helping the staff to develop into more balanced and effective workers.

Supervision may be done individually, in group, or (preferably), as a combination of both. In this way, the group learning aspects of discussing cases and issues will be made available, while still reserving a one-on-one setting for discussion of more sensitive issues. Supervision should be regarded as an integral part of staff training, not as an added "extra."

SUGGESTED TOPICS TO BE COVERED

Universal Training Topics

Some topics commonly addressed in staff training programs are placed here under three categories. First are the training topics that may be considered mandatory for staff. This category has two levels: (1) those which should be done either prior to beginning work or very soon afterward, and (2) those which might be required but can be picked up in time. Examples of training programs falling under this first category follow:

1. First level:

   • Agency orientation (personnel policies, program procedures)
   • Explanation of agency/program treatment model
   • CPR/first aid
   • Medical issues/medication management
   • Crisis intervention/restraint
   • Shadowing a member of staff (i.e., spending some number of shifts working hand in hand with an experienced staff member for on-the-job training)

2. Second level:

   • Fire/water safety
   • Behavior management
   • Depression/suicide
   • Staff as a member of the treatment team
   • Case study scenarios for discussion
   • Ongoing supervision

The second category includes clinically oriented training programs that are highly beneficial to staff. As many staff as possible should attend these. The more staff trained in these areas, the greater the effectiveness of the treatment team. The following are some examples:

   • Treatment planning
   • Group dynamics/conducting groups
   • Working with families
   • Milieu treatment techniques
   • Interviewing skills
   • Ongoing supervision

The third category includes training offered for staff development. Staff should be encouraged to attend such programs to satisfy their interests or to gain insight into areas particularly pertinent to their jobs or needs. Some examples include the following:

   • Communication skills
   • Child abuse/neglect
   • Substance abuse issues

- Cultural diversity
- Sexuality issues
- Anger management/relaxation techniques
- Designing educational programs for clients
- Skills building through milieu and recreation
- Advanced topics in conducting groups and interviewing
- Other training opportunities available in the community

Sex Offense-Specific Training Topics

A program that treats sexually abusive clients should offer training specific to this population. The following staff training scheme was taken from Lundrigan (1996a) and is divided into three modules: (1) mandatory, which would be taken by all staff; (2) optional, which would be open to all and particularly important for working with the client, and therefore highly recommended; and (3) advanced, which would help to round out the training and are especially recommended for interns and for staff whose jobs demand that they engage in greater levels of treatment. The topics are as follows:

1. Mandatory modules:

- Introduction to SO treatment in this program
- Characteristics of adolescents who sexually offend (includes behaviors to watch out for and be concerned about)
- Basic conceptual model of offending
- Etiology of sex-offending behavior

2. Optional modules:

- Sexual abuse basics
- The sexual assault cycle
- Introduction to relapse prevention planning
- Assessment of sexually offending clients

3. Advanced modules:

- General issues with adolescents who sexually abuse
- Treatment of sexual offenders (overview of techniques and options)
- Family treatment for adolescents who have sexually offended
- Staff self-care

Readers who would like further information on this program or the materials used should contact the author (see Appendix A).

THE USE, PRESENCE, AND TRAINING OF INTERNS

Programs will sometimes make use of interns (undergraduate or graduate) to provide training opportunities for these individuals and also to obtain additional services for clients. Using interns can have many beneficial effects on the program, such as introducing new ideas; injecting fresh blood and energy; helping staff, teachers, clinicians, and administrators learn by teaching others; and providing an often needed "extra pair of hands." For their part, the interns gain valuable experience not available in the classroom, and they are able to make important contacts that will serve them well when they begin their job search.

As with any member of staff, interns must receive training. In fact, in addition to providing mandatory training to help them perform the functions required of them, the program has an obligation to provide additional training to interns. They are there to learn, after all. The number of training topics mandatory for interns should be high (if this fits in with the educational plans from their school), and training should be made available to them accordingly. In addition, they should be provided with at least weekly supervision to maximize their learning experience and, in many cases, to satisfy the requirements of colleges and/or state licensing boards.

The mutually beneficial relationship between interns and programs can be a wonderfully powerful experience for interns, staff, and clients alike. Interns should be given as much responsibility as they can handle and provided with opportunities to engage in the activities that will be required of them when they enter the workforce. Since interns are given much responsibility (e.g., having graduate interns conduct individual therapy or co-lead groups), program staff are obliged to provide personal and professional support. This support can come in the form of supervision, informal check-ins, social interaction, training, advice, and kind words. It is easy to focus on the clients and neglect staff and interns. We owe it to ourselves and our clients to help interns maximize their experience and grow into the professionals of tomorrow.

Chapter 16

General Resident Education

GENERAL RESIDENT EDUCATION AS A COMPONENT

Why Have Such a Component?

In a sex offense-specific program with a mix of clients, only some of whom have sexually offended, a resident education program that targets all residents can be a very helpful addition to the program's treatment regime. When a program contains a mixture of clients who have a history of sex offending and those who do not, some problematic situations may result. Sometimes a degree of enmity will develop between the offenders and others, and sometimes staff will exacerbate a separation of the two populations by their own actions. There may be suspicions or resentments about the "special" treatment regime that sex-offending clients participate in, and/or nonoffending residents may be lied to by offenders regarding the true nature of some of their behaviors. This results in an unequal power balance between the offenders and their less informed peers.

Furthermore, many "locker room" myths about offending and those who commit sexual offenses can play out in the development of prejudices and the persecution of offenders. Sometimes in juvenile correctional settings, residents often want to set up a pecking order of offenses (such as is found in prisons); the result is that the offenders are given (by approved custom) the lowest rank. On the other side of the coin, residents who do not know about some of the specifics of offending may be skillfully manipulated by offenders into sexually acting-out behavior. In addition, these residents may fail to identify offenders' behaviors that are problematic and should be reported to staff. They may also fall prey to these behaviors if they progress to the point of acting out.

One Program's Experience with This Component

In one facility, a resident was able to offend several youths (sometimes with others present) without any information being transmitted to the staff. After one resident disclosed what was happening to his therapist, the entire situation became known. At a full program group, many residents spoke about the enmity present between clients with sexual behavior problems and others, their lack of understanding of sex offending, and their inability to decide if they should have come forward with the information they had. After some education and processing, the residents were much more receptive to the presence of offenders and were able to drop the "prison" way in which to view and treat clients who have committed a sexual offense. In addition, many of the barriers that had prevented the residents from sharing their concerns with staff were removed. For the offenders, this forum had two primary benefits: (1) it helped them to see the reality of how they were viewed (and would continue to be viewed) by a majority of society, and (2) it helped them to feel safer in talking about their issues in open program groups.

As a result of this experience, a general resident education program (GREP) was developed and implemented as a component of the facility's sex offense-specific treatment. This component improved the cohesion of the treatment community, increased safety by bringing sex offending out into the open, and enhanced the sex offense-specific nature of the program milieu.

Assumptions Underlying the Use of Such a Component

A GREP may operate under the following assumptions:

- Education of all residents on the sex offense-specific treatment regime and on the basics of sexual offending is as necessary for the non-sex-offending residents as it is for the staff.
- Providing an open forum for discussion would help to alleviate prejudices, dispel myths concerning offending and those who offend, and reduce anxieties and possible harassment of offending clients by other clients.

- Giving some information to the residents in general would make them (in a way) part of the treatment team and would help them to participate more fully in open psychotherapy groups when a client introduces his sex-offending issues.
- Informing all residents about the dynamics of offending would make it easier for them to note when something "is not quite right" with a client's behavior.
- Openness and encouragement would prompt residents to share concerns with staff, thus aiding the staff in gaining information concerning the resident's day-to-day thoughts and behaviors in the milieu. This hopefully will assist in more effective treatment planning and help to reduce the possibility of sexually acting-out behaviors.
- Residents who had sexually offended would benefit from such an intervention by becoming more comfortable with discussing their issues in mixed population groups, by learning more about how sex offenders will be viewed and treated by society, and by engaging in a group activity that would reinforce some of the educational material learned in their sex offense-specific group.

A MODEL GENERAL RESIDENT EDUCATION COMPONENT

This model component (developed for the program mentioned earlier) consisted of psychoeducational groups for all residents in the program and used a custom-designed curriculum. The component was designed to educate all residents in a manner that was consistent with the larger goals of the program and the sex offense-specific treatment regime, while being careful to remain applicable to all clients regardless of their issues.

Goals of This Component

The goals of this component, as stated in Lundrigan (1996a), are as follows:

- Provide a forum in which sex-offending can be discussed openly and away from private communication that encourages misconceptions, lies, and manipulations

- Increase the understanding of SO issues and dynamics for the clients who do not abuse, and reduce prejudices and unnecessary fears
- Minimize the ability of potential offenders to manipulate, groom, coerce, or sexually act out by exposing the secretive dynamics of these behaviors to the general population
- Inform all residents as to what behaviors are indicative of residents progressing in their assault cycle so that they can bring these behaviors to the attention of staff and clinicians
- Give the clients who have offended a perspective on how nonoffenders view them (vis-à-vis their offending behavior) so that offenders will be better prepared to face hostile views of sex offenders and their behaviors

The Format of the Sessions

Each of the sessions (which were conducted on a monthly basis) followed this format:

1. Standard Introduction Module:
   a. State the purpose of the component and why it is in place. In the model program, this included an explanation of the reasons for the component's implementation:
   - Need identified by resident abusing others and tensions in the program.
   - Residents requesting more information.
   b. Briefly summarize the goals of the component.
   c. Request that residents ask questions and not let concerns go unsettled. They should speak their minds.
2. Educational Module:
   a. One of a rotating series of six topics would be presented. These presentations were generally a combination of didactic material and discussion.
   b. Use videotapes, statements made by clients in offense-specific treatment, and role-plays to liven the discussion. One module employed a "quiz show" format to present material in a more interactive and less threatening way.
3. Questions and Wrap-Up:
   a. Residents are given the opportunity to ask questions about previous discussions or any other aspect of offending. Time is set aside to discuss answers.

b. Concluding comments are made (same ones each session):
- Any questions that people feel uncomfortable asking in the group can be asked privately anytime.
- If you are feeling uncomfortable about the conversation or behavior of a resident, bring this to staff or clinicians. You will not get him in trouble if he is not doing anything wrong. You cannot go wrong by just asking. You cannot take another's word that it is not necessary to bring your concern to staff. Trust your gut.
- If you think that it is unimportant to bring these things up and let them slide, you could be helping to create an unsafe situation. It is everyone's responsibility to maintain safety. If you do not want people to act out, then you must keep behavior in the open.

The Session Topics

The educational modules of this component were as follows:

1. SO Treatment at the Program
2. The Trauma Outcome Process
3. The Sexual Assault Cycle
4. Why Do People Sexually Abuse?
5. Myths About Sex-Offending Behavior
6. Grooming Behaviors in the Milieu

For more details regarding these modules or for information on obtaining materials used for the presentations, please contact the author (see Appendix A).

Topics may require more than one session to cover, or the program may need to interject educational modules to address specific needs. The point is to create a forum for the discussion of the sex-offending issue and to use this component to educate clients and positively influence the peer culture.

Afterword

Treating youth who sexually abuse is a challenging field of work. However, it does not need to be an endeavor taken up by an individual or a program in isolation. The construction of a comprehensive continuum of care; the availability of appropriate programs; the use of proven and effective treatment strategies; consistency, communication, and networking within and among programs; and ongoing support for workers at all levels—all help to make this difficult work a bit less arduous.

It is my hope that through reading this book the reader has gained both some useful information that will help him or her in the work of sex offense-specific treatment and avenues of further study to pursue in order to deepen his or her understanding of the issues raised in this book. The field is continuing to evolve. New insights and approaches that deserve attention are being developed all the time. At the dawn of a new century, we are poised to look back at all we have learned and to gaze forward to that which we still can learn.

With God's help, let us meet the challenge. Let us take it upon ourselves to remove the scourge of sexual assault from our society. Let us do this work to make our country and the world a safer place for all people. Let us not give up for lack of apparent success but rather try to recognize the positive impact that our work has had and will have. For those who believe, all things are possible.

APPENDIXES

Appendix A

Sources of Additional Information

AUTHOR CONTACT INFORMATION

The author is available to assist readers in any way possible. Contact information is as follows:

Stephen Lundrigan
AdCare Hospital
107 Lincoln Street
Worchester, MA 01605
(508) 453-3079

RESIDENTIAL STANDARDS

A recent two-year effort by a task force of experts has produced the document "Standards of Care for Youth in Sex Offense-Specific Residential Programs" (The National Offense-Specific Residential Treatment Task Force, 1999). This document, published by the New England Adolescent Research Institute Press (NEARI Press), represents the most current thinking in the field on the residential treatment of youth in offense-specific residences. It is a must for all those who currently operate or are planning to operate such a program.

An order form and additional information regarding the standards may be found online at <http://www.saperi.com/orderfrm.html>. Questions regarding these standards may be directed to The National Offense-Specific Residential Treatment Task Force, 70 North Summer Street, Holyoke, MA 01040, Phone: (413) 532-1713, Fax: 413-532-1795, E-mail: SBengis@aol.com.

RESOURCES AND CONTACTS FOR PROGRAM MODELS

The most up-to-date information regarding sexual abuse treatment programs nationwide is *The 1996 Nationwide Survey of Sexual Abuse Treatment Providers and Programs,* by Burton and colleagues (1996). This excellent resource lists the information gained from an extensive survey of sex offense-specific treatment programs (including treatment modalities and methods used, distribution by state, distribution according to type of setting and special populations served, etc.).

In addition, the *Nationwide Survey* contains a list of people (complete with addresses) that the reader may contact for further information and guidance. A copy of the latest edition of the survey may be obtained from Safer Society Press, P.O. Box 340, Brandon, VT 05733-0340, Phone: (802) 247-3132.

Appendix B

Sample Day and After-School Program Schedules

The following schedules are examples of how various intensive out-patient programs could be structured. These schedules could also be of help to group care providers who are looking to add a sex offense-specific treatment regime to their program schedules. The author may be contacted concerning personnel requirements, staffing patterns, space and resource needs, and cost projections for operating any of these programs out of an outpatient clinic or mental health center.

AFTER-SCHOOL PROGRAM

Time	Mon	Tue	Wed	Thurs	Fri
3:00 - 3:15	Weekend Check-In Group	Gathering Group	Gathering Group	Gathering Group	Gathering Group
3:15 - 3:30		Sex Offense-Specific Education Group	Level/Stage Group	Life Skills	Social Skills Group or Recreational Activity
3:30 - 4:00	Business Meeting				
4:00 - 4:30	Snack/ Socializing	Snack/ Socializing	Snack/ Socializing	Snack/ Socializing	Snack/ Socializing
4:30 - 6:00	Process Group	Anger Management or Substance Abuse Group	Topic Group (experiential)	Sex Offense-Specific Group	Recreational Activity

DAY PROGRAM

Time	Mon	Tue	Wed	Thurs	Fri
10:00 - 10:30	Socializing and Gathering Group	Socializing and Gathering Group	Socializing and Gathering Group	Socializing and Gathering Group	Socializing and Gathering Group
10:30 - 11:30	Weekend Check-In Group, Application of Concepts, and Relapse Prevention Strategies	Life Skills Activities	SO Education/ Sexuality Group	Level/Stage Group	Supervised Free Time or Recreational Activity (on a field trip day)
11:30 - 12:30			Program Business Meeting	Family Issues or Social Skills Group (alternating weeks)	
12:30 - 1:30	LUNCH	LUNCH	LUNCH	LUNCH	LUNCH
1:30 - 3:30	Recreational Activity	Recreational Activity	Recreational Activity	Recreational Activity	Recreational Activity
3:30 - 4:00	SNACK	SNACK	SNACK	SNACK	SNACK
4:00 - 5:30	Anger Management or Substance Abuse Group	SO Group	Process Group	Drama Therapy	Topic Group (experiential)
5:30 - 6:00					Weekend Planning Group

COMBINED DAY AND AFTER-SCHOOL PROGRAM WITH PROVISIONS MADE FOR SERVICING OTHER OUTPATIENT CLIENTS

Time	Mon	Tue	Wed	Thurs	Fri
9:00 - 10:00	Staff Coordination, Planning, Paperwork, Telephone Calls, Individual Sessions, etc. *Day Program Clients Begin to Arrive*				
10:00 - 10:30	Weekend Check-In Group, Application of Concepts, Prerelapse Prevention	Check-In Group	Check-In Group	Check-In Group	Check-In Group
10:30 - 11:00		Social Recreation	Social Recreation		
11:00 - 11:30		Sexuality/ Dating/ Relationships Group	Family Issues or Social Skills Group (alternating)	Drama Therapy Group	Supervised Free Time
11:30 - 12:00	Social Recreation (at group's end)				
12:00 - 1:00	LUNCH	LUNCH	LUNCH	LUNCH	LUNCH
1:00 - 3:00	Recreation (athletic)	Recreation (hobby)	Process Group (day program clients)	Recreation (reading/ drawing/art)	Recreation (organized)
3:00 - 3:30	*Arrival of After-School Clients,* SNACK, Brief Group				
3:30 - 4:00	Life Skills	Education Module (variety)	Recreation (movie)	Education Module (SO)	Level/Stage Group
4:00 - 4:30			At the same time a full staff meeting and/or training session for staff not supervising clients		
4:30 - 5:00	Topic Group (experiential)	Sex Offense-Specific Groups (one full-range, one aftercare)		Process Groups (clients divided into two groups)	Anger Management or Substance Abuse Group
5:00 - 6:00					
6:00 - 7:00	*Day/After-School Program Ends—Clients Depart for Home or Foster/Group Home* Clinicians on evening shift make preparations for groups				
7:00 - 9:00	Standard Outpatient Full-Range SO Group	Multiple Family Therapy Group	Multiple Family Therapy Group	Standard Outpatient Aftercare SO Group	N/A

Notes: From 4:00-6:00 clinicians not involved in activities of the day/after-school programs are conducting individual therapy sessions, and two SO groups (one full-range, one aftercare) during the course of the week for standard outpatient clients. Outreach workers are actively on shift seven days/week 8 a.m. to 11 p.m. and are on call at night.

Appendix C

Sex Offense-Specific Group Materials

GROUP RESOURCES

The following is a brief list of some workbooks and other books that contain helpful materials for use in SO groups. Some of these are adult workbooks, but the reader will note that much of the material is applicable and usable with adolescents by making slight alterations. Complete publication information for these books can be found in the Reference section.

Breaking the Cycle: Adolescent Sexual Treatment Manual, Loyal F. Marsh, Patrick Connell, and Ellen Olson (1988).
Empathy and Compassionate Action: Issues and Exercises—A Guided Workbook for Clients in Treatment, Robert Freeman-Longo, Laren Bays, and Evan Bear (1999).
How Can I Stop? Laren Bays, Robert Freeman-Longo, and Diane Hildebran (1999).
Maintaining Change: A Personal Relapse Prevention Manual, Hillary Eldridge (1998a).
A Manual for Structured Group Treatment with Adolescent Sexual Offenders, Ineke F. Way and Thomas J. Balthazor (1990).
A Model Residential Juvenile Sex-Offender Treatment Program: The Hennepin County Home School, Joseph W. Heinz, Suzanne Gargaro, and Kevin G. Kelly (1987). *** *Out of Print* ***
Pathways: A Guided Workbook for Youth Beginning Treatment, Timothy J. Kahn (1990).
The Relapse Prevention Workbook for Youth in Treatment, Charlene Steen (1993).
Tell It Like It Is: A Resource Guide for Youth in Treatment, Alice Tallmadge with Galyn Forster (1998).

Who Am I and Why Am I in Treatment? Robert Freeman-Longo with Laren Bays (1999).
Why Did I Do It Again? Laren Bays and Robert Freeman-Longo (1999).

REPRODUCIBLE SO GROUP MATERIALS

Included in this section are the handouts, worksheets, and homework questions that were produced by the author and mentioned in Chapter 7. To save space, worksheets that had a series of questions separated by spaces for responses have been shortened to a list of questions. The reader is free to use any of these materials.

Group Contract

The Sex Offense-Specific Group is designed for those clients who have been involved in sexually inappropriate or abusive behaviors. The group's goal is to help the client understand and stop these behaviors both during and after the time in the program. The group will use a variety of methods to help the client explore his thoughts, feelings, and behaviors in the context of a challenging and supportive group therapy format.

Client Responsibilities

1. What is said in group stays in group.
2. Clients are expected to actively participate in group. Participation involves not only actively and *honestly* talking about your issues and feelings but also giving one another feedback and confronting lying and manipulation.
3. Clients who mislead the group, lie, or fail to disclose offenses honestly are expected to correct these errors as soon as possible.
4. No laughing at others or putting them down.
5. No sidetracking group discussions.
6. No interrupting others. One person talks at a time.
7. Clients must complete all homework assignments. Assignments not done properly must be redone.
8. No inappropriate, abusive, or threatening behavior will be tolerated in group.

Group Leaders

Group leaders will maintain regular contact with other clinical staff in the program. They will discuss what they think is necessary to properly coordinate treatment. New or unknown offenses that are disclosed will be reported. Resident progress and level of participation will be discussed with caseworkers and appropriate staff and will be summarized in regular written evaluations. Information revealed that involves the safety of clients, staff, family members, or the community will be discussed with the appropriate persons. Whenever possible, all such communication will be discussed with the client beforehand.

Group leaders will make themselves available to help clients who are genuinely in need of extra assistance outside of group. Leaders will write special requested reports or appear in court or at meetings, if this is possible. Leaders are responsible for preparing for each group and doing their "homework."

I have read, understand, and agree to follow this contract:

Client: _____   Date: _____

Group Leader:_____

Offense Cycle Assignment #1

Based on the beginning of the Sexual Assault Cycle, identify for yourself the following:

1. What experiences *in the past* made you feel victimized, abandoned, rejected, hurt, helpless, or powerless?
2. What situations *in the present* bring up these same feelings again?

Offense Cycle Assignment #2

Build on the feelings and situations that you wrote about in the last assignment:

1. What did you do *in the past* to deal with these feelings? Make sure you include both thoughts and behaviors.
2. How do you deal with these feelings *now?* Again, make sure you include both thoughts and behaviors.
3. Is there a difference between how you deal with these feelings now and in the past? What is the difference (if any)?

Victim Questions Assignment

Please answer the following questions as if your victim were asking you directly. Use a separate sheet of paper, and write out each question followed by a detailed answer. If you have more than one victim, pick one to ask the questions.

1. Why did you do those things to me?
2. Why did you pick me? What did I do?
3. Should I trust you anymore? Why?
4. Did you ever think I was scared? How did you think I felt?
5. How do you think the abuse has affected my life?
6. Didn't you feel guilty about what you did, and tell yourself not to do it again? Then why did you keep doing it?

Writing Out Offenses

Write a description of one of your offenses. Be sure to talk about thoughts and feelings you experienced before, during, and after the offense.

Relapse Prevention Questions (Part 1)

Answer the following questions on a separate sheet of paper:

1. What things were happening for you (physically, mentally, emotionally, and in your environment) before committing your offenses?
2. What choices did you make that led to committing your offenses?
3. Describe situations in the past that put you at risk to reoffend. How did these situations put you at risk to reoffend?
4. How did you try to stop yourself from offending? Why did/didn't it work?

Relapse Prevention Questions (Part 2)

Answer the following questions on a separate sheet of paper:

1. What things could be signs for you that you may be moving to a potential offense (include physical feelings, thoughts, emotions, things going on around you, etc.)?

2. What do you need to change (in the way you think, your behavior, sexual thoughts, relationships, family, the way you deal with your emotions, etc.)?
3. What situations would put you at risk to reoffend?
4. What can you do to stop yourself from reoffending?

Deciding If a Sexual Act or Fantasy Is Appropriate

Please see Figure C.1.

Sexual Relationships

Answer the following questions:

1. What makes a relationship a sexual relationship?
2. Name some relationships that clash with a sexual relationship. Why do they clash?
3. Are male-male and female-female sexual relationships appropriate?
4. What is the male's role in a sexual relationship? What is the female's role?

Fantasy Assignment #1

Describe what goes on in your nonsexual fantasies. Why do you use these fantasies? What purpose do they serve for you mentally and emotionally? For example, "I sometimes picture myself as an NBA all-star. I am able to make incredible plays and sink every shot; everyone cheers." The purpose here might be to make me feel like I can do things right and to make people look up to me. Or, "I fantasize about getting into a fight with my brother. I beat him down, and he begs me to stop." The purpose here might be so that I can feel like I can get back at him—he's too big to do it for real; it makes me feel powerful.

Fantasy Assignment #2

1. Describe your most common sexual fantasies. Is there coercion, force, inappropriate persons, manipulation, etc.? (Notes: No need to be graphic. Include both present fantasies and those active before your offense. If you have any questions about what to include, ask one of the group leaders.)

FIGURE C.1. Sexual Act or Fantasy Decision Chart

DECIDING IF A SEXUAL ACT OR FANTASY IS APPROPRIATE

To decide if a fantasy or sexual activity between two persons is appropriate two important questions should be considered: (1) *Who* is the person? and (2) *What* is going on (the actions)? Each of these questions has at least two parts. For the act or fantasy to be appropriate, it must fit in the "appropriate" category *on all four of the following points.*

PERSON

AGE OF THE PERSON

Appropriate: For an adolescent, another adolescent two to three years from your age. For an adult, another adult is okay.

Inappropriate: Large age gap between adolescents (a bigger gap is okay with adults over twenty-five or so). Adults with anyone under eighteen. Children (up to age twelve years) with anyone.

RELATIONSHIP OF THE PERSON

Appropriate: No conflicting relationship.

Inappropriate: The two people have a relationship with each other that does not allow for sexual behavior between them (e.g., mother-son, brother-sister).

ACTION

IS THERE CONSENT?

Appropriate: There is consent, and there are *no* manipulations, bribes, tricks, threats, mind games, or other coercion present.

Inappropriate: There is limited consent or no consent. Some form of coercion, tricks, bribes, threats, or manipulation is being used. Also if the person is unable to give consent (too young, retarded, drunk/high, asleep).

WHAT IS THE SEXUAL ACT?

Appropriate: "Normal" sexual acts for your age group.

Inappropriate: Acts that are not "normal," are harmful to another, or are socially unacceptable.

2. What "fantasy rules" have you put in place so far? What rules do you need to add to set boundaries about what is okay to fantasize about?

Preoffense Pattern Assignment

1. First take some time to look at the diagram of the preoffense pattern.* Make sure you understand it. If you do not understand, ask a group leader to help you.
2. Take one of your offenses. Start by talking about what things were going on for you before you began your preoffense pattern. Then move into what inappropriate fantasies you were having. Finally, tell how you moved through each step in "breaking down the wall" and abusing. Talk about what you were thinking, feeling, and doing.

Pattern Interruption Assignment

1. Discuss where you are now in your preoffense pattern. What pre-offense behaviors are you doing (whether they are leading to an offense or not)?
2. Are you offending now? If you are not, what is keeping you from offending?
3. What inappropriate fantasies are you having?
4. Where do you see yourself "cruising" for victims or "collecting" fantasy material? What types of "grooming" behaviors are you using now? With whom?
5. How could you control your inappropriate fantasies? How could you deal with them if they began to increase?
6. What would you do if you noticed you were "cruising," "collecting" material for inappropriate fantasies, or "grooming"? Discuss what you could do to interrupt all three.
7. What would you do if you began to plan an offense or inappropriate sexual interaction?

Family Relations and Reactions

1. List the significant members of your family: those who live with you and/or those who do not. Include both those you get along with and those you do not.
2. Describe your relationship with each of the people in question 1.

---

*This diagram was developed for the conceptual model of the program the group was using. For more information on this and other charts of the model, please contact the author (see Appendix A).

3. How did your family members react when they learned about your offenses?
4. What do they think about you and your offenses now?

Urge Control Questions

1. Explain "thought stopping."
2. Explain how "covert sensitization" works.
3. Identify for yourself thoughts you have that
   a. put you down, and make you feel bad about yourself,
   b. support thinking errors of the Sexual Assault Cycle,
   c. justify unhealthy behaviors, and
   d. are part of your Maintenance Behaviors.

Appendix D

Family Treatment Component Materials

CONTENTS OF THIS APPENDIX

This appendix contains materials that were created by one program for use in the parent education groups discussed in Chapter 8. The reader is free to copy, adapt, or otherwise use any of these materials in the construction of an education group for a family treatment component.

Explanation of the Family Treatment Component for Parents

A handout given to parents at their orientation to the education and therapy groups that explains the specifics of the family treatment in more detail than the general overview of the sex offense-specific treatment regime.

A Parents' Guide to the Sex Offense-Specific (SO) Group

A simple explanation of the SO group that was used in an education group.

The Stages of Loss

A diagrammatic representation of Pithers and colleagues' (1993) verbal adaptation of Kübler-Ross's stages of loss.

The Parents' Role in Treatment

A handout used to guide the discussion by the same name in one parent education group.

The Dynamics of Sexual Offending

A thumbnail sketch of the dynamics of offending for parents to read and reflect upon.

How Do I Feel About What My Son Has Done?

A discussion guide for use in a parent education group.

EXPLANATION OF THE FAMILY
TREATMENT COMPONENT FOR PARENTS

What Is the Component All About?

The Parent Education and Involvement Component of our program's sex offense-specific treatment was developed to fill an important gap in the treatment of these young men and their families. This component seeks to help the parents of these clients participate more fully in their sons' treatment, and to understand more fully the nature of their behaviors.

Many parents of children who have committed sexually abusive or inappropriate behaviors struggle to understand why their son developed this means of dealing with his emotions. Also, many parents blame themselves (sometimes unjustly), are embarrassed or ashamed at what has happened, and wish that they could make the problem go away. This program works to educate parents in the dynamics (the "how it works") of sexual abuse and in the challenges your family must face as you help your son to work on his issues and remain free from abusing in the future.

You will most likely be your son's primary means of supervision after he has left the program, and it is very important for you to understand what makes him offend, what his triggers (or "red flags") are, and how you can help to keep him from offending either inside or outside your home.

The issues we will be discussing are difficult ones to deal with (especially if one of the victims is a member of your family). You will have a tendency to want to deny many of the situations that are shown to be present in your family, or to deny that your son could have done what he did. It is important to come to an acceptance of the reality of your son's behavior so that you can clearly see the impact of the offenses, and so that you can correct situations in the family environment that could unknowingly support further abusive behavior by your son. It is important for you to know that no one is here to point a finger in blame. The goal is to understand what happened and why, and to figure out how to prevent it from happening again.

The Parent Education Groups will take place during the Multiple Family Therapy Group time and will take approximately thirty minutes each week. The remainder of the time in the therapy group will be used to work on the other issues that are important to your family.

Goals of Family Treatment

1. Provide support for the youth as he works on his treatment
2. Identify and interrupt patterns that may have allowed or supported the sexual abuse
3. Improve family relationships, enhance family communication, and maximize family strengths
4. Provide information needed for the family to participate in Relapse Prevention Planning
5. Support the family as it goes through the process of treatment and works to resolve long-standing family issues
6. Provide a place where families can learn from one another, teach one another, and support one another
7. Provide a setting where families can safely bring up concerns they have been unable to address previously

Expectations

1. Parents and clients are expected to actively participate in the program and in the Education and Involvement Component.
2. Parents will be asked to meet for an information gathering interview as part of their sons' assessment process. Other meetings will be discussed at that time.
3. Clients are expected to disclose their offenses to their parents. After their son has disclosed to them, parents are required to speak (briefly) with their son's therapist to discuss the disclosure. Disclosing offenses in the Multiple Family Group is a *family* decision; you or your sons will not be required to disclose the specifics of the offenses in the groups.
4. Clients must keep their parents updated on the work they are doing in treatment. Parents should provide some time for this during the course of the week's encounters.
5. Parents must take an active role in the development of their son's Relapse Prevention Plan when he reaches the final stage of his treatment.

Topics of the Education Groups

The following list of topics was developed to guide our work in the Education Groups. We will move through these topics, taking as much time as necessary. You will be provided with additional handouts and other materials to help you more fully participate in the work. The list of topics is as follows:

- Sex Offense-Specific Treatment at the Program
- The Stages of Loss
- The Parent's Role in Treatment
- Why Do Children Abuse?
- How Do I Feel About What My Son Has Done?
- The Sexual Assault Cycle
- Normal Sexual Development
- Thinking Errors
- Roadblocks to Progress in Treatment
- Myths About Sexually Abusive Behavior
- The Preoffense Pattern
- Caring for Yourself

If you are unable to attend a family group, you may contact the program to ask about what we discussed and to get copies of any handouts distributed. Some of the sessions will take place without the boys present so that the parents can discuss more freely some of the topics we will cover.

We want you to have all the information you need or want. If you would like copies of additional reading, if you would like to discuss things in more detail, or if you have *any* questions, please do not hesitate to call.

A PARENTS' GUIDE
TO THE SEX OFFENSE-SPECIFIC (SO) GROUP

Who Is in Sex Offense-Specific Treatment at Our Program?

Clients who have been involved in sexually abusive and/or inappropriate behaviors are enrolled in the program's sex offense-specific treatment. Contrary to what you may think at first, the other boys in sex offense-specific treatment are not much different from your son in many ways. They have many common problems and look like a great many other boys that you might know.

How Big Is the Group and When Does It Meet?

One of the most important parts of the sex offense-specific treatment is the sex offense-specific group that is attended weekly by each client who has a history of sex offending. The group is kept to a small number (four to eight clients) and provides very intensive and individualized treatment. The group meets for two and a half hours per week.

What Happens in the Sex Offense-Specific Group?

The sex offense-specific group uses a combination of teaching, discussion, exploration of thoughts and behaviors, disclosing, directing, and confrontation of thinking errors that support abuse. The group is challenging and is designed to work on the clients' issues on a variety of levels. The group is led by a male-female team and uses many different types of activities and methods to help clients. Clients receive homework assignments each week that help to prepare them for group and encourage them to think about and work on their offending issues between group meetings. Part of each group is spent reviewing these assignments. The remaining time is split between activities (such as educational presentations, role-plays, discussions, group exercises, videotape viewing and discussions, etc.) and individually focused work by the group with one or more boys.

What Is Required of My Son in This Group?

All the boys are expected to *actively* participate in the group. Each boy signs a contract before entering group (a copy of the contract is attached to this sheet). This contract lists the responsibilities of the clients and group leaders. All residents make a full disclosure of their offenses to the group at their first group and redisclose each time a new client is added to the group. The clients are required to keep confidential the disclosures of other residents and other material discussed in this group. This group is the main place that the client works on his offending issues and progresses through the stages of treatment.

What Is the Pattern of the Group?

To deal effectively with the range of issues that the group explores, the group runs through a series of focus topics. It takes about three months to make a cycle through the topics. To offer a variety in homework and exercises, and to come at each topic from a variety of ways, three distinct cycles of the group are used to address all the topics listed. It would take a client

THE STAGES OF LOSS

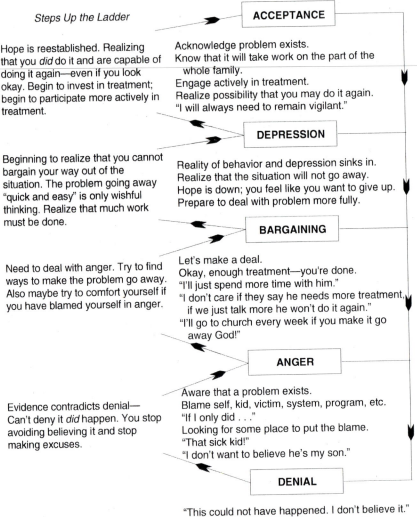

Steps Up the Ladder ➤ ACCEPTANCE

Hope is reestablished. Realizing that you *did* do it and are capable of doing it again—even if you look okay. Begin to invest in treatment; begin to participate more actively in treatment.

Acknowledge problem exists. Know that it will take work on the part of the whole family. Engage actively in treatment. Realize possibility that you may do it again. "I will always need to remain vigilant."

DEPRESSION

Beginning to realize that you cannot bargain your way out of the situation. The problem going away "quick and easy" is only wishful thinking. Realize that much work must be done.

Reality of behavior and depression sinks in. Realize that the situation will not go away. Hope is down; you feel like you want to give up. Prepare to deal with problem more fully.

BARGAINING

Need to deal with anger. Try to find ways to make the problem go away. Also maybe try to comfort yourself if you have blamed yourself in anger.

Let's make a deal. Okay, enough treatment—you're done. "I'll just spend more time with him." "I don't care if they say he needs more treatment, if we just talk more he won't do it again." "I'll go to church every week if you make it go away God!"

ANGER

Evidence contradicts denial— Can't deny it *did* happen. You stop avoiding believing it and stop making excuses.

Aware that a problem exists. Blame self, kid, victim, system, program, etc. "If I only did . . ." Looking for some place to put the blame. "That sick kid!" "I don't want to believe he's my son."

DENIAL

"This could not have happened. I don't believe it." "They are exaggerating what happened." "It was not *sexual assault*."

Source: Based on Pithers et al., 1993, pp. 3-6.

from nine to twelve months to complete the three cycles. The main topic areas are as follows:

- The Sexual Assault Cycle
- Family Dynamics and Issues
- Sexuality
- Victim Empathy
- Specifics of Own Offense and Offending Dynamics
- Preoffense Patterns
- Relapse Prevention Planning Preparation

The goal is for the client to learn about why he has used sexual abuse in order to get his needs met, how this behavior has become part of his thinking and acting, and how to change these thoughts and behaviors. In addition, the group works with other groups in the program on areas that are important to these boys, such as assertiveness training, social skills, anger management, negotiation, appropriate male and female roles, and expressing feelings appropriately. Sexual offending is a complex problem and involves much more than sex— sex is just a weapon, a tool. *Remember: Sexual offending is not just about sex. It is about getting your needs met in relationships.*

THE PARENTS' ROLE IN TREATMENT

1. Be present, available, and participate in Family Treatment.
2. Work to increase communication with your child as he works to do the same.
3. Honestly look at yourself and the family and carry that honesty into interactions with your son.
4. Be a positive role model for your son by doing work on family issues.
5. Learn about sexual offending and why your son offended. Some key concepts are

   - thinking errors
   - internal and external barriers
   - maintenance behaviors
   - preoffense patterns
   - preconditions
   - grooming behaviors
   - offense cycle
   - relapse prevention

6. Be willing to see the reality of your son's problem. Recognize the reality of what he did, and what he is capable of doing. Avoid the tendency to minimize and deny.
7. Learn to be a "lookout" for behavioral signals from your son.
8. Help in the development of your son's Relapse Prevention Plan.
9. Support your son's therapy. Be positive about the program. Help him to stay invested.
10. Be prepared to follow up with helping your son to keep to his Relapse Prevention Plan after he completes the program.

THE DYNAMICS OF SEXUAL OFFENDING

Sexual offending is a complex problem. It can be very difficult to understand why a person uses sexually aggressive or exploitative behaviors to get his way if you are looking at it from a purely *sexual* point of view. Sexual offending is primarily about getting needs met within relationships. These may be needs for power and control, being liked, gaining respect, feeling more intelligent or competent, wanting to have a person close to you who will not leave, feeling less lonely and rejected, feeling more like a "man," trying to get rid of past feelings of abuse, working through sexual confusion, taking out feelings of anger or revenge on another person, and a whole list of other possible reasons. Others simply wish to satisfy their sexual desires and do so whether the other person wants to or not.

The typical young person who has committed a sex offense has developed, as one of his ways of dealing with painful feelings, patterns of thought and behavior that include sexual behaviors with other persons. For the young man, the need to deal with the feelings through the sexual behaviors overrides the wishes of the other person. He cares more about doing what he believes will make him feel better than he does about the feelings of the other person involved. But *why?* Why does he not seek to get his needs met in appropriate and nonabusive ways that do not hurt others? Furthermore, if he is going to hurt another, why does he choose a sexual way?

The young man could just as easily have developed patterns of physical violence, intimidation, mental torture, defiance, manipulation, mind games, and/or domination of others to deal with his feelings. In fact, these behaviors are *extremely* common among those who offend and are found in the behavior surrounding their offenses, and in their everyday lives as well. What makes the adolescent who commits sex offenses unique is that he has developed the use of *sexual* means of violence, intimidation, torture, defiance, one-upmanship, and domination. The sexual act is seldom the real (underlying) goal of the behavior. The true goal of the behavior often lies in feelings of power, control, superiority, emotional connection, and strength that result from the behavior. The sexual act is not the end in itself—it is a *means* to the end of trying to counteract feelings that the youngster cannot or does not deal with appropriately. But how does this all fit together and work in a young person's thinking and acting?

Diagrams such as the "Sexual Assault Cycle" help show how feelings are triggered and follow a pattern of ineffective ways of coping that eventually lead to sexually acting out. Studying such a cycle will help you to gain a better understanding of why a particular young man has sexually offended. As he applies the cycle to himself, he can see how his patterns of dealing with the feelings did not really work but actually made the feelings worse, leading to sexually acting out. The cycle and the specifics of sex-offending dynamics (the "how it works") can be a bit complicated and take some time to digest and understand. Further study of the cycle will help you to better understand how a simple event is able to trigger a lot of old feelings, and how the boy's attempts to deal with the situation (although they seem logical and work to some degree) actually do not deal with the *real* problem.

In addition, the cycle shows how his anger and sense of powerlessness can become transferred to other people whom he begins to blame for his problems. In his retreat into fantasy, he plans how he will deal with the problem. What happens during this fantasy is that lots of things get mixed together in his head, such as anger toward others (whether they deserve it or not), the need to feel more competent and superior, the need to be loved and nurtured, ways that he thinks he can behave with others that will make him feel good, sexual thoughts and feelings, and many other errors in thinking. All this mixing of thoughts over time allows the idea of a sexual offense to develop. This idea may kick around for a long time before the slow eroding effects of thinking errors (e.g., "It's really not so bad to do it," "It won't hurt anyone," "I can stop anytime," "She or he will really like it," "She or he really wants to do it with me," etc.) bring down the barrier that usually prevents people from acting on such thoughts. The result is a sexual offense.

It is very important to note that no one formula can explain why these boys offend. For different reasons, each boy has developed this way of acting and thinking. However, many similarities and common themes seem to apply to all boys who sexually offend, no matter how different they are. That is why special treatments that have been developed are known to be effective with this group.

As you continue to explore why your son offended, you will have to learn the specific issues and problems that your son was not dealing with effectively, and what patterns of thinking he used to justify what he did. You will need to explore with him what distorted thinking told him it would be acceptable to hurt someone else. You need to see with him what was going on in his head when he felt that a warm, loving relationship meant two people linked together by tricks, intimidation, and sexual acts. You need to realize what was behind his learning to do this, and that these old patterns die hard and *are still present* in some form. You need to understand what allowed him to cross a line that others may think about crossing but do not.

You may be saying to yourself, "I'm not too sure I want to know all this." That is okay. You will have to trust that we will work with you to give you only what you want, need, and are able to deal with at any given time. There is much that you should know to be better able to help your son, but some things you may not feel ready to know. Please let the therapists know about this as we go along, so that this time of treatment can be helpful and rewarding without being overwhelming.

Sex offending is about getting needs met in relationships. It is about people who learn to deal with their feelings by using other people for their own purposes. It is about thinking errors that make it all seem logical and okay. It is about a boy hurting other people to feel better and perhaps not caring about it as long as he gets his needs met. For most, it is about guilt and shame for what they did, and about feeling powerless to stop themselves. It is about a boy who is running scared and running deeper into the cycle that has a hold on him. It is about someone desperately in need of help (although he seems to look just fine on the outside). It is about secrets, and covering up, and fear of being caught, and manipulation. It is about not wanting people to find out the truth, yet, for many, hoping that someone will. It is about engaging in behaviors that bring up the very feelings they are supposed to banish. For these boys now in treatment, it is about breaking this cycle! And if they are not working to break the cycle, they are keeping it alive.

HOW DO I FEEL ABOUT
WHAT MY SON HAS DONE?

As you work through you own "stages of loss" and come to accept the reality of your son's behavior, many feelings can set in. These can involve anger, denial, shame, regret, fear, confusion, sadness, pain, and many other feelings. If you are still in the process of working toward acceptance (as are most parents in your situation), you may find yourself experiencing many of these emotions.

If you shy away from dealing with these emotions, then you might be more inclined to enter denial and ignore problems as a way of avoiding your own painful feelings. It is important to be honest with yourself about what you feel so that you can clearly and honestly address the issues that are still unsettled surrounding the abuse that your son has committed.

Other feelings you may have (or had) may involve the way you feel *about* your son. You may at times feel disappointment, disgust, fear, hatred, anger, and perhaps even want to take revenge on your son for all the pain his actions have caused to the family. You may be conflicted about feeling this way about your own son. You may also have more complicated feelings if the victim was one of your own children or another member of the family. It is important again to be honest with yourself and to work through these feelings in family treatment.

These feelings are normal; they are not uncommon among parents in your situation. If you do not deal with these feelings, you may develop an "I don't want to know" stance that will block your learning the truth about what your son did and is *still* capable of doing. If you do not deal with these feelings, you may continue to harbor resentment toward your son that will affect your relationship with him, and this can cause painful divisions in the family. Finally, you may refuse to look at your son's continued risk to offend in order to avoid painful feelings.

One big obstacle to looking at and dealing with these feelings is thinking that what you feel about your son is "bad" or "wrong." Feelings are not bad or wrong. What your son did has affected the lives of many people. You, as a parent, have been affected and must take care of yourself; you must attend to your own personal issues while your son is getting help. Try being less hard on yourself and resolve to be honest. We do not need to point fingers in blame; we need to work to ensure that this abuse does not happen again.

Questions to Think About

1. How did you feel when you first learned what your son had done? How did those feelings change over time?
2. How did the abuse affect other members of the family?
3. What feelings or thoughts did you have that you were ashamed of?
4. Did you blame yourself or feel responsible?
5. How do you feel now?
6. Do you or anyone else in the family need to do more work in order to deal with leftover feelings and to accept the reality of your son's offending?
7. What support do you need at this time? Where can you get this support?

Appendix E

Pretreatment Intervention Monthly Assessment Form

I. Cooperation/Participation

    A. Cooperation (Completes Tasks and Homework Assigned; Attends Group)
1. Fully cooperates with all aspects of pretreatment, almost without exception
2. Cooperates extremely well; has had one or two noncooperative episodes
3. Cooperates most of the time/Very good yet mostly insincere cooperation
4. Inconsistent or intermittent cooperation
5. No cooperation at all

    B. Participation (Involves Self in the Activities of the Pretreatment)
1. Appears to be sincerely participating for own personal growth; takes initiative, requests additional work to aid in preparation; takes a leadership role in group; openly shares of self and seems to wish to positively engage in future treatment
2. Participates extremely well; sets positive example; seems to be genuinely trying to work and learn
3. Goes through the motions; only participates to avoid consequences
4. Poor participation/Sets negative example/Is hostile to group process
5. Does not participate at all/Has been suspended from group (indicate which)

II. Degree of Acceptance of Responsibility for Offense(s) (Acceptance of responsibility is seen to go beyond the accurate disclosure of the offense of record and admitting that it happened. Responsibility is seen to include accepting responsibility for such aspects of offending as premeditation, harm caused to the victim, fantasy, frequency of offending—including unknown offenses, intention to offend, etc.)

   A. Level of Acceptance of Responsibility
1. Presents with no apparent outward denial of aspects of responsibility
2. Continues to be in some degree of denial of responsibility (explain)
3. Is in complete denial of known offense(s) and accepts no responsibility

   B. Changes in Client's Account of the Offense(s) Since Last Report
1. Has altered story, accepting increased responsibility for offense(s)
2. Has changed some details of his account
3. No changes in client's account of the offense(s)
4. Has altered story, taking less responsibility for offense(s)
5. Other (explain)

III. Feelings/Thoughts

   A. Degree of Empathy
1. Appears to display accurate empathy; constantly able to place self in victim's shoes without taking the victim role himself; seems to feel genuine remorse for effects his offending behavior has had on his victim
2. Displays empathy for victim; does not blame victim for the offense; appears to understand how the victim could have been harmed by his offenses
3. Shows a small degree of empathy for victim/Believes victim has been harmed
4. Other (explain)

   B. View of Victim
1. Sees victim as equal participant in the offense/Believes victim enjoyed offense
2. Places significant responsibility for the offense on the victim/Does not believe the victim has been harmed in any way
3. Is hostile toward the victim/Believes he has been the victim of his offense(s)
4. Other (explain)

IV. Assessment of Progress

    A. Overall Progress
        1. Has made substantial progress since last report
        2. Has made a moderate degree of progress
        3. Very little progress
        4. No progress since last report
        5. Has regressed

    B. Group Progress Areas (Provide a yes or no response)
        1. Is retaining educational material
        2. Is able to apply the material to real-life situations
        3. Is able to use the material to explore his own offense(s)
        4. Shows that he is moving beyond the mere learning of material
        5. Uses group to begin working on his treatment
        6. Shows increased investment in working on his treatment
        7. Speaks about his sexual behavior in an open manner
        8. Speaks about his offending in an open manner
        9. Recognizes the seriousness of his offending and situation
      10. Recognizes his potential to reoffend

V. Summary

Appendix F

Aftercare Component Materials

CLIENT INFORMATION SHEET

What Is the Aftercare Component?

As a resident in the final stage of your sex offense-specific treatment in our program, you will be enrolled in the Aftercare Follow-Up Component. Through involvement in the component, you will develop an aftercare plan, define therapy and support services, and have at least one session with your next therapist prior to graduation. For three months after graduation, you are required to make follow-up contact with the program. Also, clinical staff from the program will maintain at least monthly contact with your next treatment provider and send a packet of information about you to that provider to help your transition to the community.

What Do I Need to Do?

You must do the following *before* graduation:

- Finish all treatment requirements for graduation
- Complete your aftercare plan
- Have therapy and support services in place
- Meet at least once with your next therapist
- Set up a follow-up contact schedule (part of your aftercare plan)

This sheet is given to clients to help them and their families understand the workings of the aftercare component.

You must do the following *after* graduation:

- Follow through on your treatment plans that have been set up
- Make the required follow-up contact with the program
- Cooperate with your next treatment provider
- Follow your Relapse Prevention Plan

What Role Do the Follow-Up Contacts Play?

The follow-up contacts are in place for two main reasons: (1) to give us a chance to talk to you to see how you are doing after graduation and to get feedback from you on how we can improve the program for future clients, and (2) to make your transition smoother by giving you familiar people as a support while you build a relationship with your next therapist. These contacts are not for you to get "counseling time" or to interfere with your work with your next therapist. We are interested in you and how you are doing, and we want to do everything we can to help you to make it. You know that we will always be here as a support as long as you need us, but you also need to have a strong network around you in the community. We do not want to get in the way of you building that network.

AFTERCARE PLAN

Resident:_____   Date:_____

I. Therapy

                        <u>With Whom</u>   <u>Address/Phone</u>

    1. Individual

    2. SO group

    3. Family therapy

    4. Other

II. Follow-Up Contact with the Program

    1. Calls (schedule):
    2. Planned visits (may include participation in Aftercare Group or MFT)

III. Educational/Vocational Plan

IV. Support Services (list supports and contact information)

V. Other Plans

    1. Follow my Relapse Prevention Plan
    2. Give copies of my plans to:
    3. Other plans (use back of sheet if needed):

    This plan is a contract between myself and [name of program] that I will follow this plan to the best of my ability. I realize that it is expected that I will follow up with the program for at least three months after graduation. I know that [name of program] will always continue to support me for as long as I need.

        Signed:_____

    This form is a basic layout for an aftercare plan that could accompany the client's relapse prevention plan.

SAMPLE RELEASE OF INFORMATION FORM

I, _____, hereby authorize _____ to exchange, obtain, and/or disclose information on my son/myself _____ with, from, or to the following:

_____

_____

_____

I authorize that these exchanges may include information regarding progress and/or content of therapy sessions, the results of assessments and/or evaluations, and other pertinent information exchanges needed to facilitate my son's/my continued treatment. I realize that the purpose of authorizing this release is to allow information exchanges (verbal or written) that will assist in the effective coordination and continuity of treatment between [name of program] and other service providers.

This consent may be revoked by me at any time, except to the extent that action has already been taken to comply with it.

_____   _____
Client   Witness

_____   _____
Parent   Date

_____

This is a sample release of information, allowing the program to have open contact with the next treatment provider. Minors would have parents sign the form; adults can sign themselves. A release should be obtained for all persons/agencies that you might need to interface with during the aftercare period.

SAMPLE LETTER SENT TO NEXT TREATMENT PROVIDER

[Date]

[Service provider and address]

Re: [Client name]

DOB: [Client date of birth]

Dear [Name],

As part of the sex offense-specific treatment at [program name] all clients are automatically enrolled in an aftercare follow-up component for at least three months following graduation. The activities of this component are designed to help smooth the transition from a structured residential setting to outpatient treatment, and to provide support needed to assist this transition. The component is also in place for the purpose of collecting data on the progress of graduated residents in order to learn how we may better treat future clients. Please understand that these services are not meant to interfere with your treatment or your role as primary service provider, or to foster a continued dependence on [program name]. We would like to be able to work with you to ensure as much continuity of services as possible, to provide whatever support that we can, and to learn from you how we could have better prepared this youth to return to the community.

Follow-up services began before our initial contacts with you and are being continued by us through the enclosed packet of materials. In this packet, we have included: (1) information on the sex offense-specific treatment at [program name], (2) a summary of the client's course of treatment in sex offense-specific therapy, (3) a final program progress assessment, (4) a copy of the client's relapse prevention plan, (5) a copy of the client's aftercare plan, and (6) copies of releases allowing us to communicate with you and share information on this case. If you require any further information, please let us know.

As part of our aftercare follow-up, we would like to be able to call you once monthly for the first three months to inquire as to the client's progress (for data collection purposes) and to be available as a resource to you. We would also like to make six-, nine-, and twelve-month calls, if this is agree-

---

This is a sample of a letter that could accompany the packet of information that would be sent to the next treatment provider. It helps to establish a connection and explain somewhat the aftercare component.

able to you. In addition to these contacts, the client's aftercare plan contains follow-up contacts with our program. These are in place in order to collect data and to allow the client to comfortably separate from relationships he has had for a year or more at our program. The client is aware that providers from both programs will communicate with one another, and that we plan to inform you immediately of anything that the client tells us that you should know. If you have any concerns regarding us contacting you or the resident contacting us, please let us know so we can modify our plans to accommodate your concerns.

If you have any questions or would like to speak to us for any reason, please do not hesitate to contact a member of the treatment team.

Sincerely,

[Provider's name]

References

Abbott, B. R. (1992). Group therapy for adult incest offenders and adolescent child molesters. In M. McKay and K. Paleg (Eds.), *Focal group psychotherapy* (pp. 359-417). Oakland, CA: New Harbinger Publications.

Abel, G., Mittleman, M., Becker, J. V., Rathner, J., and Rouleau, J. L. (1988). Predicting child molesters' response to treatment. In R. A. Prentky and V. L. Quinsey (Eds.), *Annals of the New York Academy of Science* (pp. 223-235). New York: New York Academy of Science.

Association for the Treatment of Sexual Abusers (ATSA) (1997). *Ethical standards and principles for the management of sexual abusers* [Brochure]. Breverton, OR: Author.

Baker, D., Sullivan, P., Kessler, E., Prete, N., and Johnson, R. (1999, April). "Intensive treatment with incarcerated sex offenders." Workshop presented at the First Joint Conference on Sex Offense-Specific Assessment, Treatment and Safe Management of Children, Adolescents, and Adults, Marlborough, MA.

Barbaree H. E, and Cortoni, F. A. (1993). Treatment of the juvenile sex offender within the criminal justice and mental health systems. In H. Barbaree, W. Marshall, and S. Hudson (Eds.). *The juvenile sex offender* (pp. 243-263). New York: The Guilford Press.

Barbaree, H. E., Marshall, W. L., and Hudson, S. M. (Eds.) (1993). *The juvenile sex offender*. New York: The Guilford Press.

Barbaree, H. E. and Seto, M. C. (1997). Pedophilia: Assessment and treatment. In D.R. Laws and W. O'Donohue (Eds.), *Sexual deviance: Theory, assessment, and treatment* (pp. 175-193). New York: The Guilford Press.

Bays, L. and Freeman-Longo, R. (1999). *Why did I do it again? Understanding my cycle of problem behaviors*. Holyoke, MA: NEARI Press.

Bays, L., Freeman-Longo, R., and Hildebran, D. (1999). *How can I stop? Breaking my deviant cycle*. Holyoke, MA: NEARI Press.

Beck, A. J. (1989). *Recidivism of prisoners released in 1983*. Washington, DC: U.S. Department of Justice, Bureau of Justice Statistics.

Becker, J. V. (1996). Outpatient treatment of adolescent male sexual offenders. In M. Andronico (Ed.), *Men in groups: Insights, interventions, and psycho-educational work* (pp. 377-388). Washington, DC: American Psychological Association.

Becker, J. V. and Hunter, J. A. (1992). Evaluation of treatment outcome for adult perpetrators of child sexual abuse. *Criminal Justice and Behavior, 19*(1), 74-92.

Becker, J. V. and Kaplan, M. S. (1993). Cognitive behavioral treatment of the juvenile sex offender. In H. E. Barbaree, W. L. Marshall, and S. M. Hudson (Eds.), *The juvenile sex offender* (pp. 264-277). New York: The Guilford Press.

Bengis, S. M. (1986). *A comprehensive service-delivery system with a continuum of care for adolescent sexual offenders.* Orwell, VT: Safer Society Press.

Bengis, S. M. and Cuninggim, P. (1997, December). "Treating adolescent sex abusers in residential placements: Making it work." A training presented through the New England Adolescent Research Institute, Framingham, MA.

Berlin, I. N. (1997). Attachment theory: Its use in milieu therapy and in psychotherapy with children in residential treatment. *Residential Treatment for Children and Youth,15*(2), 29-37.

Bergman, J. (1995). Life, the life event, and theater: A personal narrative on the use of drama therapy with sex offenders. In B. K. Schwartz, and H. R. Cellini (Eds.), *The sex offender: Corrections, treatment, and legal practice* (pp. 17-1–17-24). Kingston, NJ: Civic Research Institute, Inc.

Bingham, J. E., Turner, B.W., and Piotrowski, C. (1995). Treatment of sexual offenders in an outpatient community-based program. *Psychological Reports, 76*(3, pt. 2), 1195-1200.

Blackburn, R. (1993). *The psychology of criminal conduct: Theory, research, and practice.* New York: John Wiley and Sons.

Blanchard, G. T. (1997, April). "Getting past denial and resistance." Paper presented at the annual convention of the National Adolescent Perpetrator Network, Cherry Hill, NJ.

Blanchard, G. T. (1998). *The difficult connection: The therapeutic relationship in sex offender treatment.* Brandon, VT: Safer Society Press.

Borduin, C. M., Henggeler, S. W., Blaske, D. M., and Stein, R. J. (1990). Multisystemic treatment of adolescent sexual offenders. *International Journal of Offender Therapy and Comparative Criminology, 34*(2), 105-113.

Brake, S. (1996, Summer). "Pre-treatment" of offenders in denial. *The Forum, 8*(2).

Brake, S. and Shannon, D. (1997). Using pretreatment to increase admission in sex offenders. In B. K. Schwartz, and H. R. Cellini (Eds.), *The sex offender: New insights, treatment innovations and legal developments* (pp. 5-1–5-16). Kingston, NJ: Civic Research Institute, Inc.

Bribitzer, M. P. and Verdieck, M. J. (1988). Home-based, family-centered intervention: Evaluation of a foster care prevention program. *Child Welfare, 67*(3), 255-265.

Burton, D., Fiske, J. A., Freeman-Longo, R. E., and Levins, J. (1996). *The 1996 nationwide survey of sexual abuse treatment providers and programs.* Brandon, VT: Safer Society Press.

Casella, D. A. (1990, April). "Treatment of the adolescent sexual offender: Residential treatment and aftercare." Training given in an unknown location.

Cellini, H. R. (1995). Assessment and treatment of the adolescent sexual offender. In B. K. Schwartz, and H. R. Cellini (Eds.), *The sex offender: Corrections, treatment, and legal practice* (pp. 6-1– 6-12). Kingston, NJ: Civic Research Institute, Inc.

Christensen, D. N. (1992). Family involvement in sexual offender treatment. *Treatment Quarterly, 1*(2), 12-17.

Cohen, F. (1995). Liability and negligent release. In B. K. Schwartz and H. R. Cellini (Eds.), *The sex offender: Corrections, treatment, and legal practice* (pp. 27-1–27-13). Kingston, NJ: Civic Research Institute, Inc.

Corder, B. F. (1994). *Structured adolescent psychotherapy groups.* Sarasota, FL: Professional Resource Press.

Cotter, L. P. (1996, Spring). Further reflections on denial. *The Forum, 8*(1), 3.

Crenshaw, D. A. (1988). Responding to sexual acting out. In C. E. Schaefer and A. J. Swanson (Eds.), *Children in residential care: Critical issues in treatment* (pp. 50-76). New York: Van Nostrand Reinhold Company.

Cumming, G. and Buell, M. (1997). *Supervision of the sex offender.* Brandon, VT: Safer Society Press.

Cusack, J. (1994, May). "Treatment of the adolescent sex offender." Workshop presented at The Pilgrim Center, Braintree, MA.

Cusack, J. (1999, April). "Deviant/offending/relapse cycles and clocks: Their past, present, and future." Workshop presented at the First Joint Conference on Sex Offense-Specific Assessment, Treatment and Safe Management of Children, Adolescents and Adults, Marlborough, MA.

Cutler, P. G. (1997, April). "Cognitive corrections: A psychoeducational curriculum for adolescent sexual offenders." A poster presented at the annual convention of the National Adolescent Perpetrators Network, Cherry Hill, NJ.

Dayton, T. (1994). *The drama within: Psychodrama and experiential therapy.* Deerfield Beach, FL: Health Communications, Inc.

Dougher, M. J. (1995). Clinical assessment of sex offenders. In B. K. Schwartz and H. R. Cellini (Eds.), *The sex offender: Corrections, treatment, and legal practice* (pp. 11-1–11-13). Kingston, NJ: Civic Research Institute, Inc.

Durrant, M. (1993). *Residential treatment: A cooperative, competency-based approach to therapy and program design.* New York: W. W. Norton and Company.

Eastman B. J. and Carpenter, D. R. (1997, April). "The essential link in treatment: The role of family therapy in adolescent sex offender treatment." A paper presented at the annual convention of the National Adolescent Perpetrators Network, Cherry Hill, NJ.

Edmunds, S. B. (Ed.) (1997). *Impact: Working with sexual abusers.* Brandon, VT: Safer Society Press.

Ehrenberg, M. and Ehrenberg, O. (1988). *The intimate cycle: The sexual dynamics of family life.* New York: Simon and Schuster, Inc.

Eldridge, H. (1998a). *Maintaining change: A personal relapse prevention manual.* Thousand Oaks, CA: Sage Publications.

Eldridge, H. (1998b). *Therapist guide for maintaining change: Relapse prevention for adult male perpetrators of child sexual abuse.* Thousand Oaks, CA: Sage Publications.

Farrenkopf, T. (1992). What happens to therapists who work with sex offenders? *Journal of Offender Rehabilitation, 18*(3/4), 217-223.

Finkelhor, D. (1984). *Child sexual abuse: New theory and research.* New York: The Free Press.

Freeman, A. M. (1979). Planning community treatment for sex offenders. *Community Mental Health Journal, 14*(2), 147-152.

Freeman-Longo, R. and Bays, L. (1999). *Who am I and why am I in treatment?* Holyoke, MA: NEARI Press.

Freeman-Longo, R., Bays, L., and Bear, E. (1999). *Empathy and compassionate action: Issues and exercises—A guided workbook for clients in treatment.* Holyoke, MA: NEARI Press.

Freeman-Longo, R. and Blanchard, G. T. (1998). *Sexual abuse in America: Epidemic of the 21st century.* Brandon, VT: Safer Society Press.

Friedman, S. (1991). *Outpatient treatment of child molesters.* Sarasota, FL: Professional Resource Exchange, Inc.

Goyette, A., Marr, K., and Lewicki, J. (1995). The family and community in milieu treatment: Challenging the parameters of residential treatment. *Journal of Child and Youth Care, 9*(4), 39-50.

Graham, K. R. (1996). The childhood victimization of sex offenders: An underestimated issue. *International Journal of Offender Therapy and Comparative Criminology, 40*(3), 192-203.

Green, R. (1995a). Community management of sex offenders. In B. K. Schwartz and H. R. Cellini (Eds.), *The sex offender: Corrections, treatment, and legal practice* (pp. 21-1–21-8). Kingston, NJ: Civic Research Institute, Inc.

Green, R. (1995b). Comprehensive treatment planning for sex offenders. In B. K. Schwartz and H. R. Cellini (Eds.), *The sex offender: Corrections, treatment, and legal practice* (pp. 10-1–10-9). Kingston, NJ: Civic Research Institute, Inc.

Green, R. (1995c). Psycho-educational modules. In B. K. Schwartz and H. R. Cellini (Eds.), *The sex offender: Corrections, treatment, and legal practice* (pp. 13-1–13-10). Kingston, NJ: Civic Research Institute, Inc.

Green, R. (1995d). Sex offender treatment program evaluation. In B. K. Schwartz, and H. R. Cellini (Eds.), *The sex offender: Corrections, treatment, and legal practice* (pp. 9-1–9-11). Kingston, NJ: Civic Research Institute, Inc.

Greer, W. (1991). Aftercare: Community integration following institutional treatment. In G. Ryan and S. Lane (Eds.), *Juvenile sexual offending: Causes, consequences, and correction* (pp. 377-390). Lexington, MA: D. C. Heath and Company

Groth, A. N., Hobson, W. F., Lucey, K. P., and St. Pierre, J. (1981). Juvenile sexual offenders: Guidelines for treatment. *International Journal of Offender Therapy and Comparative Criminality, 25*(2) 265-275.

Gwynn, C., Meyer, R., and Schaefer, C. (1988). The influence of the peer culture in residential treatment. In C. E. Schaefer and A.J. Swanson (Eds.), *Children in residential care: Critical issues in treatment* (pp. 104-133). New York: Van Nostrand Reinhold Company.

Halvorson, V. M. (1992). A home-based family intervention program. *Hospital and Community Psychiatry, 43*(4), 395-396.

Happel, R. M. and Auffrey, J. J. (1995). Sex offender assessment: Interrupting the dance of denial. *American Journal of Forensic Psychology, 13*(2), 5-22.

Hare R. D. (1993). *Without conscience: The disturbing world of the psychopaths among us.* New York: Pocket Books.

Heinz, J. W., Gargaro, S., and Kelly, K. G. (1987). *A model residential juvenile sex-offender treatment program: The Hennepin County Home School.* Syracuse, NY: Safer Society Press.

Heinz, J. W., Ryan, G., and Bengis, S. (1991). The system's response to juvenile sex offenders. In G. Ryan and S. Lane (Eds.), *Juvenile sexual offending: Causes, consequences, and correction* (pp. 185-198). Lexington, MA: D. C. Heath and Company.

Hunter, J. A. and Figueredo, A. J. (1999). Factors associated with treatment compliance in a population of juvenile sexual offenders. *Sexual Abuse: A Journal of Research and Treatment, 11*(1), 49-67.

Hunter, M. (1990). *The sexually abused male.* Lexington, MA: Lexington Books.

Ingersoll, S. and Patton, S. (1990). *Treating perpetrators of sexual abuse.* Lexington, MA: Lexington Books.

Jenkins, A. (1990). *Invitations to responsibility: The therapeutic engagement of men who are violent and abusive.* Adelaide, South Australia: Dulwich Centre Publications.

Jensen, S. and Jewell-Jensen, C. (1998). Why license sexual offender treatment providers? Because it's the responsible thing to do! *Sexual Abuse: A Journal of Research and Treatment, 10*(3), 263-266.

Kahn, T. J. (1990). *Pathways: A guided workbook for youth beginning treatment.* Brandon, VT: Safer Society Press.

Kahn, T. J. (1992, October). "Adolescent sex offenders: Assessment and treatment." Training presented at the Brightside Series, West Springfield, MA.

Kennedy, H. G. and Grubin, D. H. (1992). Patterns of denial in sex offenders. *Psychological Medicine, 22*(2), 191-196.

Knight, R. A. and Prentky, R. A. (1993). Exploring characteristics for classifying juvenile sex offenders. In H. Barbaree, W. Marshall, and S. Hudson (Eds.), *The juvenile sex offender* (pp. 45-83). New York: The Guilford Press.

Knopp, F. H. (1982). *Remedial intervention in adolescent sex offenses: Nine program descriptions.* Brooklyn, NY: Faculty Press Inc.

Landgarten, H. B. (1981). *Clinical art therapy: A comprehensive guide.* New York: Brunner/Mazel, Inc.

Laws, D. R. (Ed.) (1989). *Relapse prevention with sex offenders.* New York: The Guilford Press.

Lundrigan, S. E. (1994). "A home-based outreach program for troubled families with adolescents." Unpublished manuscript. Assumption College, Worcester, MA.

Lundrigan, S. E. (1996a). "Alpha omega sex offender specific treatment component manual." Unpublished manuscript.

Lundrigan, S. E. (1996b). "Education and treatment for families of adolescent sexual offenders." Workshop presentation at the annual convention of the Massachusetts Association for the Treatment of Sexual Abusers, Worcester, MA, October.

Lundrigan, S. E. (1997, April). "The use of a specialized aftercare follow-up component following residential treatment of adolescent sexual offenders." Paper presented at the annual convention of the National Adolescent Perpetrators Network, Cherry Hill, NJ.

Lundrigan, S. E. (1999). Multi-component residential treatment for adolescent sexual offenders: A pilot program evaluation. *Journal of the National Association of Forensic Counselors, 1*(1), 112-130.

Lundrigan, S. E. and Breault, J. C. (1999). "Pre-treatment" of incarcerated adolescent sexual offenders: A pilot study." Manuscript submitted for publication.

Maletzky, B. M. (1991). *Treating the sexual offender.* Newbury Park, CA: Sage Publications, Inc.

Maletzky, B. M. (1996). Editorial: Denial of treatment or treatment of denial. *Sexual Abuse: A Journal of Research and Treatment, 8*(1), 1-6.

Mandell, J. G. and Damon, L. (1989). *Group treatment for sexually abused children.* New York: The Guilford Press.

Margolin, L. (1983). A treatment model for the adolescent sex offender. *Journal of Offender Counseling, Services and Rehabilitation, 8*(1/2), 1-11.

Margolin, L. (1984). Group therapy as a means of learning about the sexually assaultive adolescent. *International Journal of Offender Therapy and Comparitive Criminology, 28*(1), 66-72.

Marques, J. K., Day, D. M., Nelson, C., and Miner, M. H. (1989). The sex offender treatment and evaluation project: California's relapse prevention program. In D. R. Laws (Ed.), *Relapse prevention with sex offenders* (pp. 247-267). New York: The Guilford Press.

Marques, J. K., Day, D. M., Nelson, C., and West, M. A. (1994). Effects of cognitive-behavioral treatment on sex offender recidivism: Preliminary results of a longitudinal study. *Criminal Justice and Behavior, 21*(1), 28-54.

Marsh, L. F., Connell P., and Olson. E. (1988). *Breaking the cycle: Adolescent sexual treatment manual.* Beverton, OR: St. Mary's Home for Boys.

Marshall, W. L. (1994). Treatment effects on denial and minimization in incarcerated sex offenders. *Behaviour Research and Therapy, 32*(5), 559-564.

Marshall, W. L. and Barbaree, H. (1988). The long-term evaluation of a behavioral treatment program for child molesters. *Behaviour Research and Therapy, 26* (6), 499-511.

Marshall, W. L. and Barbaree, H. (1990). Outcome of comprehensive cognitive-behavioral treatment programs. In W. L. Marshall, D. R. Laws, and H. E.

Barbaree (Eds.), *Handbook of sexual assault: Issues, theories, and treatment of the offender* (pp. 363-389). New York: Plenum Press.

Marshall, W. L., Earls, C. M., Segal, Z., and Darke, J. (1983). A behavioral program for the assessment and treatment of sexual aggressors. In K. Craig and R. McMahon (Eds.), *Advances in clinical behavior therapy.* New York: Brunner/Mazel.

Marshall, W. L. and Pithers, W. D. (1994). A reconsideration of treatment outcome with sex offenders. *Criminal Justice and Behavior, 21*(1), 10-27.

Mayer, A. (1988). *Sex offenders: Approaches to understanding and management.* Holmes Beach, FL: Learning Publications, Inc.

Mayer, R. S. (1995). Treatment of the very difficult sexual abuse survivor. In M. Hunter (Ed.), *Adult survivors of sexual abuse* (pp. 83-97). Thousand Oaks, CA: Sage Publications.

McCord, W. M. (1982). *The psychopath and milieu therapy: A longitudinal study.* New York: Academic Press.

McGovern K. B. (1991).The assessment of sexual offenders. Guest chapter in B. M. Maletzky. *Treating the sexual offender* (pp. 35-66). Newbury Park, CA: Sage Publications.

McGrath, R. J. (1993). Preparing psychosexual evaluations of sex offenders: Strategies for practitioners. *Journal of Offender Rehabilitation, 20*(1/2), 139-158.

Meloy, J. R., Haroun, A., and Schiller, E. F. (1990). *Clinical guidelines for involuntary outpatient treatment.* Sarasota, FL: Professional Resource Exchange, Inc.

Miller, W. R. and Rollnick, S. (1991). *Motivational interviewing: Preparing people to change addictive behavior.* New York: The Guilford Press.

Monto, M., Zgourides, G., and Keenan, T. (1998). Empathy, self-esteem, and the adolescent sexual offender. *Sexual Abuse: A Journal of Research and Treatment, 10*(2), 127-140.

Mullen, L. R. (1998). *Society and sex offenders.* Houston, TX: Emerald Ink Publishing.

Murphy, J. J. (1996). Treatment of denial in sex offenders. *The Forum, 7*(4), 4-5.

Murphy, W. D. (1990). Assessment and modification of cognitive distortions in sex offenders. In W. L. Marshall, D. R. Laws, and H. E. Barbaree (Eds.), *Handbook of sexual assault: Issues, theories, and treatment of the offender* (pp. 331-342). New York: Plenum Press.

Naar, R. (1986). *A primer of group psychotherapy.* New York: Human Sciences Press, Inc.

The National Offense-Specific Residential Treatment Task Force (1999). *Standards of care for youth in sex offense-specific residential programs.* Holyoke, MA: New England Adolescent Research Institute Press.

Nelson, K. E., Landsman, M. J., and Deutelbaum, W. (1990). Three models of family-centered placement prevention services. *Child Welfare, 69*(1), 3-21.

Northeastern Family Institute (1994, August). *Perpetrators of sexual abuse caucus.* Notes of the proceedings of the Perpetrators of Sexual Abuse Caucus. Danvers, MA: Author.

Northey, W. F. (1997, April). "Examining the use of coercion in the treatment of adolescents accused of sexual offenses: Therapeutic implications and consequences." Paper presented at the annual convention of the National Adolescent Perpetrators Network, Cherry Hill, NJ.

O'Connell, M. A. (1986). Reuniting incest offenders with their families. *Journal of Interpersonal Violence, 1*(3), 374-386.

O' Donohue,W. O. and Letourneau, E. (1993). A brief group treatment for the modification of denial in child sexual abusers: Outcome and follow-up. *Child Abuse and Neglect, 17*(2), 299-304.

Oster, G. D. and Gould, P. (1987). *Using drawings in assessment and therapy: A guide for mental health professionals.* New York: Bruner/Mazel, Inc.

Pare, B., Casella, D., Eckard, A., and Prehl, L. (1994, November). "Working with the families of abusing youth." Panel presentation at the annual conference of the Massachusetts Adolescent Sex Offender Coalition, Worcester, MA.

Pence, E. and Paymar, M. (1990). "Power and control: Tactics of men who batter." An educational curriculum of the Duluth Domestic Intervention Project, Duluth, MN.

Perry, G. P. and Orchard, J. (1992). *Assessment and treatment of adolescent sex offenders.* Sarasota, FL: Professional Resource Press.

Perry, G. P. and Paquin, M. J. (1987). Practical strategies for maintaining and generalizing improvements from psychotherapy. In P. A. Keller and S. R. Heyman (Eds.), *Innovations in clinical practice: A source book* (Volume 6, pp. 151-164). Sarasota, FL: Professional Resource Press.

Pithers, W. D. (1990). Relapse prevention with sexual aggressors: A method for maintaining therapeutic gain and enhancing external supervision. In W. L. Marshall, D. R. Laws, and H. E. Barbaree (Eds.), *Handbook of sexual assault: Issues, theories, and treatment of the offender* (pp. 343-362). New York: Plenum Press.

Pithers, W. D., Gray, A. S., Cunningham, C., and Lane, S. (1993). *From trauma to understanding: A guide for parents of children with sexual behavior problems.* Brandon, VT: Safer Society Press.

Prendergast, W. E. (1991). *Treating sex offenders in correctional institutions and outpatient clinics.* Binghamton, NY: The Haworth Press, Inc.

Prochaska, J. O. (1984). *Systems of psychotherapy: A transtheoretical analysis.* Pacific Grove, CA: Brooks/Cole Publishing Company.

Proulx, J., Pellerin, B., Paradis, Y., McKibben, A., Aubut, J., and Ouimet, M. (1997). Static and dynamic predictors of recidivism in sexual aggressors. *Sexual Abuse: A Journal of Research and Treatment, 9*(1), 7-27.

Quinsey, V. L., Lalumiere, M. L., Rice, M. E., and Harris, G. T. (1995). Predicting sexual offenses. In J. C. Campbell (Ed.), *Assessing dangerousness: Violence by sexual offenders, batterers, and child abusers.* Thousand Oaks, CA: Sage Publications.

Rasmussen, L., Burton, J., and Christopherson, B. (1992). Precursors to offending and the trauma outcome process in sexually reactive children. *Journal of Child Sexual Abuse, 1*(1), 33-48.

Redl, F. (1959). The concept of a "therapeutic milieu." *American Journal of Orthopsychiatry, 29*(4), 721-736.

Rice, M. E. (1997). Violent offender research and implications for the criminal justice system. *American Psychologist, 52*(4), 414-423.

Rogers, R. and Dickey, B. (1991). Denial and minimization among sex offenders: A review of competing models of deception. *Annals of Sex Research, 4*(1), 49-63.

Ross, J. (1994). "Workshop: The adolescent sexual offender." Workshop given at an unknown location.

Ross, J. and Loss, P. (1991). Assessment of the juvenile sex offender. In G. Ryan and S. Lane (Eds.), *Juvenile sexual offending: Causes, consequences, and correction*, (pp. 199-252). Lexington, MA: D. C. Heath and Company.

Roush, D. W. (1984). Contributing to the therapeutic milieu: Integrating key theoretical constructs. *Child Care Quarterly, 13*(4), 233-249.

Ryan, G. D. and Lane, S. L. (1998). *Juvenile sexual offending: Causes, consequences, and correction.* Lexington, MA: D. C. Heath and Company.

Saunders, E. B. and Awad, G. A. (1988). Assessment, management, and treatment planning for male adolescent sexual offenders. *American Journal of Orthopsychiatry, 58*(4), 571-579.

Schaefer, C. E. and Swanson, A. J. (1988). *Children in residential care: Critical issues in treatment.* New York: Van Nostrand Reinhold Company.

Schladale, J. (1993). "A collaborative approach for treatment with juvenile sex offenders and their families." Unpublished manuscript. University of Louisville, Louisville,KY.

Schlank, A. M. and Shaw, T. (1996). Treating sex offenders who deny their guilt: A pilot study. *Sexual Abuse: A Journal of Research and Treatment, 8*(1), 17-23.

Schlank, A. M. and Shaw, T. (1997). Treating sex offenders who deny—A review. In B. K. Schwartz and H. R. Cellini (Eds.), *The sex offender: New insights, treatment innovations and legal developments* (pp. 6-1–6-7). Kingston, NJ: Civic Research Institute, Inc.

Schneider, S. and Cohen, Y. (1998). Potential space in milieu therapy with children and adolescents. *Therapeutic Communities: International Journal for Therapeutic and Supportive Organizations, 19*(2), 81-88.

Schwartz, B. K. (1995a). Group therapy. In B. K. Schwartz and H. R. Cellini (Eds.), *The sex offender: Corrections, treatment, and legal practice* (pp. 14-1–14-15). Kingston, NJ: Civic Research Institute, Inc.

Schwartz, B. K. (1995b). Theories of sex offenses. In B. K. Schwartz and H. R. Cellini (Eds.), *The sex offender: Corrections, treatment, and legal practice* (pp. 2-1–2-32). Kingston, NJ: Civic Research Institute, Inc.

Seelig, W. R., Goldman-Hall, B. J., and Jerrell, J. M. (1992). In-home treatment of families with seriously disturbed adolescents in crisis. *Family Process, 31*(2), 135-149.

Sefarbi, R. (1990). Admitters and deniers among adolescent sex offenders and their families: A preliminary study. *American Journal of Orthopsychiatry, 60*(3), 460-465.

Seghorn, T. K. (1986). "The challenge of the adolescent sexual offender: A proposed strategy." Unpublished manuscript.

Seto, M. C. and Barbaree, H. E. (1999). Psychopathy, treatment behavior, and sex offender recidivism. *Journal of Interpersonal Violence, 14*(12), 1235-1248.

Skaggs, R. (1997). Music-centered creative arts in a sex offender treatment program for male juveniles. *Music Therapy Perspectives, 15*(2), 73-78.

Smith, R. C. (1995). Sex offender program planning and implementation. In B. K. Schwartz and H. R. Cellini (Eds.), *The sex offender: Corrections, treatment, and legal practice* (pp. 7-1–7-13). Kingston, NJ: Civic Research Institute, Inc.

Steele, N. (1995a). Aftercare treatment programs. In B. K. Schwartz, and H. R. Cellini (Eds.), *The sex offender: Corrections, treatment, and legal practice* (pp. 19-1–19-9). Kingston, NJ: Civic Research Institute, Inc.

Steele, N. (1995b). Cost effectiveness of treatment. In B. K. Schwartz, and H. R. Cellini (Eds.), *The sex offender: Corrections, treatment, and legal practice* (pp. 4-1–4-19). Kingston, NJ: Civic Research Institute, Inc.

Steen, C. (1993). *The relapse prevention workbook for youth in treatment.* Brandon, VT: Safer Society Press.

Stevenson, H. C., Castillo, E., and Sefarbi, R. (1989). Treatment of denial in adolescent sex offenders and their families. *Journal of Offender Counseling, Services, and Rehabilitation, 14*(1), 37-50.

Stickrod Gray, A. and Pithers, W. D. (1993). Relapse prevention with sexually aggressive adolescents and children: Expanding treatment and supervision. In H. Barbaree, W. Marshall, and S. Hudson (Eds.), *The juvenile sex offender* (pp. 289-320). New York: The Guilford Press.

Stickrod Gray, A. and Wallace, R. (1992). *Adolescent sexual offender assessment packet.* Orwell, VT: Safer Society Press.

Tallmadge, A. with Forster, G. (1998) *Tell it like it is: A resource guide for youth in treatment.* Orwell, VT: Safer Society Press.

Thomas, J. (1991). The adolescent sex offender's family in treatment. In G. Ryan and S. Lane (Eds.), *Juvenile sexual offending: Causes, consequences, and correction* (pp. 333-376). Lexington, MA: D. C. Heath and Company.

Thompson, J. K. (1989). Lifestyle interventions: Promoting positive addictions. In D. R. Laws (Ed.), *Relapse prevention with sex offenders* (pp. 219-226). New York: The Guilford Press.

Ward, T., McCormack, J., Hudson, S., and Polaschek, D. (1997). Rape: Assessment and treatment. In D. R. Laws and W. O'Donohue (Eds.), *Sexual deviance: Theory, assessment, and treatment* (pp. 356-393). New York: The Guilford Press.

Way, I. F. and Balthazor, T. J. (1990). *A manual for structured group treatment with adolescent sexual offenders.* Notre Dame, IN: Jalice Publishers.

Way, I. F. and Spieker, S. D. (1997). *The cycle of offense: A framework for treating adolescent sexual offenders.* Notre Dame, IN: Jalice Publishers.

Wenhold, J., Cutler, P., Kinscherff, R., Latham, C., and Stone, K. (1994, November). "Special issues in the assessment of adolescent sexual abusers." Panel presentation at the annual conference of the Massachusetts Adolescent Sex Offender Coalition, Worcester, MA.

West, J. G. (1998). Designing an orientation program for the direct care staff of a children's residential treatment center. *Residential Treatment for Children and Youth, 16*(1), 21-32.

Winn, M. E. (1996). The strategic and systemic management of denial in the cognitive/behavioral treatment of sexual offenders. *Sexual Abuse: A Journal of Research and Treatment, 8*(1), 25-36.

Wood, S., Barton, K., and Schroeder, C. (1988). In-home treatment of abusive families: Cost and placement at one year. *Psychotherapy, 25*(3), 409-414.

Yalom, I. D. (1985). *The theory and practice of group psychotherapy* (Third edition). New York: Basic Books.

Yokley, J. M. (Ed.) (1990). *The use of victim-offender communication in the treatment of sexual abuse: Three intervention models.* Orwell, VT: Safer Society Press.

Yorker, B. (1997). Preventing institutional liability for children who molest children. *The A.P.S.A.C. Advisor, 10*(3), 9-15.

Index

Page numbers followed by the letter "i" indicate illustrations; those followed by the letter "n" indicate notes; and those followed by the letter "t" indicate tables.

Order Your Own Copy of
This Important Book for Your Personal Library!

TREATING YOUTH WHO SEXUALLY ABUSE
An Integrated Multi-Component Approach

_____ in hardbound at $59.95 (ISBN: 0-7890-0936-6)
_____ in softbound at $24.95 (ISBN: 0-7890-0937-4)

COST OF BOOKS_____

OUTSIDE USA/CANADA/
MEXICO: ADD 20%____

POSTAGE & HANDLING_____
(US: $4.00 for first book & $1.50
for each additional book)
Outside US: $5.00 for first book
& $2.00 for each additional book)

SUBTOTAL_____

in Canada: add 7% GST____

STATE TAX____
(NY, OH & MIN residents, please
add appropriate local sales tax)

FINAL TOTAL____
(If paying in Canadian funds,
convert using the current
exchange rate, UNESCO
coupons welcome.)

❑ **BILL ME LATER:** ($5 service charge will be added)
(Bill-me option is good on US/Canada/Mexico orders only;
not good to jobbers, wholesalers, or subscription agencies.)

❑ Check here if billing address is different from
shipping address and attach purchase order and
billing address information.

Signature_____

❑ **PAYMENT ENCLOSED: $**_____

❑ **PLEASE CHARGE TO MY CREDIT CARD.**

❑ Visa ❑ MasterCard ❑ AmEx ❑ Discover
❑ Diner's Club ❑ Eurocard ❑ JCB

Account # _____

Exp. Date_____

Signature_____

Prices in US dollars and subject to change without notice.

NAME_____

INSTITUTION_____

ADDRESS_____

CITY_____

STATE/ZIP_____

COUNTRY_____ COUNTY (NY residents only)_____

TEL_____ FAX_____

E-MAIL_____

May we use your e-mail address for confirmations and other types of information? ❑ Yes ❑ No
We appreciate receiving your e-mail address and fax number. Haworth would like to e-mail or fax special
discount offers to you, as a preferred customer. **We will never share, rent, or exchange your e-mail address
or fax number.** We regard such actions as an invasion of your privacy.

Order From Your Local Bookstore or Directly From
The Haworth Press, Inc.
10 Alice Street, Binghamton, New York 13904-1580 • USA
TELEPHONE: 1-800-HAWORTH (1-800-429-6784) / Outside US/Canada: (607) 722-5857
FAX: 1-800-895-0582 / Outside US/Canada: (607) 722-6362
E-mail: getinfo@haworthpressinc.com
PLEASE PHOTOCOPY THIS FORM FOR YOUR PERSONAL USE.
www.HaworthPress.com

BOF00